DETER

Also published by Jennifer Birkett

SAMUEL BECKETT: *Waiting for Godot*
THE BODY AND THE DREAM: French Erotic Fiction,
1464–1900
THE SINS OF THE FATHERS: Decadence in France and
Europe, 1870–1914

Determined Women

Studies in the Construction of the Female Subject, 1900–90

Edited and introduced by

JENNIFER BIRKETT
Professor of French Studies, University of Strathclyde

and

ELIZABETH HARVEY
Lecturer in German, University of Salford

MACMILLAN

First edition 1991

Published by
THE MACMILLAN PRESS LTD
Houndmills, Basingstoke, Hampshire RG21 2XS
and London
Companies and representatives
throughout the world

Printed in Hong Kong

British Library Cataloguing in Publication Data
Determined women: studies in the construction of
the female subject, 1900–90
1. Literature. Women writers. Special themes: Women —
Critical studies
I. Birkett, Jennifer   II. Harvey, Elizabeth
809′.89287
ISBN 0-333-44838-3 (hc)
ISBN 0-333-44839-1 (pbk)

Contents

Contents

Acknowledgements

Robin Adamson wishes to thank the Scottish Universities French Language Research Association for the grant she received for travel to Paris for research on her chapter. Jennifer Birkett wishes to acknowledge the kind assistance of the British Academy in financing the research for her chapters. Elizabeth Harvey would like to thank the Research Committee of the University of Salford for assistance with research expenses. Coral Ann Howells wishes to thank the British Association for Canadian Studies and the Research Board of the University of Reading for financial assistance in her research.

Notes on the Contributors

Robin Adamson is Lecturer in French and Director of the Language Unit at the University of Dundee. Her research has focused on computer-assisted stylistics and advanced language learning. She contributed to and edited *Le Français en faculté* (2nd edn, 1986) and *En fin de compte . . .* (1988).

Jennifer Birkett is Professor of French Studies at the University of Strathclyde and Convenor of the M.Litt. in Women's Studies. Her publications include *The Body and the Dream: French Erotic Fiction 1464–1900* (1983), *The Sins of the Fathers: Decadence in France and Europe 1870–1914* (1986) and *Samuel Beckett: 'Waiting for Godot'* (1987). She has also written essays and articles on English, American and French women writers and she is currently preparing a book on *Sexuality, Politics and Fiction in the French Revolution* and completing (in collaboration with James Kearns) *The Macmillan Guide to French Literature.*

Helga Geyer-Ryan is Associate Professor in Comparative Literature at the University of Amsterdam and has taught German literature at the Universities of Geneva and Cambridge. She has published widely on literature and feminism, popular culture and literary theory, and her major publications include *Der andere Roman: Versuch über die verdrängte Ästhetik des Populären* (1983), *Popular Literature in the Third Reich* (1980), *Literary Theory Today* (co-editor, with Peter Collier) (1990) and *Fables of Desire: Essays in Feminist Criticism* (forthcoming, 1991).

Patricia Harbord lives in Edinburgh. She has translated articles by West German feminists and has published an interview with the film-maker Jutta Brückner. She has written on the representation of femininity in the work of several East German women writers.

Elizabeth Harvey is Lecturer in German at the University of Salford. Her publications include a study of youth welfare in Weimar Germany and articles on youth unemployment during the Depression. She is currently preparing a book on *Youth and the State in Weimar Germany*.

Coral Ann Howells lectures in English at the University of Reading, where she teaches courses on British fiction and Canadian women's fiction. Her publications include *Private and Fictional Words: Canadian Women Novelists of the 1970s and 80s* (1987), *Love, Mystery and Misery: Feeling in Gothic Fiction* (1978) and essays on Ann Radcliffe, George Eliot, Margaret Laurence, Margaret Atwood, Alice Munro, Audrey Thomas and Marian Engel. She is currently completing a book on Jean Rhys, to be followed by one on Margaret Atwood.

Stan Smith is Professor of English at the University of Dundee. He has published widely on modern literature, and his books include *A Sadly Contracted Hero: The Comic Self in Post-War American Fiction* (1981), *Inviolable Voice: History and Twentieth-Century Poetry* (1982), *W. H. Auden* (1985), *Edward Thomas* (1986) and *W. B. Yeats: A Critical Introduction* (1990). He co-edits the Longman Critical Reader series, with Raman Selden.

1 Introduction

JENNIFER BIRKETT and ELIZABETH HARVEY

> *How did she end up in this madhouse? By putting one foot
> in front of the other and never taking her eyes off her feet.
> You could end up anywhere that way. . . . What, underneath
> it all, is Loulou really like? How can she tell? Maybe she is
> what the poets say she is, after all; maybe she has only their
> word, their words, for herself.*
>
> Margaret Atwood, 'Loulou, or the Domestic Life of the
> Language', *Bluebeard's Egg and Other Stories* (1988) p. 80

> *Feminism's protest is always posed in terms of women's per-
> ceptions of themselves and their status in relation to men.
> From a litany of their discontents feminism gathers an identity
> of women, and formulates the demands and aspirations that
> will transform the social relations/conditions in which women
> and men will live.*
>
> Sally Alexander, 'Women, Class and Sexual Differences',
> *History Workshop Journal*, 17 (Spring 1984) p. 130

Getting into the madhouse is easy enough: a simple matter of
following determined paths, without looking further than the ends
of one's feet. Getting out requires a different kind of determination,
harder to come by. Women who want not only to survive the
madhouse but also to change it into a house fit for human habitation
must come to terms with both meanings of the word.

Patriarchy, in its wider sense, has been defined by Gerda Lerner:
'the manifestation and institutionalization of male dominance over
women and children in the family and the extension of male dominance over women in society in general.'[1] It is maintained through
a multitude of channels. Legal and institutional mechanisms exclude
women from positions of power. Economic structures put women in
a subordinate position in relation to a society's material resources.
Linguistic conventions marginalise the female by using masculine

forms to denote humanity in general.[2] The subordination of women
is underpinned by an ideology which structures perceptions of the
male and the female in terms of 'natural' sexual difference within a
hierarchy in which primacy is given to the male. Biological sex
differences are overlaid by socially constructed categories of gender.
Notions of the 'masculine' and the 'feminine' are used to ascribe
roles and status to members of society according to their biological
sex; 'feminine' qualities are ascribed to the biologically female, and
women are relegated on the basis of their supposed 'nature' to the
domestic and sexual sphere.

Fundamental to the perpetuation of patriarchy is the way it is
inscribed in the consciousness of women and in their perceptions of
themselves from earliest childhood.[3] The psychological constraints
upon women, which are intertwined with the legal, economic and
biological dimensions of women's subordination, hinder women from
analysing their situation and redefining their role.

But an analysis of patriarchal ideology which stresses its all-power-
ful and all-pervasive nature soon encounters a paradox. How can
feminist consciousness and feminist discourse ever arise within patriarchal society? If there is no space outside patriarchy to which
women can escape, how has resistance to patriarchy been possible
both in the past and the present?[4] The paradox is only an apparent
one, based on an excessively monolithic view of patriarchy: the fact
that women occupy a subordinate position in society does not mean
that all women are entirely without power. As Linda Gordon puts
it: 'To be less powerful is not to be power-less, or even to lose all
the time.'[5] It is the task of feminist research, in Gerda Lerner's
words, 'to trace with precision the various forms and modes in which
patriarchy appears historically, the shifts and changes in its structure
and function, and the adaptations it makes to female pressure and
demands.'[6] Such research can reveal the conditions under which
women develop new perceptions of themselves and formulate
demands for change.

The present collection of essays considers, from a variety of
perspectives – historical, literary and linguistic – some of the range
of images and categories within Western culture which have constructed women's sense of themselves, and the constructions that
women have placed on their world. The exchange works both ways.
The contributors examine historical moments ranging in time from
the First World War up to the present day. The essays, focusing
geographically on Britain, France, Germany, the United States and

Canada, consider the operations of patriarchal ideology and women's experience of patriarchy in these different forms and contexts. They show how limits are set to women's development. At the same time, they explore the question of how women have perceived and responded to their situation and under what conditions the limits imposed by patriarchy have been resisted or circumvented.

The time span over which the contributions range is marked by important developments affecting the way women view their place in society and the instruments available to them to change it. The feminist campaigns of the late nineteenth and early twentieth centuries had drawn attention to obstacles which prevented women achieving economic independence and equal status with men in the public sphere, and had made some headway towards dismantling them. Gradually, improvements in women's legal status, employment opportunities and educational provision were achieved. A vital step in women's emancipation was the gaining of the vote on equal terms with men. This came about in Canada (at federal level) and in Germany in 1918, throughout the United States in 1920, in Britain in 1928, and in France, belatedly, in 1945.[7] Where the vote was won, feminist movements lost their great unifying cause and some of their momentum. Where liberal democracy itself was undermined, in countries such as Germany, feminism was crushed along with it. In the United States and Britain in the interwar period, feminist campaigning continued and diversified in new directions, but with a lower public profile than before.[8] The slackening in pace of the feminist movement in the countries where it had been strongest did not mean that feminist ideas were entirely eclipsed.[9] But the mid-twentieth century 'intermission' following the heyday of classic liberal feminism left a space into which the next great mobilisation of women in the cause of women's emancipation was to move in the 1960s, in the 'second wave' of feminist politics.

Meanwhile, the reception of the work of Marx and Freud has brought in the twentieth century a transformation of awareness in Western culture of the economic and psychological determinants of human consciousness. Women writing in the twentieth century have been able to do so with a new consciousness of how society and personality are structured by class and gender. This cultural transformation has heightened in its turn political consciousness and the awareness of possibilities for the restructuring of sexual relations and gender roles.[10]

As different points of time bring different opportunities and disadvantages, so too do different places. The periods and places reviewed in the contributions begin in interwar Europe in Germany and Britain. During this era the gains achieved in the cause of women's emancipation were revealed to be partial and vulnerable, subject to the vicissitudes of economic crisis and political upheaval. The defence of women's rights was linked to the cause of the democratic Left and of liberal democracy, ranged against Fascism and its anti-feminist backlash.

Elizabeth Harvey's essay on girls' reading in the Germany of the 1920s focuses upon a period during which women's nature and women's place were the object of fierce and politically polarised debate. The German Revolution of November 1918 brought women the vote, and the 1919 constitution of the new Weimar Republic laid down the principle of sexual equality. German women's political equality, their greater educational opportunities and their growing economic independence gave some substance to the image of the New Woman, whose aspirations and behaviour broke with prewar conventions. The growing right-wing backlash against liberalism, the Left and feminism and the economic turmoil of these years meant that the gains which were made were fragile and insecure; nevertheless, girls at this time were growing up in a new climate in which alternatives to conventional feminine patterns of behaviour were opening up as real possibilities. How eagerly such alternatives were embraced by the younger generation of Weimar women is another question. Elizabeth Harvey's essay sheds light on girls' attitudes in this period by looking at a genre of teenage fiction, the *Backfisch-buch*, which remained consistently popular, despite educationalists' attempts to change girls' reading habits and despite the growing gulf between the world portrayed in the books and the reality in which girls were growing up. Using evidence of readers' responses, the essay explores the ways in which the books were received and examines the reasons for the enduring appeal of conventional portrayals of femininity in a period marked by the rapid transformation of society, economic crisis and political upheaval. While there are signs of a certain resilience on the part of the teenage reader, who takes from a book what she wants rather than what she is told to want, the effect of the books may in the end have been to reinforce compliance with the patriarchal order, not least by the way in which they satisfy a desire for narrative closure – the neat happy ending.

The contradictions besetting the English patriarchal order in which Storm Jameson grew up in the 1910s and 1920s may have been less visible than those of Weimar Germany, but they were none the less substantial. Jennifer Birkett's essay on the fictional and autobiographical writings of Storm Jameson explores some of the opportunities and the obstacles confronting a left-wing woman writer in Britain in the interwar period. In some ways circumstances favoured an ambitious woman like Jameson, circumstances created at least in part by the campaigns of the feminist movement. Jameson herself on the whole kept a conservative distance from organised feminism, but she had good reason to be grateful for its achievements. The greater availability of university education for women in the first decades of the twentieth century transformed her future, while the efforts which she later put into her chosen political arena – the struggle for social equality and for human rights – were the more effective for being undertaken against the background, once the vote was won, of feminist campaigns to win equal rights for women as citizens and to legitimate women's activity in the public sphere. Nevertheless, Jameson was unable to free herself entirely from a sense of marginality, of not being fully part of the political movements in which she was involved. She and others of her generation were motivated to seek a public role in part by the felt need to take the place and carry on the work of the lost generation of their male contemporaries, killed in the First World War. Jameson speaks for her generation as she laments their loss, and as she expresses, less self-consciously, the guilt of the survivor, profiting from their demise. New causes emerged in the 1920s and 1930s for socialists to fight, and much of the strength of Jameson's writing derives from its being forged within a socialist context, above all as part of the struggle of the intellectuals of the 1930s against Fascism. And yet her work continues to be marked by self-doubts, generated by her recognition and internalisation of her dependent status.

If Jameson made more of the opportunities offered her than many of her fellow-countrywomen, this also had to do with her personal history. Her middle-class origins, placing her within the pale of establishment society, provided both the spur and the space for determined female ambition. But her loyalty to her middle-class origins also posed contradictions. Ultimately, it prevented her resolving the dilemmas she faced as a woman in the public sphere. Though she rejected the presumption of woman's biological destiny, she still felt called on to embrace the expected role of wife and mother.. Jameson lived, as her autobiography and novels all recount, with an irredeemable sense of pain and failure. But she was trapped in this

sense of failure by her inability to move beyond the limits of her
class. While her sympathy with the economic plight of working-class
women was absolute, she nevertheless clung in a more tribal sense
to her Yorkshire family and to her English 'family'. She swallowed
whole, not the idea of Empire, but the idea of middle-class Englishness, as a haven of liberal values and order. In the context of
short-term opposition to the more obnoxious imperialism of Nazi
Germany, her acceptance made sense. In the long run, it handed
her over, mystified, to go on reproducing, under protest, a patriarchal order that ultimately undermined her.

From interwar Europe, the point of analysis moves to the post-
1945 era, and the other side of the Atlantic. The postwar growth of
prosperity and the rise of consumer culture in the United States and
Canada provide the backdrop for studies of Sylvia Plath, Alice
Walker and three Canadian short-story writers.

The painful constraints of the ideology of domesticity are again
to the forefront in Stan Smith's essay on Sylvia Plath's novel *The
Bell Jar* (1963). Plath's book makes explicit what in Jameson's work
remains mystified and challenges women's role in the reproduction
of the patriarchal political and social order. As Smith puts it:

> In rejecting a constricted, paranoid definition of what it is to be
> an American woman – the holy trinity of maidenhead, marriage
> and motherhood – Esther is defecting, in her mind, from a whole
> Cold War one-dimensionality, shaped, in the last instance, by the
> paranoid style of politics of the McCarthy era.

What Plath's heroine Esther Greenwood experiences as devastat-
ing private and personal oppression is a general condition with
specific political and historical parameters. Esther is the product of
the 1940s and 1950s, and the context of her story is American society
in the grip of social conservatism. The return to a peacetime economy
after the upheaval and dislocation of the war years, together with
the onset of the Cold War, combined to roll back the gains made
for women's emancipation before and during the war. Models of
womanhood changed once more, and the 1950s saw the rise of
the affluent suburban housewife, whose freedom was the surrogate
freedom of consumer choice.

In *The Bell Jar*, Plath describes this low point of the 1950s, a
moment where one woman at least is beginning to perceive her
situation, but, fatally, lacks a language to describe it. Stan Smith

describes Esther's situation precisely as Plath presents it, within the limits of Esther's understanding, which has no means of moving beyond immediate experience or of connecting private distress to the disorders of the public world. The absence of interpretive tools which could turn emotion into analysis leaves Esther with no means of resisting imposed stereotypes of behaviour and normality – except for suicide, which turns out itself to be a stereotype. Plath demonstrates the power of the cultural image to transfix personality, and the particular relevance of that power to sexual politics. In *The Bell Jar*, as Smith points out, 'the subordination of the woman in marriage is strangely linked with the power of the camera over its objects'.

Writing from the perspective of the early 1960s, within a cultural environment which was shifting rapidly away from the constraints of the 1950s and which was marked by a new upsurge in the feminist movement, Plath found a language which Esther was denied. The other North American women writers discussed in this volume came on the scene still later. They were influenced by 'second wave' feminism, but they were aware too of some of the dilemmas and contradictions of feminist theory and practice and the problem of loyalties divided between feminism and other causes. Such conflicts can prove debilitating, but can also be turned to productive use in women's writing.

Coral Ann Howells's account of three short stories by Canadian women writers, written in the 1970s and early 1980s, begins by examining women's relationship to the ideology of nationalism. Canadian women, doubly determined by their sex and their national identity as a formerly colonised people, have participated in their country's refusal of its colonial inheritance (whether from Europe or the United States), but have equally rejected the patriarchal component in nationalist ideology and their own colonisation by Canadian men. From its revival in the 1960s, the feminist movement in Canada found itself in the 1970s and 1980s developing alongside the nationalist movement. Coral Howells shows how the relationship of Canadian women writers to their inheritance is problematic, but potentially fruitful. She examines, for example, how traditions of nineteenth-century women's wilderness writing are adapted by modern Canadian women writers. The image of the bush symbolises the unknown forces which modern Canadian women in their small-town suburban houses are trained to shut out. A specifically national and nationalist tradition is appropriated by the authors analysed to underline the limitations of contemporary women's lives.

The sensitivity of the Canadian women writers analysed in Coral Howells's essay to the conflict between national loyalties and loyalties to their sex sharpens their sense of their problematic relationship to established conventions of language and narrative. They write 'stories divided against themselves in an exposure of the limits of fiction and the failure of fiction and real life to coincide'. Experiments in disrupting inherited narrative forms are efforts to express these divisions and to make room for a distinctive female voice. Howells's analysis also emphasises the limits to which such written disruptions can take their authors. Writing, it seems, is a means of resistance only up to a certain point. Audrey Thomas's fictional writer has a painful struggle to get her imagined New Woman, looking for freedom, to cross the Montreal street by herself, away from her ex-lover. Women writers may redouble the efforts of their imagination, but their female subjects still have to move within man-made city limits. In imagination, they can make a break, but 'nothing ever really changes'.

The (white) American and Canadian authors analysed by Stan Smith and Coral Howells portray white, relatively affluent North American women who despite social privileges and education find limited opportunity to avoid the determining constraints of their situation. In contrast, the black American writer Alice Walker, whose work is the subject of Jennifer Birkett's second essay, foregrounds female characters whose rapid emancipatory evolution into self-awareness has radical and far-reaching effects on the world about them. Walker is committed, she says, to a belief in change: 'change personal, and change in society'. A life lived across two cultures – the American and the Afro-American – makes her conscious, Jennifer Birkett argues, of the possibility of choosing across a range of different modes of being. The double inheritance of black culture (the deep traditions of the community first made visible by the Harlem Renaissance of the 1930s, and cast into combative politics by the Civil Rights movement of the 1960s) and a white middle-class liberal education provided her with the language to unlock new forces for resistance and transformation. An active participant in the history of which her stories are made, Walker understands at first hand the manipulative operations of consumer society, the workings of stereotypes and the way in which selfhood is formed and reformed by the triple intersections of class, gender and race. The constituting context of her work includes the improved economic position of black women post-1945, which gave rise to a relative improvement in their position within society as a whole and an acute deterioration in their position within the traditional couple, as the resentments of their black partners became more deeply felt and violently articulated. Walker explores the conflict of loyalties to gender and race, producing for her contemporaries a model of distinctive black feminism.

The focus returns to Europe, to show two very different structural contexts provided for women in the 1970s and 1980s, in East Germany and in France.

Patricia Harbord's essay focuses on a text which is a crucial source of insight into the situation of women in the GDR in the 1970s and 1980s. Maxie Wander's *Guten Morgen, du Schöne* (1977), a collection of interviews with women of different ages, origins and occupations, has changed the way women in the GDR have perceived themselves and been perceived. The stories which the women tell about their lives and the way their accounts have been taken up and discussed shed light on the way in which different generations of women have experienced living in a socialist society within the Eastern bloc. As a result of the official doctrine of sexual equality upheld by the GDR's socialist regime, and the dictates of the country's economic development, women came to participate fully in a process of radical social and economic transformation, working alongside men in all spheres of society and the economy. From their position of economic independence and equal status, women have been able to formulate a positive vision of a new kind of living for both women and men. In the words of Christa Wolf, whose views on the position of women in the GDR and on the representation of women's experience are among those discussed by Patricia Harbord:

> My interest lies not so much in equality for women – legal and economic equality is guaranteed by our legislation – as in their self-realisation in a specific historical situation, since their self-consciousness, what they demand of life, goes beyond the opportunities society offers them. Women, who have been less disfigured than many men by the pressure to compete and achieve which industrial society has exerted for generations, are increasingly striving for new, more convivial ways of living, for a full and complete life (and not just for higher production figures). . . . I am fascinated by those women who recognise and seize the historical moment presented to them, no matter how difficult that

might be. They are able earlier than most men to articulate how a new way of life and a new era might feel.[11]

Patricia Harbord shows how the new forms in which women are being encouraged to speak have actively furthered this process of women's entry into self-consciousness. Working women, speaking the text of their own lives, have increasingly found themselves transforming individual into collective subjectivity. They no longer say 'I' but 'we'. They have been remade into critics of their own past lives, perceiving and condemning their previous reduction to objects. Patricia Harbord shows the part played in that process by laws and institutions, a key area being the laws applying to abortion (abortion was illegal in the GDR until 1972), and she emphasises the difference made by the 1972 abortion law reform to women's lives. But what women in recent years have increasingly sought is 'a new phase of emancipation which goes far beyond legislation in favour of the "socialist wife and mother" '. Such aspirations have parallels in the Western women's movement. Although many of those active in the debates in the GDR concerning women have been careful to retain a certain distance from the women's movement in the West, some aspects of Western feminism have found advocates in the GDR. Christa Wolf, in particular, has argued that the ideas of the Western women's movement can raise in the GDR 'questions which we had not yet asked' which will help force patriarchy from the socialist system.[12]

The penultimate essay in the collection, Robin Adamson's study of sexism in the language of car advertising in France, is concerned not with the processes of women's resistance, but with the mechanisms of two particular agencies by which patriarchal ideology is transmitted. The sophisticated advertising machinery of the 1980s identifies potential consumers and pitches precisely at those consumers' prejudices. Selling cars to a market that is 90 per cent men is a process of invoking male and female stereotypes, reinforcing men's and women's sense of woman-as-object. But it is not simply advertising, Robin Adamson argues, but the grammatical structures that carry it that are imbued with sexism. In an inflected and gendered language like French, the requirements of agreement, and the replacement of the noun by the pronoun in extended discourse, or by descriptive adjectives in the feminine, allow the type of sexist and misogynist language which is used for females to be extended to unsexed objects of feminine linguistic gender. This would not be possible had not grammatical gender, contrary to the assertions of many male linguists, already been allowed to become sex. Robin Adamson focuses here on a problem which for many French women writers is fundamental to Frenchwomen's inability to speak for themselves in their native tongue.

The last essay of the book, in contrast to the other contributions, is not located in a specific place or historical moment. Helga Geyer-Ryan explores the continuity with which certain effects of patriarchy are experienced by women in historically different times and places. Access to education has a liberating effect for women, but it also binds them more tightly into the common cultural traditions of Western society. The founding myths of Greek and Roman civilisation, buried in the proverbs and clichés of everyday life, are as potent as any advertising man's stereotype in formulating women's self-image. Helga Geyer-Ryan looks particularly at figures of women with deranged speech in Greek mythology. Their importance derives from the fact that they are handed down to us as our cultural heritage, whose social archetypes organise our constructions of the relationship between power, gender, body and voice: these are the myths by which we are invited to live. What figures such as Philomela, Echo, Xanthippe and Cassandra show in obsessively recurrent texts and icons is the mutilation by male violence of woman's capacity to speak out and free herself. Throughout history, the language of the patriarchy has materially shaped women's being, drawing them in man's image, refusing them the right of self-expression, and punishing the rebels. In male iconography, Cassandra is a figure of transgression, subversion and terrifying disruption; the woman who tries to refuse man's categories and determinations calls his whole world into question. Women's silence is the founding condition of man's speech. Male authority expresses itself primarily by its violation of the world of the Other, denying the autonomy of women's bodies and women's words. Women who are called to become subjects in a world where Cassandras are the model find their construction as subjects radically sabotaged. Helga Geyer-Ryan's analysis gives full weight to the physical violence embodied in the myths. At the same time, the myth carries within itself crucial challenges to its patriarchal authors, showing women who continue to struggle to speak for themselves, to find new forms of language outside man's authority, and to find in their silencing new conditions of speech.

The rest of this Introduction brings together some of the major themes which recur in the course of this volume. The next section, 'Setting the Limits', reviews the functions which patriarchy assigns to women in the home and in the wider economic sphere. The final section, 'Answering Back', assesses women's responses to men's pre-emption of their speech.

SETTING THE LIMITS

Wives and Mothers

A recurring theme in this collection is the way in which female identity and social place is defined by women's role in the private sphere and above all by the role of mother.

That the 'real' woman always is, or aspires to be, a mother is a universally established prejudice of patriarchy, which transcends specific economic and social conditions.

> Historically, cross-culturally, a woman's status as childbearer has been the test of her womanhood. Through motherhood, every woman has been defined from outside herself: mother, matriarch, matron, spinster, barren, old maid. . . . Even by default, mother-hood has been an enforced identity for women, while the phrases 'childless man' and 'nonfather' sound absurd and irrelevant to us.[13]

Nancy Chodorow, in her influential explanation of the way in which the category 'mother' determines what it is to be a woman, emphasises the limitations that it implies. The man is assigned to the sphere of authority, the woman to the sphere of reproduction:

> The sexual and familial division of labor in which women mother creates a sexual division of psychic organization and orientation. It produces socially gendered women and men who enter into asymmetrical heterosexual relationships; it produces men who react to, fear, and act superior to women, and who put most of their energies into the nonfamilial work world and do not parent. Finally, it produces women who turn their energies towards nur-turing and caring for children – in turn reproducing the sexual and familial division of labor in which women mother.[14]

As the channel for the transmission of femininity, the mother–daughter relationship is a key site for the reproduction of patriarchy.

Women of all times and places have experienced motherhood and
the mother–daughter relationship, but the nature of that experience
changes with specific historical and social contexts. In several of the
essays in this collection, some of the changes which have affected
the experience of motherhood and mother–daughter relationships
over the last three-quarters of a century are reflected. Real and
fictional women in a range of circumstances are shown succumbing
to the relationship with a particular mother, encountering the social
pressures to become mothers in their turn, and experiencing the
dilemmas of relationships with their daughters. The following section
traces this theme as it is dealt with in the contributions in this volume
and seeks to place it in context by sketching some of the features
determining women's experiences of motherhood since the First
World War in Europe and North America.

In the popular fiction examined in the essay on girls' reading
in Weimar Germany, motherhood is presented conventionally and
unproblematically as the goal of a girl's education. Even in the most
'modern' text discussed, the heroine does not hesitate for a moment
in abandoning her training as a doctor for marriage and motherhood.
The texts sustained the belief still widespread in Weimar Germany
that marriage and motherhood were the tasks for which a girl growing up had to be prepared. But motherhood was nevertheless emerging as a problem to which public debate and public policy increasingly
addressed themselves. The birth-rate continued to fall sharply as
many women restricted the number of children they bore or
remained – through necessity or choice – without children altogether. At the same time, assumptions that marriage and motherhood were a woman's destiny were being challenged by radical
feminist and left-wing advocates of motherhood outside the conventional family framework, and by sex reformers who sought to 'rationalise' human reproduction by making motherhood a matter of social
and individual planning.[15]

The increasingly complex reality of alternatives and choices
surrounding motherhood in interwar Britain is reflected in the experience of Storm Jameson. Jameson in her autobiography describes
how her mother sought to push her into the family mould and into
marriage, and how she in her turn attempted to escape the confines
of the maternal role and her mother's expectations. This, however,
had its price: Jameson's guilt at achieving the escape which had been
denied to her mother comes through clearly in her texts.

Full-time motherhood and the 'domestic drudgery' (in Jameson's words) which it involved were not the only options open to a woman in the Britain of the 1920s and 1930s. But for women in Britain, as in other Western countries in the interwar period, the family was still assumed to be their primary sphere. Work outside the home was for spinsters, who were seen as falling short of woman's true vocation. In Britain, girls' access to secondary education increased, but the content of their studies was differentiated along gender lines, with the assumption that marriage and motherhood should be a girl's primary ambition. Indeed, it was her civic duty. The newly enfranchised woman was not merely a citizen but a citizen-mother. Since before the First World War, eugenicists and medical experts concerned about the quality and quantity of the population had been calling for measures to encourage child-bearing and to raise the standards of mothercraft.[16] In Britain in 1933 the falling birthrate reached an all-time national low, and the population question attracted increasing publicity. Members of Parliament and learned physicians urged women to refill the nurseries to protect the future of the family, the nation and the Empire.[17] Meanwhile, governments in other countries were already implementing programmes to boost the birthrate. In France and Belgium, for instance, public policies were pursued in the interwar period to influence, encourage and supervise motherhood, while a ruthlessly manipulative and racist variant of the trend towards organising and administering human reproduction was pursued from 1933 onwards in Nazi Germany.[18]

The concern of politicians and planners about the future of motherhood was given additional impetus by the Second World War. Such concern did not necessarily translate itself into measures making motherhood easier to manage. Particularly for working mothers, conditions tended to worsen when the public child care provided during the Second World War in Britain, the United States and Canada in order to integrate working mothers more effectively into the war effort was cut back or abolished.[19] Mothers went back to juggling their double burden unaided, or retreated, willingly or unwillingly, into caring full-time for their children in the home.

At the same time, particularly in Britain and the United States, a discourse cultivating and celebrating motherhood and domesticity was making itself powerfully felt.[20] In Britain, new orthodoxies on child-care were propagated in the 1950s to emphasise the importance of full-time mothering.[21] In the States, 'bad' mothering was made to carry the can for increasing male failures of nerve: Rochelle Gatlin argues that a 'mid-century masculinity crisis', fuelled by men's fear of impotence and anonymity in the face of the new big bureaucracies and corporations, found relief for its frustrations in invective against the 'castrating' mother. A number of postwar works (for example, Marynia Farnham and Ferdinand Lundberg's *Modern Woman: The Lost Sex*, 1947), blamed mothers for the two million men rejected from military service in the Second World War for psychiatric disorders.[22] Smear campaigns in the USA associating public child care and feminism with Communism and a conspiracy to subvert and destroy the family grew with the intensification of the Cold War and the onset of the McCarthy era. In 1947 the *New York World Telegram* alleged that public child care was the invention of Communist-influenced leftists. When Simone de Beauvoir's *The Second Sex* (1949) appeared in the States in 1953, challenging the idea that motherhood was a woman's destiny and attacking the housewife–harlot role to which women were relegated, *The Nation* solemnly warned its readers against Simone de Beauvoir's 'political leanings'.[23]

The exact impact of this sort of discourse on women is hard to estimate. Sylvia Plath's *The Bell Jar* represents one perspective on the pressures upon American women in the postwar period to conform to the domestic ideal and on the difficulty of resisting them. Esther's world is pervaded by images of motherhood and of babies: even as she takes steps to avoid pregnancy, waiting in the clinic to have a contraceptive device fitted, babies' faces stare out of magazines at her. The chilling message of *The Bell Jar* is that daughters are conned into a trap with the collaboration of mothers: Esther's actual mother and other mother-figures are shown as colluding to push Esther into motherhood. Esther's mother sends her articles on chastity and presses her to marry the son of a friend; another mother-figure, the romantic novelist Philomena Guinea, pays for Esther's education and for the treatment in the psychiatric hospital, where a motherly psychiatrist presides over the successful treatment that restores Esther to 'normality'. Esther, the first-person narrator, writes as the possessor of a baby which stops her doing anything except look back at the past and the trap she has fallen into. Only dimly does Esther, and the reader, perceive that the acceptance of the conventional norms was the price of her survival.

Yet while the domestic ideal continued to be promoted unrelentingly in the United States, it was by the end of the 1950s increasingly contradicted by the reality of women's lives. The birthrate began to fall in 1957 and the proportion of mothers who looked after their

children full-time was decreasing.[24] 'Strangely enough, as the feminine mystique spread, denying women careers or any commitment
outside the home, the proportion of American women working
outside the home increased to one out of three.'[25] In 1960, 39 per
cent of married women living with their husbands with children
between the ages of 6 and 17 were working as against 26 per cent
in 1948.[26]

1963 saw the publication of three celebrated works looking back
at women's experience of motherhood in the 1950s and questioning
the maternal ideal which had pervaded that era: *The Bell Jar*, Betty
Friedan's *The Feminine Mystique* and Adrienne Rich's *Snapshots of
a Daughter-in-Law*. Friedan's analysis of the signs of a growing
problem of frustration among American housewives and mothers
quoted among its evidence the article in *Redbook* magazine three
years earlier entitled 'Why Young Mothers Feel Trapped', which
had invited responses from young mothers with the same problem
and had promoted 24 000 replies.[27] *Snapshots of a Daughter-in-Law*
expresses the frustrations of female creativity in language as frank
as Storm Jameson's. This is a mother who finds herself

> writing very little, partly from fatigue, that female fatigue of
> suppressed anger and the loss of contact with her own being,
> partly from the discontinuity of female life with its attention to
> small chores, errands, work that others constantly undo, small
> children's constant needs.[28]

By the late 1960s, the chance of opting out of motherhood was,
at least in physical terms, becoming easier. With the introduction of
oral contraceptives it became more common for women to assert
their right not only to limit the number of children they bore but
also to choose not to be mothers at all. More reliable and more
widely available contraception, and later legalized abortion, transformed women's lives in a way that later generations can find difficult
to comprehend.

This sense of transformation comes through clearly in the contribution by Patricia Harbord on the German Democratic Republic.
Like women in Western countries, women in the socialist GDR
experienced their growing ability to plan or opt out of child-bearing
as a vital extension of their freedom. This is made clear by the older
women who recall the bad old days of unwanted pregnancies.

Since the 1960s it has been easier for women to plan motherhood, or to avoid it altogether. But the task of mothering, and negotiating relationships between mothers and daughters, remains as difficult as ever. The women in the German Democratic Republic interviewed in the 1970s by Maxie Wander seem on the whole reluctant to speak of their relationships with their daughters and to express negative feelings towards girl–children. The Canadian and American women writers of the 1970s discussed in this volume show a critical awareness of the problems of mother–daughter relationships. These are portrayed from the perspective both of the daughter, and, perhaps reflecting the growing concern in the feminist movement from the mid-1970s with the mothering role, from that of the mother.

The fictional mother–daughter relationship portrayed in Audrey Thomas's 'Crossing the Rubicon' (discussed by Coral Howells) is riven by complexities. The narrator in 'Crossing the Rubicon' observes with concern her twelve-year-old daughter replicating the patterns of behaviour of her own schooldays, seeking to please the boys by baking Valentine's Day cakes. Will her daughter grow up just as trapped as the mother into dependence on male approval? Has she failed to transmit to her daughter a different set of values, and if so, why?

Margaret Atwood, in a short story from the *Bluebeard's Egg* collection, shows the breakdown of communication between mother and daughter from the daughter's perspective. Ages and worlds divide them; the daughter has broken free, while the mother remains fixed in the domestic role.

> [T]here must have been something going on in me that was beyond her: at any time I might open my mouth and out would come a language she had never heard before. I had become a visitant from outer space, a time-traveller come back from the future, bearing news of a great disaster.[29]

Remembering the stories her mother had told her, the narrator quotes her favourite:

> about a little girl who was so poor she had only one potato left for her supper, and while she was roasting it the potato got up and ran away. There was the usual chase, but I can't remember the ending: a significant lapse.
>
> '*That* story was one of your favourites', says my mother. She is probably still under the impression that I identified with the

little girl, with her hunger and her sense of loss, whereas in reality I identified with the potato.[30]

In Alice Walker's fiction, a range of oppressive mother–daughter relationships are portrayed, such as the relationship between Meridian and her mother, who is envious of Meridian and tries to thwart her plans. Cely's mother, less malicious than Meridian's, teaches her daughter by her example uncritical compliance with others' demands, from which Cely has to be saved by a whole band of sisters.

Workers, Consumers, Commodities

Not all women are mothers, but all women are affected by women's mothering role, which defines them primarily in terms of their sexual function.

In twentieth-century Western capitalism, women sustain the economy in a number of different ways, all of them determined to a greater or lesser extent by women's subordinate status in society and their domestic/mothering/sexual role. As (under-)paid workers, women find their subordination reinforced in a labour market segmented by gender. As consumers, they are defined as mothers and housewives who are persuaded to express their devotion to their families through the purchase and use of consumer goods. As commodities, women are turned into sex objects whose faces and bodies are used to promote and sell products to other women and to male consumers. In the following, we trace the way in which contributions in this volume shed light on these aspects of women's role in sustaining modern capitalist economies, placing them briefly in their historical context, and pointing to some of the implications for women's ability to determine and redefine their social identity.

In interwar Britain, opportunities for women in paid employment were expanding. But the expansion of employment opportunities for women involved a continuing process of 'horizontal segregation' of the labour market: expansion took place in the occupations defined as 'feminine' such as nursing and teaching, and above all in 'white-blouse' work in shops and offices.[31] At the same time, the 'vertical segregation' of occupations continued and even intensified, keeping women in low-status positions within each occupation or sector and reserving high-status positions for men.[32] Moreover, a marriage bar operated in many professions so that the career opportunities that did exist for women were restricted to the unmarried.[33]

The frustration of the middle-class woman with career ambitions is illustrated by the case of Storm Jameson. In her autobiography she recollects being passed over for a lecturing job at Leeds University in favour of a man who did less well in his degree exams than she had. Later, in the world of publishing, she found that women were limited to journalism or low-status jobs as literary agents. In her novels, Jameson portrays her educated heroine Hervey struggling against the odds to make her way as a woman writer in the crowded and male-dominated literary world between the wars.

The opportunities and the constraints which determined women's place in the labour market of interwar Britain had parallels in other Western industrialised countries. In Germany and the United States, an image of the New Woman was taking hold, associated most strongly with young, particularly middle-class unmarried women living in towns, employed in the growing service sector and enjoying a new financial and personal independence.[34] The New Woman was an elusive phenomenon, hard to define and harder to identify. But the growing mass of women in paid employment was a reality. Despite the Depression and the growing anti-feminist rhetoric in some countries in the 1930s, married women who worked outside the home refused to be dislodged from the 'feminine' occupations which they had come to dominate.

But if the long-term structural changes in Western capitalist economies brought a growing number of women of all classes into white-collar and professional occupations, women's subordinate position in the world of employment still endured. Only national emergencies could break down the patterns of occupational segregation, and then only temporarily. The gains which the mobilization on the home front during the Second World War brought to working women in the United States, Britain and Canada were limited: the barriers erected by employers and trade unions against women entering highly paid 'men's occupations' soon went up again after the war.[35] The interwar image of the New Woman faded. *The Bell Jar* provides a glimpse of the obstacles confronting educated white women in the USA of the 1950s: the declared ambition of Plath's heroine Esther to become a poet is ridiculed, and she is encouraged by her mother to learn shorthand.

In both the United States and Britain in the early 1960s, a decisive shift took place. Women workers were, relatively speaking, in a sellers' market, and the cause of equal rights and equal pay made corresponding progress. John F. Kennedy's President's Commission on the Status of Women, set up in 1961, and reporting in 1963, was little more than a gesture, but the USA's Equal Pay Act of 1963 and most of all the Civil Rights Act of 1964 between them put a formal end to all discrimination in employment on grounds of sex, race, colour and national origins. In Britain, Barbara Castle's Equal Pay Act was introduced and passed in 1970.[36]

For black women in the United States, access to employment had been in some ways easier than for black men or white women. Postwar affluence, producing new opportunities for blacks as well as whites, formed the new black bourgeoisie, mostly working in clerical and related occupations, where women formed the majority. The homemaker propaganda which tended to drive white women back to the stove in the early 1950s touched them too, but economic necessity blunted its effectiveness. The fact that black women's wages made a major contribution to the family economy meant that paid employment provided for black women a springboard to independence.[37] Alice Walker illustrates this in her portrayal of two female characters in *The Third Life of Grange Copeland* who gain a measure of independence through paid work: Josie through setting up her own juke joint and Mem through her job as a teacher. However, the freedom gained through economic independence is shown as having potentially explosive consequences for black women's relationships with their menfolk: Mem's new independence and the higher living standards she aspires to set up an ultimately fatal tension within her marriage.

Since the 1960s the expansion of tertiary sector jobs in nearly all Western capitalist countries has brought a further growth of paid employment for women.[38] Since the service sector has proved more resistant to economic downswings than other sectors of the economy, this distribution of women in the labour market has tended to cushion women's employment as a whole against the effects of the worldwide economic recession since the 1970s. On the other hand, since women tend to be recruited to less stable jobs – a job is often defined as 'woman's work' precisely because it does not offer stable and continuous employment – women often find themselves more vulnerable to redundancy than men within any particular sector of the economy. Thus, although condemnations of married women working, blaming them for the level of unemployment amongst men, are less common today than in the 1930s, women workers as individuals are still seen as more 'disposable' than men. To that extent, argues Irene

Brueghel, the theory of the 'reserve army of labour' and the 'greater disposability' of female labour still holds.[39]

Women's paid work outside the home – however low paid – can provide women with economic independence and counteract the personal isolation often experienced by full-time housewives, whose work, as Del Jordan, the chronicler in Alice Munro's 'Heirs of the Living Body' realises, has been invisible to society and has gone unrecorded in the chronicles written by men. The recent growth of paid work carried out in the home breaks down the familiar dichotomy between unpaid, isolated domestic work and paid work done away from the home. Paid work done at home may offer opportunities for reconstituting the nature of the domestic space and gender relations.[40] At the same time, homeworking deprives women of the very considerable benefits they gain from the solidarity of the workplace and its possibilities for organisation and protest. This more negative view is reflected in Margaret Atwood's 'Bluebeard's Egg'. Working at home gives the heroine Sally the shadow of independence but not the substance, enabling her to cling to familiar stereotypes of femininity and disregard the possibility of change.

The development of mass markets in Western industrialised economies since the late nineteenth century has depended on reshaping women's role not only as employees involved in the distribution and sale of goods but also as consumers. In their role as housewives, women 'exchanged their role of producer for that of consumer, a role which requires commitment, responsibility and organizational skills. Women quickly learned to be "rational" in the business of consumption'.[41] The process of constructing the housewife as consumer gained new momentum with the expansion of the mass market for consumer goods in all Western countries after the Second World War. Corralled in the domestic space, women were sitting targets for the new media, radio and television, as well as the older weapon of the women's magazine. Advertisements reinforced the message that women's place was in the suburban home with her 'labour-saving' devices. Such devices could cut down on drudgery, but could also perpetuate it, by making possible ever higher standards of domestic hygiene and comfort to which the housewife could aspire.[42]

Stan Smith points out the collocation in *The Bell Jar* and *The Feminine Mystique* of media images and popularised Freudian psychology, perceived by Plath and Friedan as working together to persuade women into conformity in their roles in sustaining the capitalist economy as well as the nuclear family. In the opening part of *The Bell Jar*, Esther finds herself in the world of New York women's magazines, where she has to be seen consuming the products (fashion accessories, martinis) in keeping with the glamorous image being constructed of her. In the modern mass market, women are not only the targets of attempts to seduce them into consuming. They are also the bait used in the process of seduction, selling goods both to female and to male consumers. Esther's image is turned into a commodity, just as her creativity is turned by magazine editors into a marketing ploy, made over into a stereotype to entrap other women and slotted into place among the mass of film and magazine images of women which pervade *The Bell Jar*.

Many stereotyped images of femininity in the advertising media are aimed at the male consumer. Robin Adamson's study of car adverts in contemporary France shows how adverts through the use of metaphor (car-as-mistress) sell to men the idea of possessing the perfect woman. Such adverts work on both men and women by denying women their new and hard-won freedom. 'Men are being sold more strenuously than ever the fantasy of controlling the ultimate feminine, just as their hold over real women is being resisted.'[43] At the same time, the fantasy images of the ideal feminine which advertising purveys can serve to reinforce women's sense of their own inadequacy and inferiority for failing to match up to that ideal.

The images of advertising, as Michèle Barrett has convincingly argued, are something more than rhetoric. In the area of cultural production, 'forms of representation – words and images – are governed by genres, conventions, the presence of established modes of communication and so on'.[44] But these forms are not arbitrary. Images derive their power from the historically constituted real relations to which representation is linked. The power of the gender stereotype is demonstrated by the fact that it cannot be reversed in advertising images. You couldn't, according to Michèle Barrett, sell a car to a woman by perching a scantily-clad male model on the bonnet and displaying an admiring salesman opening the door to his female client. Women's sense of the proper place of their own bodies is otherwise pre-empted:

To put the matter simply, we can understand why female models may be more persuasive to male customers than *vice versa* only if we take account of a prior commoditization of women's bodies. Why this should have been so, and how, are clearly questions for historical analysis, but the fact remains that a connection has been established in which not only have women's bodies become commodities themselves (for instance in prostitution), but the association between them and consumerism has more generally taken hold. . . . [H]owever irrational or erroneous a particular stereotype may be thought, we do not have the option of eradicating it by the voluntary substitution of a different one.[45]

The manipulation of women as consumers and the exploitation of their bodies as commodities are characteristic of the modern capitalist economy. In socialism, the problems are different, such forms of exploitation not being fundamental to the workings of the socialist economy. Instead, in the German Democratic Republic, discussed in Patricia Harbord's contribution, the doctrine of sexual equality has enjoyed the status of a ruling ideology. Together with the demand for women workers in the labour force, the ideology of women's equality has inspired policies to integrate women fully into the economy and to improve their status in society. However, as Patricia Harbord shows, stereotyping by gender has still not been entirely eradicated. Paradoxically, the legislation which aims to assist working mothers reinforces the idea that mothers are the primary carers. Women have been encouraged to aspire to a career, while remaining largely responsible for the family – and only since the abortion law reform of 1972 have women had full control over their reproduction. The East German ideal of the socialist woman who works and manages a family is in itself a stereotype which creates pressures and problems of its own: emancipation has brought with it the pressure to be an all-round achiever.

ANSWERING BACK: TAKING ON THE STEREOTYPES

Women do not necessarily experience their subordination as oppressive. 'The ropes which bind women are the hardest to cut, because they are woven with so many of our own desires.'[46] Patriarchal ideology structures women's desires and expectations in such a way that women are often prepared to accept and to support mechanisms which deny them power and autonomy. Psychoanalytic theory has helped feminists understand this process of what has been termed collusion, 'women's willing consent and their internalization of oppression'.[47]

Several of the women writers discussed in the contributions illustrate through examples of fictional characters the 'tendency of women to accept male definitions of ourselves', as Coral Howells puts it. Jameson scathingly portrays in her novels women who live only through their husbands, acquiring status and influence by proxy. Alice Walker's novels, and Sylvia Plath's *The Bell Jar*, show mothers colluding with patriarchy to enmesh their daughters in the same traps which they themselves had been caught in. Margaret Atwood examines the mechanisms of collusion in some detail: 'Bluebeard's Egg' sets out the self-deceptions involved in a wife's construction of comforting romantic fantasies about her marriage.

The cosy illusions may stay in place, or they may begin to crack. Plath shows Esther coming to reject the 'year after year of doubleness and smiles and compromise'. But even if women do – for whatever reasons – refuse to collude any longer in their subordination, they are not necessarily able to protest against their situation and define their role anew.

In extreme circumstances the conflict between women's desires and the social identity imposed upon them by their environment – the sense of being divided within oneself – can lead to a lapse into silence and madness. Plath's character Esther falls silent and, seeking to destroy the 'negative self' which society has forced her to become, attempts suicide.

But women may also be actively, violently silenced, as in the myths discussed by Helga Geyer-Ryan. The symbolic and physical violence of men consolidates male power by destroying a woman's autonomy: the portrayal of silencing is a portrayal of castration, the destruction of women's creative power. The motif of the enforced silencing of the female voice recurs in Jennifer Birkett's discussion of traditions of black writing. The black writer Richard Wright portrays a black man who realises himself through the murder of two women, and Alice Walker takes up the same theme in her novel *The Three Lives of Grange Copeland*: Brownfield first silences Mem and then kills her.

Despite the obstacles, despite the cultural processes which tend to silence them, women can under certain circumstances find a voice. The emphasis on women overcoming silence and articulating their response to their situation, finding images and words to make visible what had been invisible, has been a recurrent one for the women's movement since the 1960s: feminism is seen as 'providing both a place and power to speak'.[48] A number of the contributions to this

volume focus on the ways in which women are able to develop a
sense of themselves as subjects and find a language to express that
subjectivity. Two themes in particular recur. The first is that of
women finding a voice through speaking or writing their autobiographies; the second is women's use of existing oral or written
traditions as a point of departure for their own self-expression.

Patricia Harbord's contribution focuses on spoken autobiography,
women's oral testimony which explicitly sets out to record women's
personal experience. Her analysis shows the significance of women
speaking their biographies, including those aspects which are
intimate and personal, in order to share them with others. Speaking
her experiences enhances the self-awareness of the individual woman
interviewed and helps to constitute her as a subject. Her actual
experiences are validated, and can be set against the expectations
and models of femininity with which she has been inculcated. At
the same time, since the recorded autobiographies are published and
read by others, they can become part of a public discourse which
can lead to change.

'The women's movement has shown that shared individual experience is an important part of the social discovery of a common condition.'[49] There has been no autonomous women's movement in the
GDR until very recently, but the impact on women there of the
publishing of *Guten Morgen, du Schöne* may be compared to the
impact on women's movements in the West of the practice of
consciousness-raising – an important innovation during the upsurge of
the new feminism of the late 1960s and 1970s.

In Western feminism, the recounting of individual women's stories
has led in two important directions. First, it became linked to a
movement to collect interviews and histories based on oral testimony,
which aim to recover the suppressed individual and collective memories of 'ordinary' people and thus to uncover their collective history.
'Appropriating one's own biography and studying those of others is
particularly important for us women, condemned as we are to an
existence devoid of history.'[50] The importance of such projects is
increased when they give a voice to women whose experience has
been doubly suppressed by class and racial discrimination.[51]

The second direction in which consciousness-raising could point
was towards the production of autobiographical texts by individual
women. Speaking is for most people easier than writing, and it
may be easier for women unaccustomed to analysing their own
experiences to find language in the context of a group discussion or

an interview than in the forms of written autobiography. But speaking one's experience may be a point of departure for creating written texts. Carolyn Heilbrun sees the oral exchanges of experience in consciousness-raising as having created the potential for new forms of female narrative:

> What became essential was for women to see themselves collectively, not individually, not caught in some individual erotic and familial plot and, inevitably, found wanting. . . . I suspect that female narratives will be found where women exchange stories, where they read and talk collectively of ambitions, and possibilities, and accomplishments.
>
> I do not believe that new stories will find their way into texts if they do not begin in oral exchanges among women in groups hearing and talking to one another. As long as women are isolated one from the other, not allowed to offer other women the most personal accounts of their lives, they will not be part of any narrative of their own.[52]

Christa Wolf, quoted by Patricia Harbord, also argues that autobiographical forms have a particular appeal for women writers. Hitherto denied a voice in literature and in society, women are more likely to turn to literary forms and techniques which allow them to express their experience spontaneously and directly. Autobiographical forms enable women to define what is important about their lives rather than having it defined for them.

But critics of autobiography as a genre have pointed out the pitfalls which can limit the political usefulness of autobiography and hence its usefulness as a vehicle for a woman writer to challenge the inherited world.[53] First, it is argued, traditional autobiography is a form which emphasises the individual at the expense of the social and historical context and can thus blind the writer and the reader to processes of historical change. Secondly, traditional autobiography tends to produce an account of a life as a seamless whole and the author as a coherent subject. This, it is argued, discourages the reader from forming alternative interpretations of reality and considering possible alternative paths which events could have taken and could take in the future.

Several of the women writers discussed in this volume write fiction rooted in autobiography, Alice Walker and Storm Jameson being two obvious examples; Storm Jameson, in addition, wrote 'straight' autobiography. Both writers seek to avoid the pitfalls just described and make connections between personal experience and history. In this way, they can be part of a process of 'collective recovery', an 'act of recovery for a particular social and cultural situation'.[54] Such autobiographical writing becomes less a form which constitutes and confirms the autonomy of the individual subject and more a fragment of collective history. In Storm Jameson's case, the author does not even attempt to create an image of herself which is coherent and free of contradictions. On the contrary, she sets out to deconstruct the various personae she sees herself as having assumed in the course of her life, tackling the 'smiling fake' which she sees as her public face. Her account is never closed off by assertions of self-mastery or self-comprehension.

Both Alice Walker and Storm Jameson recount their lives in the awareness of the traditions from which they come and with which they have to engage in order to gain their identity. The conflicts that result from feeling part of a tradition and yet not fully belonging to it can be painful, but also ultimately productive. Storm Jameson struggles with her middle-class Yorkshire family tradition, into which she as an intellectual, independent woman cannot fit, seeking to resolve the conflict through creating a fictionalized chronicle of her family history. Alice Walker as a black woman writer draws her strength both from the Afro-American tradition of male writing and from white feminist thinking, but sees herself and other black women writers as being outside both traditions and having to find a space for themselves.

Other women writers discussed in this volume also define themselves in relation to a range of cultural traditions. The appropriation and subverting of traditions is central to Coral Howells's study of short stories by three Canadian authors, who write as Canadians within a European tradition and as feminists within a male-dominated Canadian inheritance. They are marginal to both, but this sense of double marginality sharpens their efforts to subvert the traditions in order to create a version of history which writes women back into the picture.

Overcoming the obstacles to articulacy leads to women creating new accounts of their experience, making women visible in versions of history and redefining their place in society. Changing consciousness is a precondition of changing social realities. But what changes are needed, and how can they be achieved? Once women begin to reject the stereotypes of femininity, they may revolt against the entire order which embodies and perpetuates them: 'The pervasiveness of controls over women suggests that, as a group, their attempts to free themselves from their unequal position in society offer a particularly strong threat to existing social arrangements.'[55] The changes they may demand in the existing order of things can be all the more radical, and all the harder to achieve.

The main focus of the contributions in this volume is the analysis of the limitations on women imposed by patriarchy. But there are glimpses in a number of the contributions of attempts to define women in new terms and to sketch out on the basis of this vision the methods and the goal of feminist action.

Two fundamentally different models for feminist action can be traced through the history of feminism since the late eighteenth century. The first model tends to reject sexual differences as artificial constructs and sees the purpose of feminist action as the removal of the restrictions placed upon women by socially defined femininity. The goal is parity between the sexes: girls and boys should be brought up to do the same tasks and society should be reformed to share labour equally between men and women. This view is what is termed by Linda Gordon the 'androgynous' strand in the history of feminism:

> The eighteenth- and early nineteenth-century Enlightenment feminists, religious *and* secular, tended toward an androgynous vision of the fundamental humanity of men and women; that is, they emphasized the artificial imposition of femininity upon women as part of a system subordinating, constricting, and controlling them, with the result that 'women', as a historically created category, had had their capacities as well as their aspirations reduced.[56]

An alternative model of feminism is what Linda Gordon has termed the 'female moral superiority' view. This view takes as its starting point the fact that women's behaviour and capacities *are* different from men – regardless of whether the differences are innate or acquired. Socially defined femininity, according to this view, is not to be rejected wholesale: certain elements of femininity are deemed worthy to be preserved and celebrated. Applauding the caring and nurturing qualities which are associated with women, 'female moral superiority' feminism seeks not to abandon these qualities but to accord to them the importance and social value which they deserve. Throughout the history of feminism both modes of thought have existed side by side, often in tension with one another.[57] In Linda Gordon's view, a shift away from a predominance of the 'androgynous' view and towards the 'female superiority view' can be traced both for the first wave of feminism (beginning in the late eighteenth century and fading after the First World War) and the second wave of feminism since the 1960s.[58]

Both of these alternative approaches to feminist action are reflected in the contributions to this volume. Speaking from the perspective of the interwar years, Storm Jameson inclined towards a view of feminism's goals based on the assumption of a fundamental humanity common to both sexes. She formulated her vision of the new society in terms of equal roles and equal treatment for women and men: 'You'll have to make your plans for a re-made society on the basis of feminine labour alongside masculine.' She was sceptical of claims that women *as* women would by participating more in public affairs transform them: instead, women and men would transform society through a common struggle for justice and peace. Later, in the ruins of postwar Berlin, Jameson glimpsed a potential model for the new society: in this situation of crisis she saw new relationships being forged and parenting being undertaken by men and women collectively outside the traditional framework of the biological family.

Many examples could be quoted of the opposite tendency in contemporary feminist thought: the celebration of femininity, and in particular a celebration of motherhood.[59] Hélène Cixous, for instance, celebrates the creative qualities in women deriving from their mothering role:

> In woman there is always, more or less, something of 'the mother' repairing and feeding, resisting separation, a force that does not let itself be cut off but that runs codes ragged . . . it is not a captivating, clinging 'mother'; it is the equivoice that, touching you, affects you, pushes you away from your breast to come to language, that summons *your* strength . . . the part of you that puts space between yourself and pushes you to inscribe your woman's style in language. . . . Eternity: is voice mixed with milk.[60]

Alice Walker could be seen as belonging to this strand of contemporary feminism. She celebrates in her 'womanist manifesto' the role of mothers and their potential for building a new society. Against the more oppressive mother–daughter relationships portrayed in her novels discussed above, she develops an ideal of the mother-figure caring for her children, guiding them in the light of her knowledge of black women's traditions. In this vision, the new world will be shaped through the dialogue between mothers and female children.

Christa Wolf also belongs to the tendency in contemporary feminism voicing scepticism about the goal of equality between men and women. Rejecting a schematic equality, which is achievable, in her view, only on male terms, she sees the human qualities assigned historically to femininity as the repository of hope for the future, the foundations on which a more humane world will be built. Her model is not that of the mother–daughter relationship invoked by Alice Walker but, taking up a common theme of 'second wave' Western feminism, the ideal of sisterliness.

Whether the new world is shaped upon the lines of equality, matriarchy or sisterhood, the task of working towards the vision involves small steps forward, judging opportunities and using whatever means are offered by the historical moment. It involves women working for change in both the private and the public sphere. Historically, feminists have often seen the cause of women being furthered through women's participation in campaigns for social reform, socialism, ethnic emancipation or national liberation. In this volume we find examples of individual women becoming involved in pacifism (Storm Jameson) or the black Civil Rights Movement (Alice Walker) and the cause of building socialism (the women interviewed in *Guten Morgen, du Schöne*). Situations of radicalisation and social upheaval can offer opportunities for women to realise demands which would be unrealisable in more stable times.

But the struggle for the building of the new world brings constraints in its wake which threaten to entrap women in a new stereotype of the heroine and martyr to the cause. Often there has been associated with any upsurge of the feminist movement a tendency to celebrate the role of women in history and to seek examples of activism and heroism to inspire the present generation of devotees to the cause. Important though such rediscovery of female heroism is for a certain stage in feminist movements, there is a danger in reclaiming the past in order to transform it into feminist myth: such myth-making can 'reinforce a sense that women deserve notice only when they are active and heroic'.[61]

For the feminist who has rejected definitions of femininity in terms of passivity and weakness, assuming the heroic mode is a new kind of temptation. Confronted with the Fascist threat in the 1930s, Storm Jameson recognised in herself the desire to be a heroine of the anti-Fascist struggle, but saw also the dangers of total, uncritical commitment to any cause, however worthy. The temptation can be fought and the role can be refused. In Alice Walker's novel, Meridian rejects active leadership for a supporting role: 'giving the tales new birth', nourishing black consciousness through stories. And the women interviewed in the GDR in the 1970s are ready to admit that they cannot be the Heroine of the Workplace, the strong socialist mothers building the new order, and to recognise that the positive heroines are only made of paper. Every movement needs its myths, but they must also be subject to revision, scrutiny and criticism. Only if all stereotypes, feminist as well as patriarchal, are resisted, can women define themselves freely and liberate themselves from the forces which determine them.

Notes

1. Gerda Lerner, *The Creation of Patriarchy* (New York and Oxford: Oxford University Press, 1986) p. 239. The concept of patriarchy has been the subject of detailed debate within feminism. Discussion of and references to further reading on the concept of patriarchy can be found in Veronica Beechey, 'On Patriarchy', *Feminist Review*, vol. 3 (1979) pp. 66–82; Michèle Barrett, *Women's Oppression Today: Problems in Marxist Feminist Analysis* (London: Verso, 1980) pp. 10–19; Sheila Rowbotham, 'The Trouble with Patriarchy', and Sally Alexander and Barbara Taylor, 'In Defence of "Patriarchy" ', both in Raphael Samuel (ed.), *People's History and Socialist Theory* (London: Routledge and Kegan Paul, 1981); Drude Dahlerup, 'Confusing Concepts – Confusing Reality: a Theoretical Discussion of the Patriarchal State', in Anne Showstack Sassoon (ed.), *Women and the State: The Shifting Boundaries of Public and Private* (London and Melbourne: Hutchinson, 1987) pp. 93–103.
2. Chris Weedon, *Feminist Practice and Poststructuralist Theory* (Oxford: Basil Blackwell, 1987) p. 2.
3. Juliet Mitchell, *Psychoanalysis and Feminism* (Harmondsworth, Middx: Penguin, 1975) pp. 364–406.
4. Rowbotham, op. cit., p. 365; Toril Moi, *Sexual/Textual Politics: Feminist Literary Theory* (London and New York: Methuen, 1985) pp. 26, 81.
5. Linda Gordon, 'What's New in Women's History', in Teresa de Lauretis (ed.), *Feminist Studies/Critical Studies* (London: Macmillan, 1988) p. 24.

6. Lerner, op. cit, p. 239.

7. See the comparative survey of the enfranchisement of women in Europe, North America, Australia and New Zealand in Richard J. Evans, *The Feminists: Women's Emancipation Movements in Europe, America and Australasia, 1840–1920* (London and Sydney: Croom Helm, 1977) pp. 211–28. Euroamerican women were enfranchised in all the Canadian provinces by 1925 except in Quebec, where women gained the vote in 1940 (ibid., p. 224). In Britain, every man over 21 years had the right to vote from 1918 onwards. Women over 30 years could vote from 1918 onwards as long as they were qualified in their own right or through their husbands on the local government franchise by owning or occupying land or premises of an annual value of £5. See Billie Melman, *Women and the Popular Imagination in the Twenties* (London: Macmillan, 1988) p. 1; C. L. Mowat, *Britain between the Wars, 1918–1940* (London: Methuen, 1968) p. 6.

8. Evans, op. cit., pp. 206–11; Denise Riley, *'Am I That Name?': Feminism and the Category of 'Women' in History* (London: Macmillan, 1988) pp. 59–61.

9. Olive Banks, *Faces of Feminism: A Study of Feminism as a Social Movement* (Oxford: Martin Robertson, 1981) pp. 153–203; Riley, *'Am I That Name?'*, pp. 61–3.

10. See in particular Mitchell, op. cit.; Juliet Mitchell and Jacqueline Rose (eds), *Feminine Sexuality: Jacques Lacan and the école freudienne* (London: Macmillan, 1982); Nancy Chodorow, *The Reproduction of Mothering: Psychoanalysis and the Sociology of Gender* (Berkeley and Los Angeles, Cal. and London: University of California Press, 1978); Hélène Cixous and Catherine Clément, *La Jeune Née* (Paris: UGE, 1975), trs. Betsy Wing, *The Newly Born Woman* (Manchester: Manchester University Press, 1986); Julia Kristeva, *La Révolution du langage poétique* (Paris: Editions du Seuil, 1974), trs. Margaret Waller, *Revolution in Poetic Language* (New York: Columbia University Press, 1984); Luce Irigaray, *Speculum de l'autre femme* (Paris: Minuit, 1974), trs. *Speculum of the Other Woman* (Ithaca, N.Y.: Cornell University Press, 1985) and *Ce sexe qui n'en est pas un* (Paris: Minuit, 1979), trs. *This Sex Which Is Not One* (Ithaca, N.Y.: Cornell University Press, 1985). The most useful account of the work of Cixous, Kristeva and Irigaray is in Moi, op. cit.

11. 'Literary Work in the GDR: an Interview with Richard A. Zipser', in Hilary Pilkington (ed.), *The Fourth Dimension: Interviews with Christa Wolf* (London and New York: Verso, 1988) pp. 75–6.

12. 'From a Discussion at Ohio State University', in Pilkington (ed.), op. cit., p. 114.

13. Adrienne Rich, *On Lies, Secrets, and Silence: Selected Prose, 1966–1978* (London: Virago, 1980) p. 261.

14. Chodorow, op. cit., p. 209, cit. and discussed in Weedon, op. cit., pp. 60–1.

15. Ute Frevert, *Women in German History: From Bourgeois Emancipation to Sexual Liberation* (Oxford, Hamburg, New York: Berg, 1989) pp. 185–96.

16. Jane Lewis, *Women in England, 1870–1950: Sexual Divisions and Social Change* (Brighton: Wheatsheaf Books, and Bloomington, Ind.: Indiana University Press, 1984) pp. 97–102.
17. Andy Low, 'Recent Developments in English Studies at the Centre: the English Studies Group, 1978–9', in Stuart Hall *et al.* (eds), *Culture, Media, Language: Working Papers in Cultural Studies, 1972–79* (London: Hutchinson, 1980) p. 252.
18. On interwar population policies in a number of European countries see D. V. Glass, *Population Policies and Movements in Europe* (London: Frank Cass, 1967 [reprint of 1940 edition]); on Nazi Germany in particular, see Gisela Bock, ' "No Children At Any Cost": Perspectives on Compulsory Sterilization, Sexism and Racism in Nazi Germany', in Judith Friedlander, Blanche Wiesen Cook, Alice Kessler-Harris and Carroll Smith-Rosenberg (eds), *Women in Culture and Politics: A Century of Change* (Bloomington, Ind.: Indiana University Press, 1986).
19. Denise Riley, ' "The Free Mothers": Pronatalism and Working Women in Industry at the End of the Last War in Britain', *History Workshop*, no. 11 (Spring 1981) pp. 71–3; Karen Beck Skold, 'The Job He Left Behind: American Women in the Shipyards During World War II', in Carol R. Berkin and Clara M. Lovett (eds), *Women, War and Revolution* (New York and London: Holmes and Meier, 1980) p. 68; Ruth Roach Pierson, 'Women's Emancipation and the Recruitment of Women into the War Effort', in Roberta Hamilton and Michèle Barrett (eds), *The Politics of Diversity: Feminism, Marxism and Nationalism* (London: Verso, 1986) pp. 129–33.
20. Banks, op. cit., p. 203; Riley, ' "The Free Mothers" ', pp. 89–101; Rochelle Gatlin, *American Women Since 1945* (London: Macmillan, 1987) pp. 1–73.
21. Riley, ' "The Free Mothers" ', p. 110.
22. Gatlin, op. cit., p. 9.
23. Ibid., p. 8.
24. Banks, op. cit., pp. 210–11; Heather Jon Maroney, 'Embracing Motherhood: New Feminist Theory', in Hamilton and Barrett (eds), op. cit., pp. 400–1.
25. Betty Friedan, *The Feminine Mystique* (Harmondsworth, Middx: Penguin, 1986) p. 47.
26. Gatlin, op. cit., p. 30.
27. Friedan, op. cit., p. 59.
28. Cit. Gatlin, op. cit., p. 13.
29. Margaret Atwood, 'Significant Moments in the Life of My Mother', in *Bluebeard's Egg and Other Stories* (London: Virago, 1988), p. 29.
30. Ibid., p. 28.
31. Lewis, op. cit., pp. 194–5.
32. Ibid., p. 163.
33. Ibid., pp. 102, 200.
34. Atina Grossmann, '*Girlkultur* or Thoroughly Rationalized Female: a New Woman in Weimar Germany?', in Friedlander *et al.* (eds), op. cit.; Banks, op. cit., pp. 180–202; on similar developments in women's

34   *Determined Women*

employment patterns in urban France in the interwar period, see James
F. McMillan, *Housewife or Harlot: The Place of Women in French
Society, 1870–1940* (Brighton: Harvester, 1981) pp. 117–19.
35. Berkin and Lovett (eds), op. cit., pp. 5–7; see also references in note
    19 above.
36. Banks, op. cit., pp. 210–23.
37. On black women in the postwar economy, see Paula Giddings, *When
    and Where I Enter: The Impact of Black Women on Race and Sex
    in America* (New York: Bantam Books, 1984) pp. 238–58, 325–35,
    344–57.
38. Irene Brueghel, 'Women as a Reserve Army of Labour: a Note on
    Recent British Experience', in Elizabeth Whitelegg *et al.* (eds), *The
    Changing Experience of Women* (Oxford: Basil Blackwell, 1982)
    pp. 114–15.
39. Ibid., pp. 107, 114–15.
40. Suzanne Mackenzie, 'Women's Responses to Economic Restructuring:
    Changing Gender, Changing Space', in Hamilton and Barrett (eds),
    op. cit., pp. 89–100.
41. Gabriella Turnaturi, 'Between Public and Private: the Birth of the
    Professional Housewife and the Female Consumer', in Sassoon (ed.),
    op. cit., p. 266.
42. Patricia Connelly and Martha MacDonald, 'Women's Work: Domestic
    and Wage Labour in a Nova Scotia Community', in Hamilton and
    Barrett (eds), op. cit., pp. 58–9; Hélène Strohl, 'Inside and Outside
    the Home: How Our Lives Have Changed Through Domestic Automa-
    tion', in Sassoon (ed.), op. cit., pp. 279–82.
43. Sheila Rowbotham, 'The Trouble with Patriarchy', in Samuel (ed.),
    op. cit., p. 368.
44. Michèle Barrett, 'Ideology and the Cultural Production of Gender', in
    Judith Newton and Deborah Rosenfelt (eds), *Feminist Criticism and
    Social Change: Sex, Class and Race in Literature and Culture* (New
    York and London: Methuen, 1985) p. 70.
45. Ibid., p. 70.
46. Sally Alexander and Barbara Taylor, 'In Defence of "Patriarchy"', in
    Samuel (ed.), op. cit., p. 372.
47. Barrett, *Women's Oppression Today*, pp. 110–11.
48. Carolyn Steedman, Cathy Urwin and Valerie Walkerdine (eds), *Langu-
    age, Gender and Childhood* (London and Boston, Mass.: Routledge
    and Kegan Paul, 1985) p. 205.
49. Jean McCrindle and Sheila Rowbotham (eds), *Dutiful Daughters:
    Women Talk about their Lives* (Harmondsworth, Middx: Penguin,
    1977) p. 9.
50. Translated from Erika Adolphy, 'Einige Gedanken zu der Frage:
    Was ist eigentlich eine normale Frauenbiographie?', in *Beiträge 7 zur
    feministischen Theorie und Praxis* (Munich: Verlag Frauenoffensive,
    1982) p. 9.
51. Beverley Bryan, Stella Dadzie and Suzanne Scafe, *The Heart of the
    Race: Black Women's Lives in Britain* (London: Virago, 1985) p. 2.

52. Carolyn G. Heilbrun, *Writing a Woman's Life* (London: Women's Press, 1989) p. 46.
53. Simon Dentith and Philip Dodd, 'The Uses of Autobiography', *Literature and History*, vol. 14, no. 1 (Spring 1988) pp. 4–22.
54. Ibid., p. 10.
55. Bridget Hutter and Gillian Williams (eds), *Controlling Women: The Normal and the Deviant* (London: Croom Helm, 1981) p. 11.
56. Gordon, op. cit., p. 26.
57. Riley, '*Am I that Name?*', pp. 2, 59.
58. Gordon, op. cit., pp. 26–7.
59. Maroney, op. cit., pp. 399–405.
60. Cixous and Clément, op. cit., trs. Wing, p. 93.
61. Berkin and Lovett (eds), op. cit., p. 3.

Bibliography

Adolphy, Erika, 'Einige Gedanken zu der Frage: Was ist eigentlich eine normale Frauenbiographie?', in *Beiträge 7 zur feministischen Theorie und Praxis* (Munich: Verlag Frauenoffensive, 1982).

Alexander, Sally, 'Women, Class and Sexual Differences in the 1830s and 1940s: Some Reflections on the Writing of a Feminist History', *History Workshop*, no. 17 (Spring 1984) pp. 125–49.

Atwood, Margaret, *Bluebeard's Egg and Other Stories* (London: Virago, 1988).

Banks, Olive, *Faces of Feminism: A Study of Feminism as a Social Movement* (Oxford: Martin Robertson, 1981).

Barrett, Michèle, *Women's Oppression Today: Problems in Marxist Feminist Analysis* (London: Verso, 1980).

Beechey, Veronica, 'On Patriarchy', *Feminist Review*, vol. 3 (1979) pp. 66–82.

Berkin, Carol R. and Clara M. Lovett (eds), *Women, War and Revolution* (New York and London: Holmes and Meier, 1980).

Bryan, Beverley, Stella Dadzie and Suzanne Scafe, *The Heart of the Race: Black Women's Lives in Britain* (London: Virago, 1985).

Chodorow, Nancy, *The Reproduction of Mothering: Psychoanalysis and the Sociology of Gender* (Berkeley and Los Angeles, Cal. and London: University of California Press, 1978).

Cixous, Hélène and Catherine Clément, *La Jeune Née* (Paris: UGE, 1975), trs. Betsy Wing, *The Newly Born Woman* (Manchester: Manchester University Press, 1986).

Dentith, Simon and Philip Dodd, 'The Uses of Autobiography', *Literature and History*, vol. 14, no. 1 (Spring 1988) pp. 4–22.

Evans, Richard J., *The Feminists: Women's Emancipation Movements in Europe, America and Australasia, 1840–1920* (London and Sydney: Croom Helm, 1977).

Frevert, Ute, *Women in German History: From Bourgeois Emancipation to Sexual Liberation* (Oxford, Hamburg, New York: Berg, 1989).

Friedan, Betty, *The Feminine Mystique* (Harmondsworth, Middx: Penguin, 1986).

Friedlander, Judith, Blanche Wiesen Cook, Alice Kessler-Harris and Carroll Smith-Rosenberg (eds), *Women in Culture and Politics: A Century of Change* (Bloomington, Ind.: Indiana University Press, 1986).

Gatlin, Rochelle, *American Women Since 1945* (London: Macmillan, 1987).

Giddings, Paula, *When and Where I Enter: The Impact of Black Women on Race and Sex in America* (New York: Bantam Books, 1984).

Glass, David V., *Population Policies and Movements in Europe* (London: Frank Cass, 1967 [reprint of original edition, 1940]).

Hall, Stuart *et al.* (eds), *Culture, Media, Language: Working Papers in Cultural Studies, 1972–9* (London: Hutchinson, 1980).

Hamilton, Roberta and Michèle Barrett (eds), *The Politics of Diversity: Feminism, Marxism and Nationalism* (London: Verso, 1986).

Heilbrun, Carolyn G., *Writing a Woman's Life* (London: Women's Press, 1989).

Hutter, Bridget and Gillian Williams (eds), *Controlling Women: The Normal and the Deviant* (London: Croom Helm, 1981).

Irigaray, Luce, *Ce sexe qui n'en est pas un* (Paris: Minuit, 1979) trs. *This Sex Which Is Not One* (Ithaca, N.Y.: Cornell University Press, 1985).

——, *Speculum de l'autre femme* (Paris: Minuit, 1974) trs. *Speculum of the Other Woman* (Ithaca, N.Y.: Cornell University Press, 1985).

Kristeva, Julia, *La Révolution du langage poétique* (Paris: Editions du Seuil, 1974) trs. Margaret Waller, *Revolution in Poetic Language* (New York: Columbia University Press, 1984).

Lauretis, Teresa de (ed.), *Feminist Studies/Critical Studies* (London: Macmillan, 1988).

Lerner, Gerda, *The Creation of Patriarchy* (New York and Oxford: Oxford University Press, 1986).

Lewis, Jane, *Women in England, 1870–1950: Sexual Divisions and Social Change* (Brighton: Wheatsheaf Books, and Bloomington, Ind.: Indiana University Press, 1984).

McCrindle, Jean and Sheila Rowbotham (eds), *Dutiful Daughters: Women Talk about their Lives* (Harmondsworth, Middx: Penguin, 1977).

McMillan, James F., *Housewife or Harlot: The Place of Women in French Society, 1870–1940* (Brighton: Harvester, 1981).

Melman, Billie, *Women and the Popular Imagination in the Twenties* (London: Macmillan, 1988).

Mitchell, Juliet, *Psychoanalysis and Feminism* (Harmondsworth, Middx: Penguin, 1975).

Mitchell, Juliet and Jacqueline Rose (eds), *Feminine Sexuality: Jacques Lacan and the école freudienne* (London: Macmillan, 1982).

Moi, Toril, *Sexual/Textual Politics: Feminist Literary Theory* (London and New York: Methuen, 1985).

Mowat, Charles Loch, *Britain Between the Wars, 1918–1940* (London: Methuen, 1968).

Newton, Judith and Deborah Rosenfelt (eds), *Feminist Criticism and Social*

Change: Sex, Class and Race in Literature and Culture (New York and London: Methuen, 1985).

Pilkington, Hilary (ed.), *The Fourth Dimension: Interviews with Christa Wolf* (London and New York: Verso, 1988).

Rich, Adrienne, *On Lies, Secrets, and Silence: Selected Prose, 1966–1978* (London: Virago, 1980).

Riley, Denise, *'Am I That Name?': Feminism and the Category of 'Women' in History* (London: Macmillan, 1988).

——, ' "The Free Mothers": Pronatalism and Working Women in Industry at the End of the Last War in Britain', *History Workshop*, no. 11 (Spring 1981) pp. 58–118.

Samuel, Raphael (ed.), *People's History and Socialist Theory* (London: Routledge and Kegan Paul, 1981).

Sassoon, Anne Showstack (ed.), *Women and the State: The Shifting Boundaries of Public and Private* (London and Melbourne: Hutchinson, 1987).

Steedman, Carolyn, Cathy Urwin and Valerie Walkerdine (eds), *Language, Gender and Childhood* (London and Boston, Mass.: Routledge and Kegan Paul, 1985).

Weedon, Chris, *Feminist Practice and Poststructuralist Theory* (Oxford: Basil Blackwell, 1987).

Whitelegg, Elizabeth *et al.* (eds), *The Changing Experience of Women* (Oxford: Basil Blackwell, 1982).

2 Private Fantasy and Public Intervention: Girls' Reading in Weimar Germany

ELIZABETH HARVEY

But there has to be a happy ending . . .

One of the most important influences in an adolescent girl's environment, according to a Halle girls' grammar school teacher in 1932, was her reading.[2] Other contemporary observers affirmed not only the importance of reading in adolescent girls' lives, but also the central role played in girls' reading habits by certain categories of popular fiction. This essay sets out to examine the reading habits of girls in their early teens in Weimar Germany. It analyses typical examples of the books they read, concentrating on the genre known as the *Backfischbuch*, and asks why such works were so popular.

The portrayal of adolescent femininity in the *Backfischbuch* is the main focus of the essay. First, the books' teenage heroines are compared with other images of femininity current in Weimar Germany, where young women's lives were changing rapidly, and girls growing up were confronted with conflicting ideas about women's role. Secondly, the essay explores the readers' response to these books and to their models of idealised girlhood, in an attempt to cast light on the mentality of girls in Weimar Germany and their attitude to the social changes they were witnessing.

Reading, that private refuge for the adolescent, had become in this period a matter for public scrutiny and concern. This public interest in what girls read provides a third focus for the essay, which looks at the way in which public authorities and professionals investigated and sought to influence girls' reading habits.

Recent work on popular literature has stressed that the way such literature works upon its readers is fluid, complex and uncertain – that it is not simply a matter of norms being imposed upon a naïve, passive readership.[3] Rather than being mere receptacles for the ideology purveyed by the texts, readers may respond actively to them, selecting, rejecting and ignoring certain aspects of the texts according to personal preference, manipulating the texts rather than being manipulated by them.[4] Analysts of popular fiction for women have focused attention on the way in which female readers relate to the fantasy portrayals of heterosexual relationships which the mass-circulation romance provides.[5] Here too, newer interpretations have moved away from a simple model according to which mass market romance diverts and stifles the discontent and the aspirations of its female readership. It has been suggested that, far from lulling their readers into a state of uncritical passivity, the pleasurable fantasies offered by pulp fiction may keep alive their readers' Utopian longings for a better world.[6] The present essay explores some of these arguments by looking at the specific case of young female readers in Weimar Germany.

GIRLS IN WEIMAR GERMANY

Girls in Weimar Germany were growing up at a time of dramatic social change. In the great metropolises, above all in the capital Berlin, new social mores and cultural forms were taking root on the basis of a modern industrial economy. Life in rural areas – about a third of the population lived in small towns and villages of under 2000 inhabitants[7] – was not transformed so rapidly, but alterations in lifestyle and patterns of behaviour, which gave city-dwellers the sense they were living in an age of innovation and upheaval, also penetrated to rural parts of Germany.

Throughout Germany, women benefited from changes in their political and legal status. The advent of the Weimar Republic saw the introduction of a number of reforms which had been demanded by the feminist movement before the First World War.[8] Some of the barriers to women's equality had been broken down in the war years, when women had virtually overnight been forced to take on responsibilities in the home and in the factories which had until then been the monopoly of men. The political collapse of the Empire and the setting up of the Republic took reform several steps further. From November 1918 onwards, women had the vote on equal terms with men, and the principle of sexual equality was laid down in the

1919 constitution. For the first time, women were elected to seats in the Reichstag and the representative bodies of the federal states and local governments.

Educational opportunities grew, above all for the middle classes: girls' secondary education expanded and an increasing number of middle-class girls went on to study at university.[9] Equipped with their new qualifications, such women moved into new spheres of employment. Access opened up to the medical and legal professions and to public service careers, and women became increasingly visible in the public sphere as journalists, writers, artists and scientists. Domestic service in urban households was on the decline, as working-class girls increasingly opted for jobs in factories and shops which gave better pay for shorter hours. At the same time, in the towns and the cities the expansion of employment in offices and shops opened up new categories of jobs for women.[10]

To contemporaries, the new job opportunities for women outside the home seemed to be part of a more comprehensive transformation of women's role in society. Portrayals of women in the media reflected these perceptions. The New Woman was economically independent and sexually liberated; her aspirations no longer centred on, though they did not necessarily exclude, the traditional goals of marriage and child-bearing. The image was a potent one and seemed to sum up what was essentially modern about postwar society. The New Woman was functional, efficient, unfettered by traditions and conventions, and she was not tied to any particular national identity: she was a symbol of a new international urban culture.[11]

Behind the image of the advertisements and magazines lay a more complex reality. The Weimar period can be seen as a 'high-water mark of classical modernity',[12] a period of experiment and creativity. But it was also a period overshadowed by economic crisis in which large sections of society experienced financial insecurity and impoverishment. If more girls and women were in employment outside the home in the Weimar period than they had been before the war, this was not simply evidence of the arrival of the New Woman seeking economic independence and personal fulfilment. Paid work outside the home was for many women an economic necessity. Middle-class families impoverished by postwar inflation could no longer afford to keep their daughters at home. Many adult women, married as well as single or widowed, were forced to earn their living, and much of the work they did was badly paid and low in status. Even in the new fields of white-collar employment, a separate sphere of relatively menial 'women's jobs' was quickly created and the opportunities for career advancement were limited. Overall, discrimination against women on the labour market in terms of wages and job opportunities continued and such discrimination was frequently reflected – despite the Weimar Constitution's commitment to sexual equality – in the employment and labour market policy of the Weimar state.[13]

The continuing pressure of traditional role expectations, together with the continual crises which afflicted the Weimar economy and labour market, limited the freedom and equality which women could achieve in practice. But even this partial emancipation was enough to alarm traditionalists. The churches and conservative parties declared that the family was under threat and that the declining birthrate would mean that Germany would be depopulated within a few generations. They called for a reinstatement of the ideal of motherhood. Mothers, they said, should be honoured for their service to society, and girls should be brought up with motherhood as their highest goal in life.[14]

A range of conflicting images of womanhood thus confronted girls growing up in this period. Images of the New Woman in her various guises – capable colleague and comrade of men, liberated sexual partner, citizen, bluestocking, sports champion – vied in the media with images of the vamp and the prostitute and with the traditional images of housewife and mother propagated by the churches and conservative organisations. Girls in Weimar Germany faced a doubly uncertain future: uncertain both in terms of what the future would bring politically and economically, and in terms of their role as women in that future. Was what girls read liable to influence them in this situation of uncertainty in a particular direction? Did girls look in their reading for guidance and orientation, or for something else?

GIRLS' READING HABITS

First, how much did girls actually read at all? Some girls clearly had more free time and money than others to spend on leisure activities. Middle-class girls who stayed on longer at school had more time at their disposal in the form of school holidays than their working-class counterparts, who usually started a job or training at fourteen and were liable to be called on to help with the housework at home.

Even so, the reduction of working hours compared with the pre-1918 period meant that most girls had some opportunity for leisure activities.

Reading was only one leisure pursuit among many, and the Weimar period was a time when a great variety of leisure activities was available for young people of both sexes. Many of these leisure activities took place outside the home: going out to the cinema or dance-hall, or taking part with a club or youth group in sports, folk-dancing, music-making, hiking or camping excursions. It was the great age of youth organisations, which attracted a growing number of girls as well as boys.[15] However, reading still remained popular with the young of both sexes, and contemporary commentators sometimes expressed surprise at the extent to which the taste for reading had not been affected by the rise of alternative sources of modern entertainment such as the cinema and the radio.

Educationalists and teachers convinced of the importance of reading habits undertook a number of investigations into what young people read, partly out of scientific interest, as part of the then prevalent fashion for studying the psychology and lifestyle of youth, but partly with the aim of influencing and channelling these interests in certain directions.

One survey was carried out on the instructions of the Prussian Ministry of Welfare and was particularly interested in establishing the extent to which young people read 'trash' or 'filth' (*Schund* and *Schmutz*);[16] other surveys, carried out by librarians and teachers on their own initiative, were more broadly interested in young people's reading habits and literary tastes.[17] The surveys collected and evaluated a variety of material: observations made by youth leaders and youth welfare workers,[18] statistics of books borrowed from children's libraries,[19] and essays and book-lists written by pupils at the request of teachers.[20]

The surveys showed that girls' reading tastes varied according to age. Up to the age of about 9 or 10, the reading preferences and habits of boys and girls emerged as broadly similar, children of both sexes enjoying children's stories of a general kind, fairy tales and adventure stories.[21] Thereafter, from the age of 10 or 11 upwards, girls' reading preferences were found to diverge sharply from those of boys. Boys tended to read adventure stories, Westerns and crime stories. Girls, while also reading these types of book, largely concentrated their attention on 'girls' stories', and in particular the type of book known as the *Backfischbuch*.

The *Backfischbuch* derived its name from the term *Backfisch*, an expression dating back to the sixteenth century meaning, literally, half-grown fish, and referring to a young adolescent girl. According to a traditional rhyme, translated here literally: 'At fourteen years and seven weeks the *Backfisch* is born, at seventeen years and three weeks the *Backfisch* age is past.'[22] The term *Backfischbuch* refers to a type of novel written in the late nineteenth and early twentieth centuries for a young female audience, featuring girls in their mid-teens and their experiences as they grow to womanhood. The plot of a novel of this sort typically entails its youthful heroine getting into scrapes and difficulties but emerging happily at the end as a poised young woman ready for marriage.

The surveys found that the reading of young girls of all social classes in the age range 11–14 years was dominated by the *Backfischbuch*.[23] Of Lippert's sample of trainee kindergarten teachers questioned between 1925 and 1928 about their earlier reading habits, only 8 out of the 94 participants had never read a *Backfischbuch*, and 14 others said that they never enjoyed them, giving them up after having read one or two.[24] Three-quarters of the sample had gone through a phase of enthusiasm for this type of book. Another survey carried out in the late 1920s of 74 female pupils at an elementary school (*Volksschule*) found that nearly half of the girls questioned said that *Backfischbücher* were their favourite reading matter.[25] Boys who read *Backfischbücher* were, while not unknown, the exception.[26]

The taste for the *Backfischbuch* tended to be relatively short-lived. In Lippert's survey, the 52 participants who gave precise details had read them for no longer than a year, mostly between the ages of 10 and 15. The taste for the *Backfischbuch* faded, according to the surveys, at about the age of 15 or 16. Older teenage girls tended to share the reading tastes of adult women.[27] These preferences ranged widely and included bestselling authors of the day such as Rudolf Herzog, Ludwig Ganghofer, Paul Keller and Agnes Günther as well as the works of Storm, Gottfried Keller and Thomas Mann.[28] However, the most common reading matter of the girls in their late teens was found to be light romantic fiction, ranging from the works of Marlitt, Heimburg and Anny Wothe to those of the prolific and phenomenally successful Hedwig Courths-Mahler.[29] In addition to these more respectable types of romance – labelled by educationalists and literary critics as 'kitsch' – older girls in some surveys admitted to reading what social reformers labelled as 'trash': novelettes with titles promising a lurid mixture of kidnap, seduction and violence such as *Banished on the Wedding Eve*, *Without Ring and Myrtle: The Tale of a Woman Betrayed*, *Röschen, the Baron's Daughter, or Immured in the Madhouse*.[30] Younger girls might share their books with their brothers, and older girls with their mothers; but girls in the key phase of early adolescence had reading tastes all of their own, centred, as we have seen, on the *Backfischbuch*.

THE *BACKFISCHBUCH* AND ITS HEROINES

In the early nineteenth century, stories for girls were conceived and written as manuals of moral instruction; their heroines were presented as models of virtue for the reader to imitate.[31] The *Backfischroman* grew out of this tradition, but it represented a new departure. Its emergence was marked by the publication of Clementine Helm's *Backfischchens Leiden und Freuden* (1863), followed over the next decades by a number of works in a similar vein, most notably Emmy von Rhoden's *Der Trotzkopf* (1885). While the moral didacticism of the earlier girls' stories was still evident in the new books, they set out to entertain as well as to instruct the reader.[32]

The style of the *Backfischbuch* moved to some extent with the times, but its distinctive features of plot and character remained constant. This can be shown by looking at three of the most popular *Backfischbücher*, which were published over a period of sixty years.

Clementine Helm's *Backfischchens Leiden und Freuden* ('A Young Girl's Sorrows and Joys') was published in 1863 and reached its 79th edition in 1919.[33] Though it was out of print by the end of the 1920s, this classic *Backfischbuch* continued to be read more than sixty years after its original publication. Its heroine is Grete, a 15-year-old farmer's daughter, who is sent to stay with her aunt in Berlin in order to be educated and introduced into 'society'. She is warmhearted, honest and affectionate, but naïve, crude and uncultivated in her behaviour, a country bumpkin who has to be told to clean her fingernails, wipe her feet and not drink out of her saucer. The other main character is drawn as a contrast. Sophisticated cousin Eugenie, daughter of a diplomat, who also comes to be educated by the aunt in Berlin, knows what is expected of her by polite society; indeed, she is precociously well-versed in the ways of the adult world. She is also selfish, bold and wilful. She blasphemes at the breakfast table, plays practical jokes and makes fun of the moralising of her aunt and cousin. But, as Grete, the narrator, emphasises, under this alarming exterior lie better qualities. 'She had the most kind and loving heart, that was only too clear, but under what layers of dross lay those grains of gold!'[34] The story shows the miraculous changes wrought in both Grete and Eugenie under the wise guidance of their aunt and through the influence they have on each other. The norms and values underpinning conventional femininity are upheld and reinforced by the teenage heroines through a process of mutual policing. Grete (eagerly) learns about dress sense, personal hygiene, good taste, deportment, correct manners and the art of conversation. Eugenie (reluctantly) learns to be considerate towards others. But Eugenie is only finally and completely tamed with help from outside the household: her transformation is hastened by the experience of falling in love and seeing her fiancé injured.[35] The 'Amazon'[36] vanishes, giving way to the loving wife and mother. Grete, meanwhile, completes her education, leaves Berlin and returns home to her parents. She becomes engaged to a man she has met in Berlin and the book ends with her getting married and leaving the village again for her new life as the wife of a civil servant. Upward social mobility through a good match is the reward for her conformity.

The plot of Emmy von Rhoden's *Der Trotzkopf* ('Stubborn Ilse'), published 22 years after *Backfischchens Leiden und Freuden*, resembles that of the earlier work in a number of obvious respects. Ilse, the 15-year-old heroine, is the daughter of a landowner; her mother is dead and Ilse has grown up on the farm as a tomboy. Her father remarries and her stepmother, after trying and failing to take Ilse in hand, decides to send her to boarding-school. Like Eugenie, Ilse is a rebel and is not in the least interested in becoming a lady. Wise teachers and kind friends teach Ilse better manners, though here too a traumatic experience – witnessing the death of a young fellow-pupil – is needed to bring out the good in Ilse's nature. The reader discovers that beneath the stubbornness lie sterling qualities. Transformed into a young lady, she parts from her schoolfriends and returns home, where she meets a young lawyer – a friend of the family – and becomes engaged. Revealing views on woman's proper vocation are expressed by Ilse and her mother on the news that Ilse's friend Nellie, too, has become engaged:

'Nellie is getting married to Dr Althoff!' exclaimed Ilse joyfully.
'Now she won't become a teacher.'

'No, she won't. Now she has a place where she really belongs,' responded Frau Macket.[37]

Der Trotzkopf was a spectacular success, running into 45 editions by 1906, continued in print throughout the 1920s, and was still, in an abridged version, in print in the 1980s; a 1979 edition had illustrations depicting girls in 'modern' dress in the style of the 1950s and replacing horse-drawn carriages with cars.[38] When it was first published, the book was praised by reviewers for the psychological realism of its portrayal of the main character.[39] The success of the book led to the publication of sequels[40] in response to readers' demand to know 'what happened next' to Ilse. The development from single book to saga, and the success of the sequels, suggests a craving on the part of readers for a reinforcement of the message purveyed by the original: that conformity brings happiness.

Trotzkopf showed the potential of the series formula, and other authors soon copied the pattern. Else Ury's 'Nesthäkchen' sequence, published in the years after the First World War, was planned from the beginning as a series taking the heroine Annemarie, known as 'Nesthäkchen' ('baby of the family') virtually from cradle to grave.[41] The high point of the popularity of the 'Nesthäkchen' series came towards the end of the Weimar Republic,[42] but the series was still in print in 1987; according to the publishers, the number of copies of 'Nesthäkchen' books sold to date is nearly 7 million.[43]

In terms of the development of the *Backfischbuch*, the key volume of the series is *Nesthäkchens Backfischzeit* ('Annemarie's Schooldays'), the fourth volume of the sequence, published in 1920. To a reader in the 1920s, *Nesthäkchens Backfischzeit* would have seemed clearly more up-to-date than *Trotzkopf* or *Backfischchens Leiden und Freuden*. Its plot and setting reflect some of the social changes brought about by the war, and the book is more firmly rooted in an identifiable political and social context. The First World War and its revolutionary aftermath, together with the economic problems stemming from Germany's defeat, impinged on the daily life of middle-class girls far more than political events had ever done in prewar days, and this fact finds expression in the book. The reader finds Annemarie and her friends battling with coal shortages, power cuts and transport problems. Pupils are admonished by their geography teacher that 'young people in particular must do all they can to restore the fortunes of the fatherland after the terrible blows it has suffered'.[44] This element of contemporary realism is also evident in the portrayal of the heroine, who takes her schoolwork seriously and makes career plans – she aims to become a doctor like her father and join him in the family practice. Instead of ending with the heroine's engagement, the book finishes with her leaving school after passing her *Abitur*.

But *Nesthäkchens Backfischzeit* still resembles the earlier *Backfischbücher* in its structure and, most of all, in the message which it purveys. Annemarie is yet another hothead needing to be tamed. The plot is structured as a series of episodes in which the heroine is revealed as brave, warm-hearted and unaffected, but at the same time impulsive, stubborn, clumsy, naïve, and the ringleader in schoolgirl pranks. Moreover, the story's apparently modern emphasis on schooling and preparation for a career is deceptive. Although Annemarie's school education and her career plans are stressed, the development of her motherly qualities and feminine attributes is equally important: she is portrayed as being naturally 'good with children', but deeply ignorant of housewifely skills. She must learn her Tacitus, but she must also learn tidiness, punctuality and how to iron baby clothes. The episodes highlighting the heroine's education in domestic accomplishments prepare the reader for the message that a woman's priorities do not lie ultimately in academic achievement. If this message is hinted at rather than spelled out in *Nesthäkchens Backfischzeit*, it is made abundantly clear in the sequel. In *Nesthäkchen fliegt aus dem Nest* ('Annemarie Grows Up'), academic goals are firmly subordinated to motherhood. Annemarie abandons her medical training and her plans to become her father's assistant in his practice in order to marry an already qualified doctor and to have children.[45]

The plots of the three *Backfischbücher* outlined above conform to a fairly simple pattern.[46] The story presents the heroine growing from girlhood to womanhood. She confronts practical problems in the outside world: the plots all involve a temporary removal of the heroine from her parental home and show her dealing with travel and unfamiliar environments. At the same time, her emotional life and social relationships go through various phases of confusion, unhappiness and collisions with authority. In these collisions, it is authority and convention which triumph.

The heroine of the *Backfischbuch* successfully surmounts the obstacles in her path and reaches the state of womanhood; however, she does so without losing the attractive qualities of her girlhood. Her initial freshness, spontaneity and exuberance are retained.

Grete, Eugenie, Ilse and Annemarie thus achieve the impossible: they change while remaining essentially the same. Expressed positively, they combine the sophistication of maturity with the naturalness of youth. Expressed negatively, they never grow up. The twin ideals of youth and of womanhood are the two poles around which the *Backfischbuch* revolves. By exploring the conflict between these two ideals and showing at the same time the possibility of their reconciliation, the *Backfischbuch* addresses, in its stereotyped fashion, a problem central to conventional female adolescent identity.

The concept of youth as a phase of life in its own right between childhood and adulthood became established in industrialised Western countries in the second half of the nineteenth century.[47] The middle classes were increasingly keeping their offspring in full-time education beyond the age at which working-class children became economically independent. This enhanced dependency of the middle-class young on their parents provided the basis for a new and ambivalent image of adolescence. On the one hand adolescence was portrayed negatively as a crisis-ridden phase of life, during which young people needed particular care and guidance. On the other hand, the idea of youth was elevated to a positive myth of spontaneity and creativity. Youth, enjoying a privileged freedom as yet unfettered by adult responsibilities, appeared to represent a force for the renewal of a jaded bourgeois world.

Girls were peripheral to the myth of youth: images of adolescence focused on the young male. Although the *Backfischroman* was one sign that the new thinking on adolescence could be applied to girls as well as to boys, the assumption was still that female adolescent existence was to follow laws different from those of the male. The heroines of the *Backfischromane* have in the course of their adolescence to internalise the conventions of the adult female role. The faults in their behaviour, presented as characteristic of girls in adolescence – tomboyishness, toughness, carelessness, a lack of self-control and lack of tact – show up as all the more crass when measured against the ideal of femininity promoted by the books. A neat and attractive appearance, a graceful and serene demeanour, a discreet, patient and tactful manner and a pure and selfless character were a woman's way to happiness. Boldness, assertiveness and rebelliousness, qualities associated with the male-biased myth of youth, fitted more easily with the conventional image of adult masculinity than with that of femininity. The process whereby adolescent heroines suppress the instincts and overcome the impulses of their youth is far more radical than the changes required to turn an untamed, rebellious adolescent hero into an adult figure of strength, authority and responsibility. Girls, implies the *Backfisch-buch*, have to put in more work than boys if they are to negotiate the transition to adulthood successfully.

The heroines' growing conformity to the female ideal brings them benefits. Paradoxically, they are shown to achieve individual fulfilment by subordinating aspects of their individuality, in return for which they gain love, social approval and success. The ultimate reward is a desirable husband.

Interestingly, some of the qualities of girlhood have to be retained. The teenager's rebelliousness gives way to the adult woman's confident assumption of her proper role, but her youthful energy has not been extinguished – just channelled in the right direction. The girlish qualities she retains – 'spontaneity', 'unaffectedness', but above all a sexual innocence which continues right up to engagement and marriage – are presented as an essential part of what makes the heroines attractive to men. In its celebration of eternal girlhood, the *Backfischbuch* refuses to be explicit, or even realistic, when it comes to depicting the relationship between heroine and future husband: the details of the love affair are left out, just as marriage itself remains a *terra incognita*. In *Backfischchens Leiden und Freuden*, the future husbands of Eugenie and of Grete are represented not as sexual beings, but as guardian angels who protect the heroines from the threat of sexuality. Baron Senft rescues Eugenie from a rampaging bull; Dr Hausmann rescues Grete from sinister 'gypsies'. Through these heroic deeds, they establish their legitimate sexual rights to the heroines.

The attempted reconciliation in the *Backfischbuch* of the ideal of youth and that of femininity produces a highly circumscribed model for its readers to follow. The feminine ideal portrayed in the books is admittedly not a purely passive one: the *Backfischbuch* insists that women should be active, energetic subjects who can take initiatives and bear responsibilities. But nor is the ideal one of authentic power. The books continually promote the idea that woman's role lies in caring for others and in 'spreading happiness' in those around them, as Trotzkopf is described as doing by her future mother-in-law.[48] The exuberant adolescent will make a cheerful, healthy mother – as Eugenie does in *Backfischchens Leiden und Freuden*. Compared to the image of the adult and powerful New Woman, the *Backfischbuch* ideal with its wholesome innocence and girlishness could – and, to at least some of its contemporary critics, did – appear positively infantile.

CRITICS OF THE *BACKFISCHBUCH*

The popularity of the *Backfischbuch* did not go unremarked by contemporary educationalists and social reformers, who on the whole found the 'addiction'[49] to the books among a large number of young readers a cause for concern.

The first widely publicised blast against the *Backfischbuch* was sounded by Heinrich Wolgast, a leading figure in the movement to reform children's literature which arose shortly before the turn of the century.[50] Wolgast rejected the *Backfischbuch* on aesthetic grounds within the context of his controversial attack on all literature written specially for children: such books, he argued, could never satisfy the criteria of genuine art.

In the Weimar period, the controversy over Wolgast's ideas continued to rage. Within the general debate over what children should and should not be reading, over how to suppress trash, discourage kitsch and encourage Art, critics were by no means united on what, if anything, was wrong with the *Backfischbuch* and what, if anything, should be done to change girls' reading habits.

Some children's book experts and teachers actually defended the *Backfischbuch*. While not works of art, they argued, such works were essentially harmless and should be tolerated. 'The addiction to the *Backfischbuch* must be allowed to work itself out naturally', argued Elisabeth Lippert.[51] The *Backfischbuch* did no lasting damage, any more than puberty itself did lasting damage to the character.[52] Another teacher went further than this and dared to assert that girls experienced 'spiritual enrichment' from reading the books, which – she pointed out – 'are all full of noble-heartedness and other exemplary moral qualities'.[53]

However, these were the opinions of a minority; the majority of commentators condemned the *Backfischbuch*. This was partly for aesthetic reasons: the books allegedly ruined the taste of their readers. The *Backfischbücher* were 'saccharine pieces of kitsch, totally lacking in authenticity'.[54] The plots were artificial and didactic, the characters were stereotypes, and the style was wordy and pretentious.[55] These features of the *Backfischbuch*, argued the critics, were also to be found in the romantic fiction beloved of adult women. A taste for the one led to a taste for the other: a craving for the adolescent kitsch of the *Backfischbuch* led to an addiction to adult kitsch – in other words, an addiction to sexual fantasy – and an incapacity to appreciate the emotional depth of good literature.[56]

More to the point, the *Backfischbuch* – in the critics' view – gave girls a false picture of society and of women's role. What was seen as false varied according to the critic's particular ideological standpoint. Some critics did not object so much to the fact that the books presented marriage and motherhood as a girl's most important goals in life as to the way in which they presented marriage and motherhood unrealistically, encouraging girls to expect that love at first sight would be inevitably followed by an engagement followed by marital and maternal bliss. Others objected to the emphasis on marriage and motherhood as such and the ways the books ignored the other roles played in society by women as citizens[57] and as workers.[58] This demand for a broader view of women's role could be based on the one hand on a feminist perception of girls' needs as individuals: girls had to take their jobs seriously in order to achieve the economic and psychological independence vital for their happiness. On the other hand, this demand for a less narrow-minded portrayal of women could stem from a more corporatist view of the duty owed by women as a group to the nation in times of adversity.

> All the heroines of these novels [*Backfischbücher*, E. H.] . . . eventually find fulfilment as wives and mothers. These duties often seem too narrow to us today. We are children of a great crisis of the fatherland and we must have many more women and girls who put themselves at the service of a cause outside and above the family.[59]

Those who condemned the *Backfischbücher* agreed that it was difficult to discourage girls from reading them. Perhaps one of the main attractions of reading for young people was its privacy and its freedom from control by adults. This was in contrast to other areas of leisure activity, which often involved constraints – for instance, many girls' clubs and groups were run by adults, and juveniles' access to cinemas and other public entertainments was regulated and restricted by law. Reading, on the other hand, was virtually impossible to control and supervise: this was what made it so potentially dangerous.

This difficulty did not deter those educationalists and social reformers who sought to promote 'good' literature for young people. Where 'trash' literature was concerned, their campaign included a drive for censorship legislation, and a law was passed in 1926 to ban books and publications liable to corrupt the innocent mind or unduly excite the juvenile emotions and imagination. But *Backfischbücher* could not be banned, since they were not deemed to fall within the categories of 'trash' and 'filth' which the censorship legislation sought to eradicate. Nor were informal bans likely to have much effect. Even if parents responded to appeals to withhold such books from their children,[60] such parental bans were likely to be ignored.

There was a consensus among critics that girls should be encouraged at school and through youth organisations to read something better: but what should that be? Some saw the final goal as the eradication of 'books for girls' altogether.[61] This goal was justified not only in the aesthetic terms used twenty years earlier by Wolgast, but also on feminist grounds. Girls' books, according to Gina Kaus, reinforced stereotypical gender roles; if girls and boys read more of the same books, this would encourage girls to see their tasks in life as similar to those of men.[62] Kaus did not believe that it would be possible in the short term to eradicate books for girls, but she thought that it was feasible in the meantime to create better products than the *Backfischbuch*.

On this point Kaus was in agreement with those who were convinced of the legitimacy of a literature targeted at adolescent girls and merely wanted to see better books on offer. Such books, they thought, would have to be better written and reflect the social changes that had taken place since the First World War.[63] A girl's job should not, as it was for instance in *Trotzkopf*, be presented as a temporary occupation to be abandoned as soon as a girl found a husband. Marriage should not be shown as a meal ticket. Kaus called upon authors to undertake a critical portrayal of the patriarchy and to make it clear to their readers that 'in an age and in a country dominated by male privilege, the very fact of being a girl poses a major problem'. A book should show life as it is, not as it should be: and a book for girls should be 'an appeal to the new generation of women that they must do things better than their elders'.[64]

Whether or not in response to such calls for an alternative to the *Backfischbuch*, some authors did set out to provide the sort of book

Kaus was calling for.[65] But to what extent was there a real demand for such alternatives to the *Backfischbuch*?

'WHAT WE WANT FROM A BOOK': READERS' OPINIONS AND RESPONSES

Wilhelm Fronemann, a children's book expert, proclaimed in 1930 that there were signs of a shift in girls' reading tastes away from the *Backfischbuch*. He welcomed this change and ascribed it to the efforts of teachers, youth workers and the youth movement to enlighten the public about the depraving effects of trash literature and to promote better reading matter.[66]

Certainly there was evidence to show that there was a minority of readers who did not like the *Backfischbuch*. As was pointed out above, a quarter of Lippert's sample of trainee kindergarten teachers had either never read the books or never liked them. Critical views from young female readers who rejected such books were to be found among the winning entries of an essay competition for 15–20-year-old girls held in 1931 by the Association of German Booksellers on the subject '*Was wir vom Buch erwarten*' ('What we want from a book').[67] A number of the winning entries expressed dissatisfaction with the *Backfischbuch* and demanded more relevant and challenging books for the modern girl.

A commercial trainee, aged 16, wrote in her essay:

A lot of girls in our class still read *Backfischbücher* which are completely out of touch with the times we live in. I would like books which show us girls who are neither stunningly clever nor amazingly beautiful, but who have to prepare themselves for a career like we do. As a commercial trainee, I would like best of all a story about the development of girl trainees like myself, similar to Otto Ernst's story *The Young Asmus Semper*. . . . I really enjoyed that book, and some of my classmates too liked it better than those old-fashioned girls' boarding-school stories.[68]

A vocational school pupil, aged 17, wrote:

I don't like books for young girls. A girl today doesn't want to be treated more softly than a boy. She has to struggle and to work, just as a young man does, she has to know just as much

as he does what the real world is like, she has to know how to
fight for herself. Those are the sort of books we need – books
that tell us these things![69]

What these two girls demanded from books was realism rather
than fantasy: practical information and guidance about the modern
world in which they lived and worked. Such demands may have
been specifically influenced by the anti-kitsch campaign waged by
the youth movement and youth organisations which condemned
sentimentality in literature. The opinions expressed by these two
girls also convey a sense of that determination and practicality which
was part of the image of the New Woman. The new ethos of hard-
headedness may have left its mark on the preferences of at least
some young female readers.

However, the readers who wanted something new and different
remained a minority. Other commentators writing in the final phase
of the Weimar Republic could find no sign of the general rejection
of the *Backfischbuch* asserted by Fronemann.[70] Sielaff, in his article
of 1933, made the explicit point that girls' lives had changed but
their reading habits had not. The more 'progressive' new books for
girls were not particularly popular with their target audience,
however favourably they might be reviewed by educationalists. On
the contrary:

> even today, girls want to read the same books as their mothers
> and grandmothers read. Their new leisure activities, such as
> sports, and their much more relaxed social contacts with members
> of the opposite sex, have not changed this taste in books at all.[71]

One way of explaining the continuing appeal of the *Backfischbuch*
would be to argue that the demand was determined by the supply:
girls read the books because they were so readily available.
Mothers, aunts and grandmothers gave their daughters, nieces and
granddaughters the books they had enjoyed when young as Christmas
and birthday presents. Girls found it easy to borrow the books from
their classmates. Indeed, there was some peer group pressure to
read them: the *Backfischbuch* formed part of the classroom culture
in the higher forms of the *Volksschule*.[72]

Ease of reading may have been a further factor. Reading the
books was enjoyable and relaxing because it was so effortless. The

contents of the book were predictable, so that the text could easily be skimmed.[73]

In addition to these factors, contemporary commentators favoured psychological explanations of the books' popularity. The growing interest in adolescent psychology which characterised the Weimar period in Germany led to observers of girls' reading habits plunging into long disquisitions on the female adolescent mind: one study began with a 26-page analysis of the psychology of pre-puberty in females.[74] Others, more usefully, extended their analysis to cover social as well as psychological factors.

One need which the *Backfischbuch* was thought to have met was a thirst on the part of pre-teenage and early teenage girls for information about the world of adults. 'The *Backfischbuch* becomes the major source of information for girls in this particular age group', wrote Lippert of the twelve-year-old schoolgirls she observed.[75] The books provided, for instance, descriptions (however inauthentic and out of date) of unfamiliar social mileux, giving working-class readers a glimpse of the world of the middle and upper classes and the life of a society lady. In the words of one working-class reader – as reported by a social researcher in a study of working-class culture published in 1933 – 'You can learn from boarding-school stories and from Courths-Mahler novels about high society, you get education, you learn how to achieve happiness!'[76]

At another level, the books offered down-to-earth advice on matters of daily life couched in an easily absorbed form 'suited to the mentality of the *Backfisch*', as one observer remarked.[77] In *Nesthäkchens Backfischzeit* and in *Backfischchens Leiden und Freuden* readers can find useful tips about travelling around Germany on one's own by train (Clementine Helm also adds useful hints on how to pack a suitcase properly), about how not to lose one's way in a strange town and generally cope on one's own in an unfamiliar environment. In addition, the *Backfischbuch* is full of observations – however banal or shallow – about psychology and behaviour. Readers learn, for instance, how unwise it is to judge people from first impressions, how experiences can transform people, how jealousy can affect friendships, how well-intentioned actions can backfire and so on.

All this does not amount to the 'realism' and relevance to modern life demanded by the girls whose essays were quoted above. The books may have satisfied a certain level of curiosity about the workings of the adult world among younger and less sophisticated readers. At the same time, since their real information content was modest and, in the cases of the older books, out of date, the more important reasons for their appeal probably lay elsewhere.

More essential than the 'hard' information provided by the *Backfischbuch* were the images and fantasies which it offered its readers. On the one hand, these images were near enough to the age and experience of the readers to enable readers to relate the content ,of the texts to their own lives. The typical 12-year-old readers could find in the *Backfischbuch* a wide range of 15- and 16-year-old female characters into whose fictional lives they could project themselves. Moreover, the individual heroine in herself offered a range of models corresponding to the various stages of development of her character. This offered something for everyone, or for the same reader according to her mood.

The way in which readers could choose how they read the text and with which heroines they identified gave them some latitude in how they interpreted the message of the *Backfischbuch*. The *Backfischbuch* puts across a definite picture of what femininity should be and of the social role to which a girl should aspire, but reading the *Backfischbuch* was not a simple process of swallowing its message whole. Readers could approach the text in different ways. On the one hand, the reader could, by projecting herself into the character of the heroine as she emerges into adulthood, identify with the image of one who has successfully achieved the ideal of womanhood and is beloved by all.[78] On the other hand, she could equally well identify and empathise with the characters as they rebel against conventional femininity, and perhaps console herself that in her own real-life failures to measure up to ideal standards of behaviour she was not alone – the lapses of the fictional heroines being, after all, far worse.

> If I had got into mischief at school and I was feeling sorry about it afterwards, I would always seize upon books like that, to see if I was perhaps at least not quite as bad as the madcap portrayed in the book. If that was the case, that made me feel better. I read *Nesthäkchens Backfischzeit* again and again for that reason.[79]

At another level, the texts were sufficiently remote from 'real life' to encourage girls to read them not only as a source of guidance but also for pleasure, as fantasies.

All these 'ideal' types of girl play jolly tricks, talk in the language of adolescent girls, make and break friendships – in short, they seem to lead the life of a true *Backfisch* such as fourteen-year-old working-class girls dream of but can never experience.[80]

As fantasy, the *Backfischbuch* could take its readers outside their social milieu and beyond the limits of their personal experience. Reading about the adventurous, carefree life of the middle-class *Backfisch* could provide for the working-class girl reader relaxation and escape. It offered her entertainment in the form of vicariously experienced grand emotions and dramatic occurrences. In the words of one reader: 'The book is fun to read and there are so many interesting things that happen in it. At home everything is always so boring.'[81]

The books could also trigger off in the reader fantasies of an alternative existence:

> If things had gone really badly for me when I was fourteen, if I had suddenly become an orphan, I would have believed that someone would have offered me a position as a lady's companion, where I would have been welcomed into the household with warmth and affection, where everything would have been delightful and that I would have then met a young lawyer or officer and got engaged and my happiness would have been complete.[82]

The fantasy recounted here combines a number of elements: the adolescent fantasy of freedom from parental control and from one's social origins (which obviously has little to do with the reality of being orphaned), the fantasy of upward social mobility (rags to riches) and the romantic fantasy of being swept off one's feet by Prince Charming in the guise of a lawyer or officer. Such a fantasy could represent a three-fold escape from the mundane existence of a working-class girl living at home and going out to work: from family pressures, from unpleasant work and from personal isolation.

CONCLUSION: POPULAR FICTION AND GIRLS'
EXPERIENCE

By the early 1930s, it was clear that efforts by educationalists to
promote alternatives to the clichéd *Backfischbücher* had failed. The
'outmoded' books were far from dead. Their appeal rested, as we
have seen, on a number of features: their insights into the adult
world, their teenage heroines with whom readers could identify,
and their highly-coloured depictions of milieux and situations remote
from the experience of the reader.

The *Backfischbücher* were popular before the Weimar period, and
after the end of the Republic in 1933 the books continued to be
reprinted; as we have seen above, some are still in print today. To
that extent their appeal can be seen as transcending historical
epochs. But their popularity in the Weimar period is particularly
significant, both in view of the public campaign at that time to
discourage the books and in view of the way in which the traditional
norms of femininity purveyed by the books were being challenged
in society as a whole.

The fact that traditional ideas about woman's role were being
challenged may actually have sustained the books' appeal. Girls
growing up in the Weimar period were faced with uncertainties
concerning their personal fortunes and their social role which
contrasted sharply with the cosy certainties of the *Backfischbuch*. It
is tempting to see the continuing popularity of the *Backfischbuch*
in this context: the books provided images of a conflict-free world
at a time of turmoil, a haven where the dilemmas of the real world
vanished.

To suggest reasons for the books' appeal is one thing: it is another
to assert that the books had specific effects on their readers. Did
the books persuade their readers to reject emancipation? Did they
reinforce the idea that girls succeeded in life through becoming not
independent New Women, but well-adjusted wives?

The evidence quoted already on readers' responses to the books
offers some clues as to the books' impact. It has been suggested
above that there was a certain openness in popular fiction for girls,
enabling the reader to read the text in a number of different ways
according to her desires and needs. The example of the girl who
read *Nesthäkchens Backfischzeit* to console herself suggests that the
books, far from encouraging the reader to work harder at conforming
to the feminine ideal, could make a reader feel better about not

conforming. Seen from this angle, the books may not have been imposing a norm of femininity very effectively at all. But readers' responses still seem to have remained within conventional parameters. The girl who got into mischief at school is confirmed by her reading that 'mischief' is wrong, and particularly bad in a girl. The girl with fantasies of cutting adrift as an 'orphan' still sees herself landing safely in marriage. The fantasies which the books might nourish were strictly circumscribed. Readers could find little in them to encourage dreams of power and freedom: the stories may have the heroines mildly flouting convention, but not indulging in serious rebellions or real adventures. Through the narrowness of the world it depicts, the *Backfischbuch* may have obstructed and deflected young women's claims for a clear identity as individuals and as citizens, as distinct from an identity defined in relation to the family. As such, they may have encouraged an acceptance of an emancipation which remained only partial and which was to be curbed once more following the collapse of the Republic.

For the fictional *Backfisch*, there are no insoluble problems and no uncomfortable decisions to be made. Everything comes easily – even (for 'Nesthäkchen') in the midst of postwar economic chaos. Girls growing up in Weimar Germany were, of course, coping with dilemmas and problems far removed from the fictional world of the *Backfischbuch*, and their outlook was shaped by such experiences as well as by their reading. However, any pragmatism born of experience seems to have co-existed with a longing for comforting fantasies.

The resulting layers of contradictory ideas which could co-exist in a teenage reader's mind are illustrated in the account by a 15-year-old commercial trainee of a book she had read. In contrast to the typical *Backfischbuch*, this (unnamed) book had portrayed some of the problems facing girls trying to make their way in the competitive modern world. The reader's response to this more 'modern' book effectively expresses the ambivalence of her views. By her own account, the book had an important impact on her life: its sobering realism proved a trigger for her to take an important decision. She acknowledges this, at the same time as she recognises her continuing longing for the world of fantasy, for the world of the *Backfischbuch* and of romantic fiction:

> Then one day I finally read the book. It was boring at the beginning. It was all about the sense of duty, about work and so on. I skimmed over the pages. Then suddenly the book began

to mean something to me. All at once. In one scene the girl said
'I want to go into films, do you hear? I want to be a film star!'
Now I was hooked by the story. I read and read, and I can still
remember just how I felt: it is your life which is here in this
book. But it all turned out disastrously. The girl went into films,
she got some parts, but she never became famous, and after a
short time she was nothing but a miserable burden on humanity.
That really shook me. Slowly I began to change my ideas and I
abandoned the fantastic dreams I had had. No one else had
managed to persuade me, but that book did: I took up a proper
job, quite cheerfully and with no regrets. Since then my favourite
books are those about young people growing up. Similar to the
one I've described. But it shouldn't always be such a sad ending.
If I had written the story the girl needn't have had such an awful
fate. Perhaps she could have returned to her family, perhaps she
could have found happiness as a woman after all. But there has
to be a happy ending . . .[83]

   The contradictions here are obvious, and they may offer important
clues to the thinking of the 'modern girl' of Weimar Germany. This
girl has ambitions to do something exciting and not just to wait for
Prince Charming. Still, influenced by her reading and her knowledge
of the real world of work, she ultimately takes a realistic view about
her chances and settles for a 'sensible' job. But beneath the
independence and pragmatism expressed here, the old patterns of
thought are still evident. If the new solutions were to fail and the
career of the New Woman end in disaster, she would like to think
that the old roles could still be waiting for her.
   The reader just quoted, juggling with her conflicting hopes and
aspirations, may represent a mode of thinking that was typical of
girls' outlook in Weimar Germany. One way for girls to react to
the contradictions facing them was to live and think in different
modes simultaneously. But if such thinking *was* a feature of girls'
outlook in the Weimar period, it was not necessarily restricted to
that time. Conventional images of girlhood in pursuit of the feminine
ideal are still among the messages which bombard girls growing up
today. In West Germany, *Trotzkopf* and *Nesthäkchen* are still being
read. Amidst the profusion of images of feminine existence available,
the teenage heroines of the *Backfischbuch* offer clear models for
girls to follow in their quest of the feminine ideal. Modern readers

may be able to appropriate these books in their own way, read them as entertainment and even read them against the grain to subvert some of their message. But in general the tendency of such books is to reassure the reader that the traditional feminine role is still an option. Changing social realities and alternative models of feminine identity seem to erode the power of that fantasy slowly, if at all.

Notes

1. *Was wir vom Buch erwarten: Antworten von 15–20jährigen Mädchen* (Leipzig: Börsenverein der Deutschen Buchhändler, 1931) p. 26. All translations into English are my own.
2. Hilde Mothes-Eilts, 'Die Umwelt des Großstadtmädchens aus der Bildungsschicht', in H. Siemering and E. Spranger (eds), *Weibliche Jugend in unserer Zeit* (Leipzig: Quelle und Meyer, 1932) p. 13.
3. Valerie Walkerdine, 'Some Day My Prince Will Come: Young Girls and the Preparation for Adolescent Sexuality', in Angela McRobbie and Mica Nava (eds), *Gender and Generation* (London: Macmillan, 1984) p. 164.
4. Jean Radford (ed.), *The Progress of Romance: The Politics of Popular Fiction* (London and New York: Routledge and Kegan Paul, 1986) pp. 14–15.
5. Ann Barr Snitow, 'Mass Market Romance: Pornography for Women is Different', in A. Snitow, C. Stansell and S. Thompson (eds), *Powers of Desire: The Politics of Sexuality* (New York: Monthly Review Press, 1983) pp. 246–7.
6. Helga Geyer-Ryan, *Der andere Roman: Versuch über die verdrängte Ästhetik des Populären* (Wilhelmshaven: Heinrichshofen, 1978) pp. 160–3.
7. In 1925, the figure was 35.6 per cent; in 1933, 32.9 per cent. J. Falter, T. Lindenberger and S. Schumann, *Wahlen und Abstimmungen in der Weimarer Republik* (Munich: Verlag C. H. Beck, 1986) p. 35.
8. On the German feminist movement, see Richard J. Evans, *The Feminist Movement in Germany, 1894–1933* (London: Sage Publications, 1976). On women in Weimar Germany see Ute Frevert, *Women in German History: From Bourgeois Emancipation to Sexual Liberation* (Oxford, New York and Hamburg: Berg, 1989) pp. 168–204; Renate Bridenthal and Claudia Koonz, 'Beyond Kinder, Küche, Kirche: Weimar Women in Politics and Work', in R. Bridenthal, A. Grossmann and M. Kaplan (eds), *When Biology Became Destiny: Women in Weimar and Nazi Germany* (New York: Monthly Review Press, 1984) pp. 33–65.
9. Kristine von Soden, 'Frauen in der Wissenschaft', in K. von Soden

and Maruta Schmidt (eds), *Neue Frauen: Die zwanziger Jahre* (Berlin: Elefanten Press, 1988) pp. 125–7.

10. Frevert, op. cit., pp. 180–4.

11. Atina Grossmann, 'Girlkultur or Thoroughly Rationalized Female: a New Woman in Weimar Germany?', in Judith Friedlander, Blanche Wiesen Cook, Alice Kessler-Harris and Carroll Smith-Rosenberg (eds), *Women in Culture and Politics: A Century of Change* (Bloomington, Ind.: Indiana University Press, 1986) pp. 62–7.

12. Detlev J. K. Peukert, 'The Weimar Republic: Old and New Perspectives', *German History*, vol. 6, no. 2 (1988) p. 139.

13. Karin Hausen, 'Unemployment also Hits Women: the New and the Old Woman on the Dark Side of the Golden Twenties in Germany', in Peter D. Stachura (ed.), *Unemployment and the Great Depression in Weimar Germany* (London: Macmillan, 1986) pp. 88–102.

14. Karin Hausen, 'Mütter, Söhne und der Markt der Symbole und Waren: Der deutsche Muttertag, 1923–33', in H. Medick and D. Sabean (eds), *Emotionen und materielle Interessen: Sozialanthropologische und historische Beiträge zur Familienforschung* (Göttingen: Vandenhoeck and Ruprecht, 1984).

15. Martin Klaus, *Mädchenerziehung zur Zeit der faschistischen Herrschaft in Deutschland: Der Bund Deutscher Mädel*, vol. 1 (Frankfurt-am-Main: dipa-Verlag, 1983) pp. 323–7.

16. Hertha Siemering, 'Was liest unsere Jugend? Ergebnisse einer amtlichen Umfrage', in H. Siemering, E. Barschak and W. Gensch, *Was liest unsere Jugend? Ergebnisse von Feststellungen an Schulen aller Gattungen und Erziehungsanstalten sowie bei Jugendorganisationen und Jugendlichen* (Berlin: R. von Decker's Verlag, G. Schenck, 1930) p. 7.

17. See, for example, Mechthildis Berchem, 'Was liest unsere heranwachsende weibliche Jugend', *Die Bücherwelt*, vol. 17 (1920) pp. 106–7; Albrecht Rumpf, *Kind und Buch: Das Lieblingsbuch der deutschen Jugend zwischen 9 und 16 Jahren aufgrund einer Umfrage*, 2nd edn (Berlin and Bonn: Ferd. Dümmlers Verlag, 1928).

18. Siemering, 'Was liest unsere Jugend?'.

19. Berchem, op. cit.; Rumpf, op. cit.

20. F. Weigl, 'Buchinteressen von Schülerinnen der Berufsfortbildungsschule', *Die deutsche Berufsschule*, vol. 38, no. 11 (1929) pp. 302–9; Erna Barschak, 'Die weibliche werktätige Jugend und das Buch', in Siemering *et al.*, *Was liest unsere Jugend?*; Lotte Schrader, 'Vom Backfischbuch', *Hamburger Lehrerzeitung*, vol. 9, no. 50 (1930) pp. 954–6; Elisabeth Lippert, *Der Lesestoff der Mädchen in der Vorpubertät* (Erfurt: Verlag Kurt Stenger, 1931).

21. Rumpf, op. cit., pp. 60–73.

22. 'Vierzehn Jahre sieben Wochen ist der Backfisch ausgekrochen, Siebzehn Jahre Wochen drei ist die Backfischzeit vorbei.' Susanne Zahn, 'Die Backfische und das Backfischbuch', appendix to reprint of Clementine Helm, *Backfischchens Leiden und Freuden* (Berlin: Weismann Verlag, 1981) p. 275.

23. Barschak, op. cit., pp. 21–2; Willy Gensch, 'Was liest unsere Jugend?

Ergebnisse einer Umfrage', in Siemering *et al.*, *Was liest unsere Jugend?*, p. 71.
24. Lippert, op. cit., pp. 77, 105.
25. Schrader, op. cit., p. 954.
26. Rumpf, op. cit., p. 67; Lippert, op. cit., pp. 100–1.
27. Weigl, op. cit., p. 306; Barschak, op. cit., pp. 26–8.
28. On girls' preference for these authors see Erich Sielaff, *Jungmädchenliteratur* (Stettin: Verlag Bücherei und Bildungspflege, 1933) p. 14; Rumpf, op. cit., p. 121; Gensch, op. cit., pp. 71–2. On Rudolf Herzog, Paul Keller and other bestselling authors of interwar period see Marianne Weil (ed.), *Wehrwolf und Biene Maja: Der deutsche Bücherschrank zwischen den Kriegen* (Berlin: Verlag Ästhetik und Kommunikation, 1986). On Agnes Günther see Dorothee Bayer, 'Falsche Innerlichkeit', in Gerhard Schmidt-Henkel (ed.), *Trivialliteratur* (Berlin: Literarisches Kolloquium, 1964) pp. 218–38.
29. On these authors see Dorothee Bayer, *Der triviale Familien- und Liebesroman im 20. Jahrhundert* (Tübingen: Tübinger Vereinigung für Volkskunde, 1963); Gabriele Strecker, *Frauenträume, Frauentränen: Über den unterhaltenden deutschen Frauenroman* (Weilheim: Otto Wilhelm Barth Verlag, 1969).
30. *Vertrieben am Hochzeitsabend; Ohne Ring und Myrthe: der Roman einer Verführten; Röschen, das Grafenkind, oder verschleppt ins Irrenhaus*, listed by Siemering, 'Was liest unsere Jugend', in Siemering *et al.*, *Was liest unsere Jugend?*, pp. 9–10.
31. Dagmar Grenz, *Mädchenliteratur: Von den moralisch-belehrenden Schriften im 18. Jahrhundert bis zur Herausbildung der Backfischliteratur im 19. Jahrhundert* (Stuttgart: Metzler, 1981) pp. 214–15; Malte Dahrendorf, *Das Mädchenbuch und seine Leserin: Versuch über ein Kapitel 'trivialer' Jugendlektüre* (Hamburg: Verlag für Buchmarkt-Forschung, 1970) pp. 34–9; Susanne Zahn, *Töchterleben: Studien zur Sozialgeschichte der Mädchenliteratur* (Frankfurt-am-Main: dipa-Verlag, 1983) pp. 101–27.
32. Else Schaeffer, 'Das Jungmädchenbuch. Einige Gedanken aus der Praxis', *Hefte für Büchereiwesen*, vol. 16, no. 1 (1932–3) p. 13.
33. C. Helm, *Backfischchens Leiden und Freuden: Eine Erzählung für junge Mädchen*, reprinted with commentary by Susanne Zahn (Berlin: Weismann Verlag, 1981). Detailed discussion of the work in Lippert, op. cit., pp. 34–43, and Zahn, op. cit., pp. 135–55.
34. Helm, op. cit., p. 91.
35. On the motif of 'tomboy-taming' in British girls' stories of the nineteenth century, e.g. the stories of L. T. Meade, see Mary Cadogan and Patricia Craig, *You're a Brick, Angela!: The Girls' Story, 1839–1985* (London: Gollancz, 1986) pp. 53–4, and Gill Frith, ' "The Time of Your Life": the Meaning of the School Story', in Carolyn Steedman, Cathy Urwin and Valerie Walkerdine (eds), *Language, Gender and Childhood* (London and Boston, Mass.: Routledge and Kegan Paul, 1985) pp. 127–8.
36. Helm, op. cit., p. 161.

64   *Determined Women*

37. E. von Rhoden, *Der Trotzkopf: Eine Pensionsgeschichte für junge Mädchen*, 86th edn (Stuttgart: Gustav Weise Verlag, 1925) p. 242.
38. Dagmar Grenz, ' "Der Trotzkopf" – ein Bestseller damals und heute', *Informationen Jugendliteratur und Medien*, vol. 34, no. 3 (1983) pp. 50–3; Zahn, op. cit., pp. 197–222; Dietmar Grieser, *Die kleinen Helden: Kinderbuchfiguren und ihre Vorbilder* (Munich: Langen Müller Verlag, 1987) pp. 191–7; example of 'modern' illustrations in E. von Rhoden, *Der Trotzkopf* (Hanover: Neuer Jugendschriften-Verlag, 1979).
39. Grenz, ' "Der Trotzkopf" ', pp. 52–3.
40. Some of these sequels were written by the model for Trotzkopf herself, Emmy von Rhoden's daughter Else Wildhagen. See Grieser, op. cit., pp. 191–7. On the sequels see Zahn, op. cit., pp. 222–63. Else Wildhagen was the author of *Trotzkopfs Brautzeit: Eine Erzählung für junge Mädchen* (Stuttgart: Gustav Weise Verlag, 1892), *Aus Trotzkopfs Ehe: Eine Erzählung für Mädchen* (Stuttgart: Gustav Weise Verlag, 1895), *Trotzkopfs Nachkommen – Eine neues Geschlecht* (Stuttgart: Gustav Weise Verlag, 1930). An 'unauthorised' sequel was written by Suse La Chappelle Roobol, *Trotzkopf als Großmutter* (Stuttgart: Gustav Weise Verlag, 1905), while Marie von Felseneck used the Trotzkopf character in *Trotzkopfs Erlebnisse im Weltkrieg: Erzählung* (Berlin: A. Weichert Verlag, 1916).
41. On Else Ury (1877–1943) see Grieser, op. cit., pp. 32–46. On the Nesthäkchen series see Zahn, op cit., pp. 263–336.
42. Grieser, op. cit., pp. 44–5.
43. Publisher's note on cover of E. Ury, *Nesthäkchens Backfischzeit: Eine Jungmädchengeschichte* (Düsseldorf: Hoch-Verlag, 1987).
44. E. Ury, *Nesthäkchens Backfischzeit: Eine Jungmädchengeschichte* (Berlin: Meidingers Jugendschriften-Verlag, 1920) p. 102.
45. E. Ury, *Nesthäkchen fliegt aus dem Nest: Eine Erzählung für junge Mädchen* (Berlin: Meidingers Jugendschriften-Verlag, 1921).
46. On the typology of the *Backfischbuch*: E. Schaeffer, op. cit., p. 12; Dahrendorf, op. cit., pp. 125–31.
47. John Gillis, *Youth and History: Tradition and Change in European Age Relations, 1770–Present* (New York and London: Academic Press, 1981) pp. 98–105.
48. von Rhoden, op. cit. (Stuttgart, 1925 edn), p. 225.
49. Lippert, op. cit., p. 79.
50. Heinrich Wolgast, *Das Elend unserer Jugendliteratur*, 4th edn (Hamburg: Selbstverlag; Leipzig: Wunderlich, 1910) pp. 183–203.
51. Lippert, op. cit., p. 97.
52. Sielaff, op. cit., p. 13.
53. Schrader, op. cit., p. 956.
54. Barschak, op. cit., p. 22.
55. Lippert, op. cit., pp. 37, 40.
56. Ibid., p. 93; Barschak, op. cit., p. 26.
57. Lippert, op. cit., p. 45; Gensch, op. cit., p. 72; Mothes-Eilts, op. cit., p. 14.

58. Gina Kaus, 'Wie ein Mädchenbuch aussehen sollte', *Die literarische Welt*, vol. 2, no. 49 (1926) p. 4.
59. Mothes-Eilts, op. cit., p. 14.
60. H. Wolgast, 'Grossobuch oder nationale Dichtung', reprinted in Jörg Becker (ed.), *Die Diskussion um das Jugendbuch: Ein forschungsgeschichtlicher Überblick von 1890 bis heute* (Darmstadt: Wissenschaftliche Buchgesellschaft, 1986) p. 39.
61. Wilhelm Fronemann, *Lesende Jugend: Reden und Aufsätze* (Langensalza: J. Beltz Verlag, 1930) pp. 233–4; Kaus, op. cit., p. 4.
62. Kaus, op. cit., p. 4.
63. Schaeffer, op. cit., pp. 16–18.
64. Kaus, op. cit., p. 4.
65. Schaeffer, op. cit., pp. 14–16, reviews some examples of 'progressive' new fiction for girls.
66. Fronemann, op. cit., pp. 233–4.
67. *Was wir vom Buch erwarten*, see note 1 above.
68. Ibid., p. 25.
69. Ibid., p. 27.
70. Schaeffer, op. cit., p. 11.
71. Sielaff, op. cit., pp. 12–13.
72. Lippert, op. cit., pp. 53–4.
73. Ibid., pp. 53, 71.
74. Ibid., pp. 7–34.
75. Ibid., p. 113.
76. G. Staewen-Ordemann, *Menschen der Unordnung: Die proletarische Wirklichkeit im Arbeitsschicksal der ungelernten Großstadtjugend* (Berlin: Furche Verlag, 1933) pp. 107–8.
77. Barschak, op. cit., p. 22.
78. Grenz, ' "Der Trotzkopf" ', p. 50; Dahrendorf, op. cit., p. 128.
79. Lippert, op. cit., pp. 57–8.
80. Barschak, op. cit., pp. 22–3.
81. Lippert, op. cit., p. 57.
82. Ibid., p. 62.
83. *Was wir vom Buch erwarten*, p. 26 (vocational school pupil, 15 years old).

Bibliography

Bayer, Dorothee, *Der triviale Familien- und Liebesroman im 20. Jahrhundert* (Tübingen: Tübinger Vereinigung für Volkskunde, 1963).
Becker, Jörg (ed.), *Die Diskussion um das Jugendbuch: Ein forschungsgeschichtlicher Überblick von 1890 bis heute* (Darmstadt: Wissenschaftliche Buchgesellschaft, 1986).
Berchem, Mechthildis, 'Was liest unsere heranwachsende weibliche Jugend', *Die Bücherwelt*, vol. 17 (1920) pp. 106–7.
Bridenthal, Renate, Atina Grossmann and Marion Kaplan (eds), *When*

Biology Became Destiny: Women in Weimar and Nazi Germany (New York: Monthly Review Press, 1984).

Cadogan, Mary, and Patricia Craig, *You're a Brick, Angela!: The Girls' Story, 1839–1985* (London: Gollancz, 1986).

Dahrendorf, Malte, *Das Mädchenbuch und seine Leserin: Versuch über ein Kapitel 'trivialer' Jugendlektüre* (Hamburg: Verlag für Buchmarkt-Forschung, 1970).

Evans, Richard J., *The Feminist Movement in Germany, 1894–1933* (London: Sage Publications, 1976).

Falter, Jürgen, Thomas Lindenberger and Siegfried Schumann, *Wahlen und Abstimmungen in der Weimarer Republik* (Munich: Verlag C. H. Beck, 1986).

Frevert, Ute, *Women in German History: From Bourgeois Emancipation to Sexual Liberation* (Oxford, Hamburg, New York: Berg, 1989).

Friedlander, Judith, Blanche Wiesen Cook, Alice Kessler-Harris and Carroll Smith-Rosenberg (eds), *Women in Culture and Politics: A Century of Change* (Bloomington, Ind.: Indiana University Press, 1986).

Fronemann, Wilhelm, *Lesende Jugend: Reden und Aufsätze* (Langensalza: J. Beltz Verlag, 1930).

Geyer-Ryan, Helga, *Der andere Roman: Versuch über die verdrängte Ästhetik des Populären* (Wilhelmshaven: Heinrichshofen, 1978).

Gillis, John, *Youth and History: Tradition and Change in European Age Relations, 1770–Present* (New York and London: Academic Press, 1981).

Grenz, Dagmar, *Mädchenliteratur: Von den moralisch-belehrenden Schriften im 18. Jahrhundert bis zur Herausbildung der Backfischliteratur im 19. Jahrhundert* (Stuttgart: Metzler, 1981).

——, ' "Der Trotzkopf" – ein Bestseller damals und heute', *Informationen Jugendliteratur und Medien*, vol. 34, no. 3 (1983) pp. 50–3.

Grieser, Dietmar, *Die kleinen Helden: Kinderbuchfiguren und ihre Vorbilder* (Munich: Langen Müller Verlag, 1987).

Helm, Clementine, *Backfischchens Leiden und Freuden: Eine Erzählung für junge Mädchen*, reprinted with commentary by Susanne Zahn (Berlin: Weismann Verlag, 1981).

Kaus, Gina, 'Wie ein Mädchenbuch aussehen sollte', *Die literarische Welt*, vol. 2, no. 49 (1926), p. 4.

Klaus, Martin, *Mädchenerziehung zur Zeit der faschistischen Herrschaft in Deutschland: Der Bund Deutscher Mädel* (Frankfurt-am-Main: dipa-Verlag, 1983).

Lippert, Elisabeth, *Der Lesestoff der Mädchen in der Vorpubertät* (Erfurt: Verlag Kurt Stenger, 1931).

McRobbie, Angela and Mica Nava (eds), *Gender and Generation* (London: Macmillan, 1984).

Medick, Hans, and David Sabean (eds), *Emotionen und materielle Interessen: Sozialanthropologische und historische Beiträge zur Familien-forschung* (Göttingen: Vandenhoeck and Ruprecht, 1984).

Peukert, Detlev J. K., 'The Weimar Republic: Old and New Perspectives', *German History*, vol. 6, no. 2 (1988) pp. 133–44.

Radford, Jean (ed.), *The Progress of Romance: The Politics of Popular Fiction* (London and New York: Routledge and Kegan Paul, 1986).

Rhoden, Emmy von, *Der Trotzkopf: Eine Pensionsgeschichte für junge Mädchen*, 86th edn (Stuttgart: Gustav Weise Verlag, 1925).
——, *Der Trotzkopf* (Hanover: Neuer Jugendschriften-Verlag, 1979).
Rumpf, Albrecht, *Kind und Buch: Das Lieblingsbuch der deutschen Jugend zwischen 9 und 16 Jahren aufgrund einer Umfrage*, 2nd edn (Berlin and Bonn: Ferd. Dümmlers Verlag, 1928).
Schaeffer, Else, 'Das Jungmädchenbuch: Einige Gedanken aus der Praxis', *Hefte für Büchereiwesen*, vol. 16, no. 1 (1932–3) pp. 11–18.
Schmidt-Henkel, Gerhard (ed.), *Trivialliteratur* (Berlin: Literarisches Kolloquium, 1964).
Schrader, Lotte, 'Vom Backfischbuch', *Hamburger Lehrerzeitung*, vol. 9, no. 50 (1930) pp. 954–6.
Sielaff, Erich, *Jungmädchenliteratur* (Stettin: Verlag Bücherei und Bildungspflege, 1933).
Siemering, Hertha and Eduard Spranger (eds), *Weibliche Jugend in unserer Zeit* (Leipzig: Quelle und Meyer, 1932).
Siemering, Hertha, E. Barschak and W. Gensch, *Was liest unsere Jugend?: Ergebnisse von Feststellungen an Schulen aller Gattungen und Erziehungsanstalten sowie bei Jugendorganisationen und Jugendlichen* (Berlin: R. von Decker's Verlag, G. Schenck, 1930).
Snitow, Ann Barr, Christine Stansell and Sharon Thompson (eds), *Powers of Desire: the Politics of Sexuality* (New York: Monthly Review Press, 1983).
Soden, Kristina von and Maruta Schmidt (eds), *Neue Frauen: Die zwanziger Jahre* (Berlin: Elefanten Press, 1988).
Stachura, Peter D. (ed.), *Unemployment and the Great Depression in Weimar Germany* (London: Macmillan, 1986).
Staewen-Ordemann, Gertrud, *Menschen der Unordnung: Die proletarische Wirklichkeit im Arbeitsschicksal der ungelernten Großstadtjugend* (Berlin: Furche Verlag, 1933).
Strecker, Gabrielle, *Frauenträume, Frauentränen: Über den unterhaltenden deutschen Frauenroman* (Weilheim: Otto Wilhelm Barth Verlag, 1969).
Ury, Else, *Nesthäkchens Backfischzeit: Eine Jungmädchengeschichte* (Berlin: Meidingers Jugendschriften-Verlag, 1921). (Reprint, edited by Gunter Steinbach, Düsseldorf: Hoch-Verlag, 1987.)
——, *Nesthäkchen fliegt aus dem Nest: Eine Erzählung für junge Mädchen* (Berlin: Meidingers Jugendschriften-Verlag, 1921).
Was wir vom Buch erwarten: Antworten von 15–20jährigen Mädchen (Leipzig: Börsenverein der Deutschen Buchhändler, 1931).
Weigl, F., 'Buchinteressen von Schülerinnen der Berufsfortbildungsschule', *Die deutsche Berufsschule*, vol. 38, no. 11 (1929) pp. 302–9.
Weil, Marianne (ed.), *Wehrwolf und Biene Maja: Der deutsche Bücherschrank zwischen den Kriegen* (Berlin: Verlag Ästhetik und Kommunikation, 1986).
Wolgast, Heinrich, *Das Elend unserer Jugendliteratur*, 4th edn (Hamburg: Selbstverlag; Leipzig: Wunderlich, 1910).
Zahn, Susanne, *Töchterleben. Studien zur Sozialgeschichte der Mädchenliteratur* (Frankfurt-am-Main: dipa-Verlag, 1983).

3 Doubly Determined: the Ambition of Storm Jameson

JENNIFER BIRKETT

A REPRESENTATIVE HEROINE

Simone de Beauvoir, lecturing in Japan in 1966 on 'Women and Creativity', spoke of the determining lack of ambition which stopped most women from pursuing a creative vocation and aspiring to genius: while boys were taught ambition from an early age, women were conditioned to supporting roles.[1] Margaret Storm Jameson (1891–1986) is one of the few exceptions to de Beauvoir's rule. From childhood she designated herself as ambitious: 'What was I at ten? Already anxious, ambitious, eager to please, something of a hypocrite and a mule.'[2] Her first novel, she said, was written out of sheer ambition for money and fame (*JN*, I, 111). She wrote not just for writing's sake, but to insert herself into the public world and establish herself in a successful career.

The ambition for which she found words was not just her own. The wider relevance of Storm Jameson's work is often masked by her own élitist gestures. She likes to picture herself as a lonely heroine, fighting her isolated cause. But equally often, she gestures sympathetically to unnumbered other women of her time who feel the stirrings of ambition but lack the scope and the experience to formulate desire and turn it into act. For all her ambivalence towards the feminism of the early 1900s, charted in *The Pot Boils* (1919) and *The Happy Highways* (1920), Jameson is, from the beginning, aware of its implications for the mass of working women.[3] In *The Pot Boils*, she satirises the naïvety and fanaticism that sours, she says, the feminist cause, and declares feminism to be another form of middle-class self-indulgence that gets in the way of more urgent social reforms. Even so, she stresses the irreversible changes the feminists have made to women's outlook, and evokes the hundreds

68

of thousands of women standing behind them, demanding an end to domestic drudgery and the right to paid work:

> You must see that you can't shove women back, no matter how you coax or abuse. You'll have to make your plans for a re-made society on the basis of feminine labour alongside masculine. (p. 192)

Militant suffragists, in her view, are wrong to press their own political priorities: 'As if they had the right, while there is one ill-paid, ill-fed working woman in England' (p. 244).

Storm Jameson's work belongs to a very particular moment of history.[4] Her writings all emphasise the private, domestic world that shaped her – the influence of family, mother, two husbands and a son – but they recognise too how that world in its turn was shaped by its historical moment. As she grew up into the 1920s and 1930s, educational opportunities widened for women of her class, and she benefited directly not only from the opening up of the universities to women, but also from the existence (in the 1920s, still minimal) of scholarship grants. Job opportunities for women increased, though men still had the plum posts: Jameson came first in her English Honours class at Leeds University but was 'fobbed off' with a research studentship, while the man who came second got a University lectureship (*JN*, I, 58). By 1918 women over the age of 30 had the vote; in 1928 women's suffrage was finally established on the same basis as for men. Jameson's writing inscribes the great historical events of the first half of the twentieth century that shifted the lives of all her contemporaries, men and women, into radically different perspectives: the First World War, marking, as she frequently comments, the beginning of the end for the liberal values and the old hierarchies of nineteenth-century Europe; the rise of organised socialism, in the unions and in Parliament; and the counter-organisation of the Right, fostering the rise of Fascism.

The upheavals of family life and private relationships traced in her autobiography and her fictions are linked to political and economic changes that affected a whole generation. Images of the edge of dawn, of new patterns of light, are repeated motifs in her work, countered by figures of collapse, burial and darkness. Like Stendhal, chronicler of the new society emerging in early nineteenth-century France and the novelist to whom she most readily turned for a model, she writes to hold up a mirror to the life that passes along the highway before her.[5] But as her Hervey Russell trilogy indicates, hers must be *A Mirror in Darkness*.[6] A woman writing in the early decades of the twentieth century cannot, in honesty, deliver a clear, coherent image.

Storm Jameson's autobiography is everybody's; more so, in one sense, than Gertrude Stein's, in that it clings on harder to the old forms while declaring its desire for the new. But within its traditional allegiances, it achieves a major reorientation by insisting on the particular – and particularly open – form of its feminine voice, declaring the repeated frustration of its desire. The account is never closed by assertions of unity achieved, self-mastery or self-comprehension. The story runs on, novel into autobiography into novel, single volume into trilogy, diversifying into short stories. Jameson asserts feminine difference by setting out her own hesitations and contradictions, gestures of defiance, acts of conformity incomprehensible to their author: 'With both hands I destroyed myself, denaturing my senses, tearing out energies, desires, greeds, the innocent with the corrupt. I *tamed* myself. Why?' (*JN*, II, 315). She sees herself as possessing double gender like the best of her female characters: Athenais, for example, student heroine of *The Pot Boils*, whose mind is 'curiously masculine in most respects' (p. 48). The focus of her writing is double: an obsessive circling of her guilt at the first failed marriage and her regular abandonments of her son, Bill, and her longing for a career and a life of her own. Ambition plunges her into a 'double life' (*JN*, II, 380). Finally, the act of writing itself produces doubleness:

> The very act of writing, of turning pain, grief, joy, into words, creates the Doubles of these feelings, so that innocently the writer places between himself and reality a charming or dreadful mask. . . . [T]he truth is exactly that which can't be got into words. We are forced to lie, a little or, if we are inferior, much.
> (*JN*, II, 375)

For all its 'lies', writing, for Jameson, is a way of slipping through the determining mesh of 'reality'. The subject made by history remakes it in her turn, recalling and restating subverted versions – subversions – of her own past to place the present in fresh perspective. Every event in Jameson's life is written out, transforming the humiliating powerlessness of a woman in private life into the indictment of published script. After recording in her autobiogra-

phy a particularly bruising encounter with her husband, she records
also how she retired to her room to write down every word of the
exchange (*JN*, I, 178), which then reappears in her fictions. And
beyond the personal conflicts, Jameson's versions of her story also
write the public world into a new form, in which domestic detail and
political event can for the first time exist on the same level, inscribing
women into history. Still on the margins, they can at least see
mirrored their marginality.

Some women are, of course, less marginal than others. Jameson's
work breaks new ground in that it finds space for working-class as
well as middle-class women, but even so that space is relatively
limited. To see herself as determined by gender, rather than class,
requires a conscious effort. In the first volume of *Journey from the
North*, Jameson defines her sense of selfhood as a product of three
distinct historical and political moments, marked most of all by her
middle-class origins:

> [My] life spans three distinct ages: the middle-class heyday before
> 1914, the *entre deux guerres*, and the present. . . . I can excavate
> two finished stages in society, since I remember sharply the one
> I rebelled against while continuing to live blindly by more than
> one of its rooted assumptions: that people of my class do not
> starve, that reticence in speech, and clean linen, are bare necessi-
> ties, that books exist to be read. (*JN*, I, 15)

When focused, as it often is, on the decline of middle-class Englishness, Jameson's work loses much of its dynamism. Her aim then is
not to make room for the new but to reinstate the already dead.
The archaeological metaphor recurs as she describes her nostalgic
and, she confesses, outdated recreation in her first trilogy, *The
Triumph of Time*,[7] of merchant-adventurer capitalism and its cult of
possessive individualism:

> It took me three novels to write the life of Mary Hansyke, who
> became Mary Hervey, from her birth in 1841 to her death in
> 1923, and follow shipbuilding from sail to steam to turbines to
> her sell-out at the height of the war boom in shipping. This was
> something I knew about. The three novels are like prehistoric
> animals reconstructed in a museum from clay and a few real
> bones. (*JN*, I, 245)

A dutiful daughter devotes herself to preserving the family house. Jameson defines her life as a transaction with her Yorkshire inheritance, deep-rooted in the small sea-town of Whitby, in a close family with a much-loved but authoritarian mother and an often absent, ineffectual sea-captain father. Whitby's harbour leads out to the open sea, but its face is turned firmly to its own centre, the church where adventurer-sons have traditionally come home to be buried. This pattern of rupture and return is one which Jameson sees herself re-enacting, caught in the trap that holds ambitious daughters fast. The new life she made for herself in literary London was punctuated by flights back to her origins, in a panic search for an essential core to all her 'dissimilar I's', forced to acknowledge the authority of the past: 'Only a life starting from centuries of familiarity with the same few fields and streets is better than fragmentary' (*JN*, i, 15–16). As the child of her mother's family, she internalises the guilt-written limits of a dying world.

Yet if she turns to see herself as woman, she becomes the iconoclast, breaking with the values of family and class, seeking to resist the limitations of continuity: 'All I could do to destroy the pattern, I have done' (*JN*, i, 16). At such times, she confesses with a pleasurable sense of treachery that these 'traditions' by which she defines herself are fictions. She acknowledges the bankruptcy of middle-class history and values – and consequently of herself, resting in dead values and living by empty symbols. Novels and autobiography alike are caught between the desire to act the heroine, possessor of a unitary self, and the recognition that the sense of wholeness, translated from Mary Hervey's time to the modern world, is a delusion. The language of self that Jameson uses is fixed in its rationalist origins, but the impulse it translates is entirely modern. Modern subjects, men and women, cannot know a sense of self-possession. The best that they can know is the nature of their own lie:

> Nothing would have been easier for me than to write one of those charming poetic memoirs which offend no one and leave a pleasant impression of the author. I am trying to do something entirely different. Trying, in short, to eat away a double illusion: the face I show other people, and the illusion I have of myself – by which I live. Can I?
> It is true that what one sees from the inside is the seams, the dark tangled roots of feeling and action, which may be just as

misleading, as partial, as the charming poeticized version I am trying to reject. But it is a truth – known only to me (*JN*, I, 16)

Storm Jameson's work is driven by a double ambition: to succeed and to be truthful. Success can only come from the creation of a 'pleasant impression', conceding the image of a self which others have fabricated; her own 'truth', in contradiction, can only be cast in a language entirely her own, written 'from the inside', which tries to resist alien determinations. The rest of this essay will explore the old inhibitions, and the new freedoms, to which her double ambition leads.

'THE DARK TANGLED ROOTS OF FEELING AND ACTION'

Not the least of Storm Jameson's double impulses is her need to accommodate both a masculine and a feminine allegiance. The 'roots of feeling and action' of which she speaks have grown in patriarchal soil, and the ambition to succeed can only be satisfied in the male world. Politics and writing, the activities in which her ambition found expression, are traditionally male discourses. As long as she tackles them in their own language, that language masks her own. Hervey Russell, writer-heroine of *The Mirror in Darkness*, has always to choose between truth and success: writing what she wants to write, or telling the male publishers and critics who control the writing world what they want to hear and can understand. Her choices, to a large extent, are pre-determined.

Jameson's own political and authorial identity owes much to masculine moulds. She claims her socialist enthusiasm was, originally, entirely her own, angry adolescent response to poverty: 'a violent anger when I thought of children growing up in cancerously mean streets' (*JN*, II, 312).

But the enthusiasm first took coherent shape at university, in Leeds and then in London, where in 1912 she shared rooms with childhood friends, the Harland brothers, and Archie White, discussing social justice, freedom and perpetual peace (*JN*, I, 65) and sharing their admiration for A. R. Orage, the socialist critic. In March 1913, she published an essay in Orage's *New Age* and later, in 1932–3, reviewed for his *New English Weekly*. Orage, H. G. Wells and Anatole France were, she said, the major influences on her first novel (*JN*, I, 84).

Her early anger at injustice carries through into the positions she took in the 1930s, along with most writers of her generation: 'There really was a stench. On one side Dachau, on the other the "distressed areas" with their ashamed workless men and despairing women' (*JN*, I, 293).

Confronted by the need to take sides, as a writer, for socialism or Fascism, Jameson distinguishes her choice from that of her male counterparts. She claims to have seen through the political illusions that fellow-writers swallowed whole. She is scathing about 'that liberal humanism under whose banner I had enlisted' (*JN*, I, 295), and about the British democracy she was defending, 'which allowed me freedom to write and other women freedom to live starved lives on the dole' (*JN*, I, 293). At the same time she was, she claims, more aware than most of being used by the socialist and Communist forces she had sided with. To have kept her distance from absolute commitment in the 1930s is an important component of the persona created by her autobiography.

This differentiation of her own position has, as she presents it, nothing to do with being a woman. She justifies her detachment from the enthusiasms of the men of the 1930s by reference back to the higher ideals of other men, those of 'Class 1914', the generation of the Harlands and of her own much-loved brother, who vanished in the First World War. She reports a dream in which the dead heroes laugh at her efforts and tell her they are doomed to failure: their prewar world is gone, 1930s' socialism is tainted, and this new age is condemned to unreason (*JN*, I, 298). She is left to struggle on, in the awareness that she is a poor substitute for her dead heroes. There is a double movement here. On the one hand, the values Jameson pursues are undeniably her own, and she speaks boldly on their behalf. On the other, without the authority she borrows from the war heroes – Class 1914 – her speech would not be heard. In this world the only voices allowed a hearing are those speaking within the masculine discourse of war. Hence the sense of failure expressed in her dream: the need to borrow a voice in order to wrest a measure of power concedes her powerlessness. At the very moment when she most lucidly distinguishes herself from her contemporaries, Jameson's success is undermined by her equally lucid acknowledgement that the real distinction belongs to others.

The borrowed political voice, inevitably, often sounds hollow and contrived. In her novels, Jameson can put flesh and blood round the aspirations and frustrations of characters caught in a world changing too fast for their understanding; and there she writes from first-hand experience of the bewilderment of a generation. The books and pamphlets in which in the 1930s she systematises political ideas culled from the Harlands, Orage, Wells and the Christian radical R. H. Tawney blend feudal nostalgia, anti-technological rant, revolutionary rage at social injustice, and banally impractical suggestions for action. Sincerely felt, but devoid of any sense of political realities, they have an air of artifice which is missing from the best of Jameson's fictions.

The Decline of Merry England (1930), influenced by Tawney's *Religion and the Rise of Capitalism*, is a strange little book, mourning the death of small Elizabethan village communities, with their jolly peasants and 'full-blooded' aristocrats, ruled and protected by the monarch.[8] The pamphlet *The Soul of Man in the Age of Leisure* (1935), bringing together ideas scattered through her novels, is driven by the same nostalgic delusions.[9] Society, she argues, has fallen prey to a small élite of profiteering financiers, served by middle-class dependants and workers whose minds have been enslaved by the machine-culture that claimed to liberate them. The nation, to be restored, needs to rediscover its vital links with the past, severed by hasty industrialisation and the introduction of mass production. Everyone must have equal shares in drudge-work and cultural activity. Jameson wants an end to serfdom, a classless society, the revival of regionalism and a happy life for everyone. A later pamphlet, *The End of This War* (1941), recasts the same ideas into a vision of a future socialist order for Europe, won on the battlefield.[10]

The End of This War is one of the rare texts in which Jameson concedes any sense to war. Against the patriarchal jingoism that twice in her lifetime raised its ugly voice, she opposed as long as she could the language of pacifism. As president of the English Centre of PEN from 1938 to 1944 she wrote, spoke and organised to save the lives of European refugees, in the face of the British government's inertia and the anti-Semitic prejudices of much of the British populace. While the patriarchs of England were quietly ditching their much-vaunted 'English' values – love of freedom and justice, hatred of tyranny – Jameson held desperately to the idealism of Class 1914.

In writing, as in politics, Jameson looked only to men for models.

In doing so, she made some unfortunate options. Recognising this at a later date, she regrets deeply her failure to see the substantial difference between a Balzac and a Joyce, or a Proust, the one primarily interested in realist chronicle, the others primarily concerned with the possibilities of language, 'the growing impulse to break the traditional mould, achieve a new fluidity, new and personal symbols for human experience' (*JN*, I, 244–5).

For a mixture of motives – conservatism and careerism, but also humanist principle and socialist fervour – Jameson rejected outright the modernist experiment, which was already making room for new voices to break into monotone patriarchal discourse. James Joyce was the enemy of language and civilization, 'a purely disintegrating force' (*JN*, I, 245). A direct consequence of her refusal to look more closely at Joyce's innovatory prose is her despair of finding an equivalent in language for her own moments of intense feeling:

> The pain and ecstasy of youth, the brief happiness, the long uncharted decline, can be summed up in the tune of a once popular waltz, of no merit, or the point in a country lane where the violence and hopelessness of a passion suddenly become obvious, or the moment when a word, a gesture, nothing in themselves, gave the most acute sensual pleasure. None of these can be written about. (*JN*, I, 16–17)

The novella *A Day Off* (1933),[11] 'the only genuinely imaginative book I have written' (*JN*, I, 285), which evokes with brilliant intensity the self-deception, delusions and disillusionment of a woman at the turning-point of late middle-age, was a lonely experiment in 'a new and truthful way of writing', following 'my own narrow ravishingly subjective (egotistical) road' (*JN*, I, 300). Out of tune with the times, it was a publishing failure, and Jameson abandoned the experiment as a self-indulgence.

Some of the modernist experiment still finds recognition in her work under the aegis of T. S. Eliot, presenting its conservative face – evoking fragmentation, repression and despair, where Joyce sees chaotic, abundant energy. *No Time Like the Present* (1933), an early autobiography whose account of the materialism of modern society is pure Eliot in its despair, quotes abundantly from *The Waste Land*.[12] Eliot seems an obvious source for the snatches of music, gesture and unattributed voices that force their way into Jameson's 1930s' fictions; perhaps also for the suddenly convulsive syntax and the collapse of punctuation in, for example, *Company Parade*. But more often, Jameson bound herself to the best-selling 'neo-naturalism' (*JN*, I, 301) of Arnold Bennett and H. G. Wells, doyens of the literary salons to which her publishing job took her, and in consequence confined her struggle to express her own truth within frustratingly conservative limits. Inevitably, the truth she finds herself repeating is the near-impossibility of foregrounding a feminine voice in traditional masculine forms.

Her theoretical explorations of the problems of writing a novel of contemporary life never address the question of the gendered voice. In an essay of the 1930s,[13] the question is rather how to be as objective as possible; and the answer, a new style of reportage, where the writer renounces direct personal interventions for simple presentation of facts, lit from a new angle. The novelist's aim must be to situate the fact coherently in the complex of social and historical relations that gives it its meaning, emulating, in effect, the documentary film. In her 1930s' fiction, however, Jameson's sense of the specific problems of the female writer finds more scope. *Company Parade* is constructed around the difficulty of writing an honest novel, presented specifically as the problem of a female author. Confronted with the discordant mass of material that constitutes consumer society in the 1920s, Hervey Russell wonders how to produce an account that is both her truth and the truth of the whole. David Renn has an answer: every account is an intervention, and that intervention must be a strong socialist polemic on behalf of all the poor and oppressed:

> 'Don't you know you haven't any right to write novels unless you put into it this slum and those black troops being used to bully Germans? . . . Whether you know it or not, you're being used. You're either soothing or rousing people.' (p. 324)

Jameson in the 1930s is in sympathy with Renn's point. She makes it again in 1938, in *The Novel in Contemporary Life*.[14] Objectivity is always the aim:

> [T]o do his work properly the novelist must be a receiving station for the voices coming from every corner of the society he lives in. . . . Everything depends on the novelist being sensitive enough to detect the past and the future existing together in the

present, and honest enough to turn the light on it, without caring what it reveals. (pp. 14–15)

But objectively, the writer must acknowledge that what will be revealed is oppression, in a society where:

A man's work is only connected with his life by his pay envelope. Nor can he believe that he is building his life into the future of his country. The future has shrunk to a narrow personal fear. Tomorrow I may be out of work. Tomorrow there may be war. (p. 15)

Company Parade spells out the multiplicity of points of vision in this darkened landscape, and makes visible a range of alternative orientations. Recurrent in the text is the image of the airman overflying Britain, picking his way through the darkness by the clusters of lights from towns, factories, homes – some there for generations, others new configurations. The airman's path is dictated by the hard economic realities inscribed in the bright new lights of the landscape. Hervey believes there must be more than that. She makes a conscious choice to write for those left in darkness, the victims, mainly women, of harsh economic fact – poor women, landladies, society's waiters-on – and to speak for them: 'Is life nothing but bells and stairs and trays of food? Is the grave quiet?' (p. 299). Renn is right to emphasise the overriding socialist imperative; but within that imperative, there is opportunity to speak out for the female victim, and Hervey seizes it.

Both Hervey and Jameson write another new dimension into their work, which is their personal experience of oppression within sexual relationships. Jameson's miserable first marriage appears in *Company Parade* in terms very similar to those in her autobiographies. The events of contemporary history are lit from the new angle of sexual politics: deceptions and compromise in private life are seen to mirror and highlight the deceit and compromises of the public State. Made sensitive by her private suffering, Hervey reacts with the same intensity to public wrongs. She cannot focus her denunciation of class exploitation and nationalist cruelty as directly as David Renn advocates. But presented through her own experience, obliquely, and from the margins, her indictment can be no less 'rousing'.

Disowning *The Mirror in Darkness* in the 1960s, Jameson speaks of its 'flawed conception', falling between the two stools of human comedy and *roman fleuve*, so that none of the novels has a clear centre: 'At times the mirror itself – identified with that Hervey Russell who is and is not myself – supplied the images and ideas; at others, a character unfolded independently, alone or in a web of action' (*JN*, I, 301). She understands part of the reason for the incoherence:

> No earlier novelist, when he looked attentively at the life of his time or when he strained his ears to catch the note of the future, was faced by chaos. There were fixed points, or which seemed fixed. Language itself did not break in his hands. Words had not been emptied of their meaning . . . . (*JN*, I, 302).

What in her self-flagellation Jameson fails to recognise is the additional element of the gendered viewpoint – the critical feminine vision – which compounds chaos, and adds also a distinctive energy which distinguishes those early political novels from her later, more technically polished works. When Hervey later decides to dedicate herself to motherhood and resign her ambitions to become an authorial centre, Jameson's political novels certainly become more clearly focused, but at the price of concentrating on male personae and male perspectives. Their punch is as hard, but it is different: and what they say most clearly is that 1930s' women, worn out by the fight, must content themselves, for the time being, with the margins.

LIVING IN OCCUPIED TERRITORY: THE HEROISM OF RESISTANCE

The fact that women write and speak from the margins is a key theme of Jameson's work. The best image for Hervey's, and Jameson's, situation is provided in *Journey from the North*, where Jameson describes her experience as a child:

> [A] child does not try to understand the behaviour of his masters. The truth is, he does not think of himself as a child and of his elders as adults; he thinks in terms of rulers and ruled, helpless and powerful. Very much, I suppose, as the inhabitants of an

occupied country feel towards an occupier, however benevolent. (*JN*, I, 31)

Women, like the child, live on sufferance, under rules laid down by an alien power. *No Time Like The Present* describes a world defined by war, where men struggling for power kill and are killed, and women are required to watch:

> War robs [women] of their identity, and they cease to be clever, competent, intelligent, beautiful in their own right, and become the nurses, the pretty joys, and at last the mourners of their men. (pp. 211–12)

Jameson's novels, from the *Mirror in Darkness* trilogy onwards, give an account of the unworthy inheritors of Class 1914, sold-out scientists, bureaucrats, power-hungry businessmen, venal Labour politicians and weak trade unionists, lining up together to plunge the world into a second war. When that war is over, the same characters reappear to threaten the new life struggling from under the ruins.[15] Their success depends on stifling the 'feminine' virtues. In the world of *In The Second Year*, Jameson's chilling fantasy of a Britain fallen to a military coup, run by a National State Party, with all left-wing politicians, union militants and intellectuals consigned to a concentration camp, women are almost entirely absent.[16] Fascism and patriarchy fuse into a single oppressor. In *Before the Crossing*, Julian Swan, the crippled secretary-organiser of wealthy Thomas Harben's anti-Communist Economic League, rejects *en bloc* socialism, democracy and their 'woman-ridden culture' (p. 131).

The women in Jameson's stories live on the margins of men's violence. In *Love in Winter*, Delia Hunt, knocked about by her drunken husband, one of Swan's Fascist thugs, dies in silence, unable even to speak the name of her aggressor. Marie Duclos, cold and starving in the ruins of France, is casually picked up, used and brutalised by Tim Hunt (*Before the Crossing*). Other women survive war and peace by knowing acts of collusion. Jameson lays on their shoulders much of the responsibility for men's continuing oppression, both of women and of other men. Emily Lambton (*The Single Heart*, 1932), lives vicariously through her lover, makes a political career for him, tolerates his infidelities, and traps both herself and him in an enslaving dependency.[17] In *The Green Man* (1952), which covers the 1930s and 1940s, Emmy Daubeny is still doing the same for her

husband Matthew Daubeny who would, he declares, if circumstances
required it, treat with Hitler, and whose son Mark becomes a Jew-
baiting Fascist.[18] In *No Time Like The Present*, Jameson attacks the
women who second men's exploitations. This is a dereliction of duty
to self, sex and society:

> Women have not naturally the same attitude as men to all that
> touches breeding, marriage, and destroying life. . . . If civilis-
> ation as we know it ends in poison gas, the fault will be in part
> ours, because we have taken a hand in the game only as following
> and competing with men; and have not tried consciously to redress
> the imbalance of a social system shaped and directed by men.
> There is a strange irony in all this – since women are only free to
> have minds of their own in a society which is sufficiently advanced
> not to need all of them for housekeeping and breeding. Any
> relapse into a more barbarous state will make drudges of most of
> us. (pp. 229–32)

Against the immoral majority, Jameson sets a few women characters who resist, with varying degrees of success, the careers mapped
out for them. The most successful are often those whose resistance
to patriarchal authority in their own lives is joined to the resistance
of socialism to Fascism, and of exploited poor to greedy rich. In
Jameson's work the oppressions of sexual politics are a mirror that
reflects the general political darkness of the times. Holding up this
particular mirror to capitalism is not just an act of indictment. It is
also an active intervention in a world of broken and bad connections
that women are required to remake. A pattern emerges. Women's
ambition appears to founder in impotence. That impotence can then
be redefined as freedom from determination. It is the hand that
holds power in a system that is tied to the mechanisms that produce
that power. The powerless are free to benefit from the catastrophic
change that history will always bring.

Mary Hervey, owner of the Garton shipyards, Hervey Russell's
grandmother, and heroine of *The Triumph of Time*, is an unlikely
candidate for recruitment to socialist causes. Based, presumably, on
Jameson's shipowner grandfather, George Gallilee (*JN*, i, 20–4), she
is used to rewrite the origins of twentieth-century capitalism with a
feminine inflexion, to show the degree of difference that might be
made by a woman to economic and political change. The degree
is slight, since female shipowners are few, and their gains easily

incorporated in the short term into the patriarchal flow of history. But the form of Jameson's writing – trilogies, sequences, based on recurring characters and series of generations – hoards each small change until in the end the flow itself can be transformed. The metaphor – an act of faith, as much as fact – is enshrined in *The Hidden River* (1955): two women, both trapped by duty into unhappy marriages, unable to escape, hear in the river that flows by their family house a sudden new note, 'a pulse beating at a great depth: some current, starting from the sea, had reached this point'.[19] The limits and the direction of the flow may seem unchanged, but below the surface unseen resistances can start fresh movement.

Hervey Russell, like her grandmother, begins in an unhappy marriage, repeating the older woman's disabling discovery of her partner's incompetence and infidelity. Unlike her grandmother, she finds no compensation in a successful career. Struggling to make her way as a writer in a world that presses her to be a mother, Hervey represents the first generation of ordinary middle-class women attempting to take command of their own lives. *The Mirror in Darkness* charts her failure to achieve what the world counts success in a woman. She cannot be the daughter her mother wants, the pliant wife her husband wants, or the mother she thinks her child needs. Nor can she be the strong career woman she herself would like. Her socialist idealism is constantly belied by her conservative acts. She conceals her political commitments in order to keep her job. She works for the General Strike, but falls ill before the end and can't see it through. What saves her finally is her complete inability to function successfully in any conventional mode. Her husband abandons her when she is destitute, relieving her of all her irrational feelings of guilt towards him. She is left to experience the liberation of setting out empty-handed into the unknown.

The story gives Hervey no daughters to carry on her inheritance. But her capacity for endurance is complemented in the trilogy by that of Sally Rigden, the working-class wife of an ex-soldier. There is no direct contact between Hervey and Sally, who simply pass by each other briefly in the course of the General Strike. Jameson's is not a world of easy developments or simple connections. In the flow of history, the point is to become aware of parallel destinies, set apart by class, but shaped by the same political, economic and personal pressures. Hervey and Sally share one point of identity: mothers of a child who needs to be protected, they have to survive for the child's sake. Almost, with the Strike, there is a chance for identity to become solidarity – but the men fumble it.

Sally devotes to husband and family the same energy that Hervey devotes to her work. Unlike Hervey in her inarticulacy, she expresses her devotion by cleaning and caring. Her strength is tested in *None Turn Back*, with the failure of the General Strike. Her husband loses his job, and the dereliction of union and Labour leaders leaves the family with nowhere to turn. Hervey, in the same book, recovering at the end from an operation for cancer, feels herself absolved by her physical weakness from the need to carry on fighting. She and her son are protected; she has a devoted second husband, with money of his own, and a secure place in the world. Middle-class Englishness can still live on its capital. Sally has no choice but to go on living out the harsher destiny of working-class women. Hervey can turn aside; Sally cannot. Sally is caught in a collective nightmare:

> She was with other women, walking across an endless stretch of ground. They were all afraid, because they were in danger, and they were without food or homes. She had the little girl with her, grown a few years older. In some queer way she was the child, and thought as the child, while she was still herself. In their flight they came to a well; it was empty and as they stood round it the temptation seized her to throw the child into the pit, so that she would no longer have her dragging at her arms and crying for food. . . . She awoke shaking with terror. (pp. 244–5)

Class deals out different limits and challenges, and these texts recognise the fact. Darkness in *None Turn Back* presents a much more intractable problem than in earlier texts. This is not the isolated struggle of a middle-class woman to satisfy ambition in a patriarchal world. This novel refuses to concede freedom to one woman, as long as the mass of women (and men) remain imprisoned. Sexual politics and class politics come together. The darkness in this world is not just that of night, and of sleep, with the chance of a happy dawn, but the darkness of coal mines and underground galleries, in which workers and women are trapped by the inequitable distri-bution of labour and profit. The worker priest dreams he is caught in a mine, in a rockfall, and suddenly realises his body must stay there crushed forever, to stop the surface of the earth above from giving way and unsuspecting others falling into the pit (p. 131). Hervey, burying herself in domesticity for her son's sake, 'piled heavier earth on the body of her reckless, violent, disorderly self, and trod it down' (p. 151). She identifies her suffering with that of the miners preparing to strike:

> I want a new order; I want the parts of the design to shift, and release all the trapped and maimed creatures, caught between past and future. Her mind darkened, and sank with her into the passages under the earth; she saw the walls of the earth shift and fall together, squeezing the breath and blood out of the men bowed there, as paint is squeezed from a tube. Even the bone crumbled between her fingers and was scattered like dust into the pit. (p. 178)

Jameson is modest about her ability to speak out for a class to which she does not belong. But the sparse language of her portrait of Sally Rigden manages without sentimentality to convey the working-class woman's growing perception of the limits of her abilities, and her gathering anger. Sally's response to Frank's misery when he loses his job is cast entirely in the limiting language of her domesticity. But it transcends those limits, in a first act of rebellion against a system that sets its face against the family:

> She was thinking, almost without words, that he was like the boy when he tore his new coat across. On the boy's face as he came in was the same look of helplessness and misery. Eh, but why? she thought: why must they? And for the first time it seemed to her wrong that a torn coat could fill a little boy with despair because he knew coats are hard to come by. (p. 314)

The portrait of Rose in *A Day Off* similarly reproduces, in Rose's own language, the woman of the working class, forever seduced, exploited and disappointed by the world in which she must struggle to get by. Jameson reviews the armoury with which Rose defends herself: coarse laughter, aggression and insult, petty theft, and exploitation of women weaker than herself. These weapons are powerless in the end against age and loneliness. There are no words for Rose to express her desolation. All she has is the language of her body:

When she thought of herself, penniless, left, her heart thumped, the walls of her mouth dried up, and she felt empty. But she had no words at hand to describe her state. So far as she was concerned no words for it had ever existed.   (p. 263)

Her identity is a collage of make-up, coldcream and nylons, focused on fashion shop windows and popular music. In Rose's sudden intimation of her imminent collapse, Jameson brilliantly catches the untidy waste of her life and the emptiness of her 'choices' – keep house, or keep accounts for consumer society:

Suddenly the surface of her life split across and its days poured out in an untidy crumpled heap, like clothes emptied from a drawer. She could not tell one from the other. All she knew was that something terrible had happened, something she couldn't have prevented – (she thought confusedly, I might have done something, kept the room cleaner and tidier, I could have taken a course in book-keeping at that college, they say they guarantee a good post, nothing grand I daresay but better than nothing) – and now the walls of her room were giving way, dissolving, before her eyes.   (p. 210)

The most powerful female figure in Jameson's writing is the Mother, whose mediations of the patriarchal world determine not only the shape of her children's destinies but also the shape of their potential resistance. Jameson sees in the Mother the key to the reconstruction of society. The problem is the ambivalence of the figure, who ensures the survival of the child and the continuity of collective values, but who also teaches the child disabling dependencies and conformisms. Jameson's demand for a career of her own, resisting the single biological 'destiny' of women, opens the possibility of a fresh mother-image.

That this image is never fully realised is largely due to the influence on Jameson of her own mother (herself married too young, to escape from her father's house) who gave her the restlessness, the rage and the initiative to make the break with domesticity possible, but also imposed on her the strong sense of bounds and duty that tied her to the family. Jameson's texts, an account of the daughter's struggle with the mother's inheritance, offer a sustained critical analysis of the mother's power and its abuse.

Journey from the North pinpoints three areas where Mrs Jameson shaped her daughter's gender identity. The contempt she openly expressed for her husband liberated her daughter from the authority of the Father. At the same time, Mrs Jameson's preference for her son, who died in the First World War, returned Margaret to her secondary status. Finally, the mother's interventions to force her daughter into all the unwanted conventionalities of marriage and to stop her from accepting a post on *The Egoist* closed the trap (*JN*, I, 87–8).

With autobiographical distance, Jameson recognises that she internalised her mother's imperatives:

> Years ago I said Yes when I should have said No. That Yes took me out of my way. But it was I who said it. And I who, long before that moment, encouraged the birth of the smiling fake other people, beginning with my mother, drew out of me to take my place. I *am* my choice. I am what I made of my original condition. (*JN*, II, 380)

Models of 'good' women committed to domesticity, her mother and her sister, both loved and resented, shaped Jameson's torn creativity. Childbearing, she believes, is what debars a woman from genius (*JN*, II, 379–80); and yet women are taught that they owe it to the community to focus their creativity on 'children and houses'.

The self-denial Jameson imposes on herself is a guilty reflex at the acknowledgement of the self-denial life imposed on her mother, in whom she sees, thwarted, all her own ambition (*JN*, I, 19 and 32). In *None Turn Back*, Hervey's confrontation with the guilt her mother inspires coincides with the diagnosis and treatment of her cancer. Her most important recognition is that the guilt by which her mother intensified her daughter's dependency is what later made the daughter vulnerable to her husband's domineering demands (pp. 164–5). There is a collusion between mothers and men, which disables daughters in their resistance to patriarchy. While mothers and the men they serve work together to preserve the established order, the daughter's future – and the chance of a better future for the next generation – disappears:

> [Hervey] saw herself as a child, and as a girl, each separate, isolated by the darkness, seeking without finding, she saw the woman looking at her child's toys, hearing his voice, the voice coming from every man at least once during his life, Mother,

mother, these men are hurting me; she saw her own mother, indomitable and defeated, her eyes, blue and empty with staring, turned to the past. The eyes, too, of Swan and T. S. Heywood, turned romantically to the past, the last with despair, the other in senseless fear and hatred of the future. . . . And I? Hervey thought. I am not even there, in the generation certain to pay bitterly for their silence. (pp. 179–80)

Mothers are, as the Fascist industrialist William Gary says, the source of authoritarian practice:

What [all men] want, perhaps without knowing it, is to obey. They want to obey some power that they can accept with the same trust and confidence each felt when he was a child for his mother. (p. 280)

Hervey, struggling back to life after her operation, reduced to simple emotional and habitual responses, has not the strength to break with her conditioning. Her earlier perceptions of how mother-guilt compromises freedom are forgotten. The General Strike no longer seems her concern. Under the pressure of pain, she slides back willingly into memories of the maternal embrace:

Her mind slipped easily and comfortably into the past. It clung to the image of her mother. At once the living world of her childhood sprang round her, closing her between its vivid skies and secure earth as deeply and steadily as if she were present in it. . . . In everything she did in those days she was in part obeying Sylvia Russell's hard will and jealous masterful energy. She knew how often now her voice echoed hers. . . . A heavy footstep outside her room made her start, the pain licked her with its rough tongue. She laid her hand on it lightly, saying to herself aloud: 'I am the mother.' (pp. 316–17)

That retrogression into nostalgia and infantilism has dangerous implications:

Death shall have nothing of me but my bones, she said to herself, with an exultance which followed her into sleep, now that she was not afraid to sleep. An exultance – unbidden but welcomed, the sudden answer of her blind patience to the challenge of fear

and weakness. It answered as instinctively as a soldier, a mercen-
ary no doubt, but an English one. She was no one, obscure,
taught by pain. In identifying herself with the common earth of
Danesacre she was not far out of her rights.   (p. 319)

This febrile grasping at the roots of Englishness, an 'instinctive'
relaxing into mindless, mystical populism, is far too close to the
ideologies on which Gary, Swan and the Economic League are
building. While Hervey, enfolded at last in the security of convention, declares herself marginal to the narrative of the conflict between
Fascism and socialism, her world is falling into the hands of the
enemy.

Whether Jameson realises the implications of her character's
option is hard to tell. If anything, the lyricism of the writing here
endorses Hervey's position. It is the insights and values provided
over the whole of the trilogy that suggest to the reader that there is
a possible counter-reading that puts Hervey's good faith into question. *The Mirror in Darkness* ties the crucial problem of the political
implications of Motherhood into a knot of interpretation that resists
unpicking. The text here suggests, perhaps, its author's as well
as its characters' entrapment in ideologies of class and gender.
Interestingly, with her acceptance of the matriarchal role, this is the
last appearance of Hervey.

REDEFINING AMBITION

The strongest character of all in this body of work is the authorial
persona it projects. The mature Jameson does not think of herself
as a success politically, nor as a writer, in the terms she set for
herself at the beginning of her career. The sense of failure underpins
her autobiography: 'The story of a young woman raising herself from
obscurity to a shadowy success . . . a chain of failures' (*JN*, II, 382).

But in her effort to write out her torn subjectivity, expressing the
double voices of gender and class which she claims as her inheritance,
she marks a major achievement. The mother in Jameson may seem
to settle, in the end, for the consoling illusions of wholeness provided
by the familiar city:

Time to settle the account. To arrange to make a friend of the knowledge that wherever you go in the short time left you will find yourself in the same street, the same place, landing in the same harbour. (*JN*, II, 371)

The daughter remains free. The body of Jameson's texts, autobiography and fictions, remains to show the fragmentations of selfhood, wounds received and never healed, signposted by guilt or silence. 'Failures' honestly articulated become a kind of success, a confession of the truth of oneself. Jameson's 'abandoning' of her child and her 'failure' to make her first marriage work are moments of crystallisation repeatedly returned to in her texts, where they become the pretext for numerous other narratives. At the very end of the last autobiography, they are still there: the dream of a novel never written, based on a woman's guilt at losing her child (*JN*, II, 353–4) and the reiterated error of her first disastrous marriage (*JN*, II, 380). Jameson is prepared to define these acts in conventional language, as betrayals of the primary social function of women. They were hard and selfish, failures of love (*JN*, II, 382). But out of her hardness has come the whole story of her resistance.

The price has been high. Aiming to succeed in both private and public spheres, she ends by constructing herself into frustration:

But why? Why construct round myself something more intricate than any abstract sculpture, and again and again, sitting silent and unmoving, hammer on it in impotent rage, shout unheard, weep inwardly tears as bitter as gall? Why? (*JN*, II, 380)

Part of the reason is Jameson's inability to separate female sexual activity (being a woman) from bearing children (being a mother). This is a burden shared with her generation. Two world wars demanding cannon fodder, and two after-war periods in which women were forced to vacate jobs to accommodate returning heroes, required reinforcement of an already potent ideology in which women's role in the relations of production was primarily the reproduction of the workforce.[20] Female sensuality is a topic on which Jameson's writing is silent. *That Was Yesterday* blames 'A Victorian upbringing with its insistence on a polite reticence towards the body (and quite right too)' (p. 27). In this text, a rare evocation of youthful sensuality, framed in fear and self-disgust, reproduces a moment in a buttercup meadow when Hervey thinks of Penn's body lying alongside hers:

> Her senses were for a moment fully roused, ripples of excitement rising slowly in her and dying slowly away. She was familiar enough with this experience, which was always and only the product of her uncontrolled imagination. It was the only form of purely sensual pleasure she knew. No doubt there was an unclean beast living in her mind. How it came there first she had no idea. But she believed that she was the only person in the world who habited with a beast, and she concealed the fact of its existence and its secret shameful ravages from everyone, and especially from Penn. (p. 24)

Marriage is no liberation from repression. The clumsiness of Hervey's husband destroys all her pleasure in sexual experience, and his subsequent cruelties and infidelities make it impossible to recuperate a relationship marked by lingering illness and two attempted abortions, one successful. Yet marriage and motherhood remain fixed points in Jameson's ideology. An alternative is offered by Lilo Linke, Jameson's German refugee friend, met in the early 1930s, a rare attractive example of female freedom, who sees sex as interesting but marginal to her political activity. Jameson contrasts with Lilo Doris Lessing's version of the liberated woman, commenting that: 'No human being was ever less free than these women struggling in the sticky web of their sexual needs like flies in a pool of treacle' (*JN*, I, 309). But one Lilo, for Jameson, is enough. Too many such women, she declares, dedicated to childlessness, would seal the fate of the human race (*JN*, I, 310). Less significant here, perhaps, than her concern for the human race is Jameson's own fear of freedom, and the sexual possessiveness she inherits, she says, from her mother. In all her texts the space left by the absence of sexual fulfilment is filled with the pain of jealousy.

The daughter, then, seems powerless, caught between contradictory ambitions. Out of her confession of weakness, a solution arises. If women cannot change their roles, then men must invent new ones. A happy second marriage with Guy Chapman, one of the few survivors of Class 1914, enabled Jameson to imagine new possibilities. For women to exercise 'masculine' privileges, men must accept 'feminine' responsibilities. In *The Black Laurel*, David Renn, another member of Class 1914, put in charge of the British sector of Occupied Berlin, takes on himself the responsibility for finding a lost child and its mother (Marie Duclos, victim of the English Fascist Hunt). For Renn, as for Jameson, the future of Europe has now to be left to the children. The way for Jameson's generation to live down its crimes – Dachau, unemployment, violence against women – is to cut its losses, and sacrifice its own life to the survival of the new life to come. Renn finds the lost child and consecrates himself to it in the language of the maternal role:

> [H]e understood that he had attached himself again to the world by this child. He would have to work for it and its survival, and bring it up. He laughed at himself, but almost kindly, as if he were at last going to forgive himself – for what? Never mind all that, he thought, lightly; the only thing is to go on. Not on as if it were a duty. To begin to learn existence from the beginning – in the humbler existences: of the child's toys, or of herbs, pots, jugs, rooms: and, so small and weak yet, of the child. (p. 349)

Marie Duclos, having handed to Renn the child she cannot care for, makes, almost unremarked, a fresh start in America.

Before the Crossing and *The Black Laurel* sketch Utopian images of the new, feminised man, rising from the ruins of Berlin, set against the harsh self-seeking of Fascist patriarchs, English and German, in temporary retreat. In *Before the Crossing*, Arnold Coster, a young Air Force mechanic, comforts an abandoned child. In *The Black Laurel*, Heinrich Kalb, a German Jew, searches through the Berlin rubble for child survivors: ' "Come. I'll shelter you all." He opened his skinny arms widely' (p. 47). Even the hard Russian commander, Kalitin, and Gustav Leist, the German art historian looting Europe for the Nazi command, accept responsibility for a little girl whose parents have been slaughtered. The new men and women, together, form new couples and, more important, new collectivities. In the ruined cellar of an old convent in Berlin, Renn finds a whole group – the Mother Superior, Kalb, an American, a Czech priest, a Polish woman out of Ravensbrück – all 'looking for children who have been lost' (p. 131). In the breathing space after the catastrophic collapse of a rigid old order, with the brief abolition of categories of nation, gender, class, it becomes possible to work towards a better world.

For all her 'backsliding', it is Jameson's refusal to relinquish either

Determined Women

element of her double ambition, to be both woman (wife and mother) and writer, successful in the private and the public spheres, that is the source of the strength of her writing. In her day, it was impossible for a woman to be both. By refusing the impossibility, she reflects back into the wider community the responsibility for resolving the contradiction. If political catastrophe has sometimes to be accepted, in order to build a better order, then so too has private catastrophe. It may well be that the best a woman can do for her society and herself is to refuse to reproduce the prison.

Notes

1. Simone de Beauvoir, 'Women and Creativity', trs. Roisin Mallaghan, in Toril Moi (ed.), *French Feminist Thought: A Reader* (Oxford: Basil Blackwell, 1987) p. 20.
2. Storm Jameson, *Journey to the North*, 2 vols (London: Collins and Harvill Press, 1969–70; rpt. London: Virago Press, 1984) vol. II, p. 353. Hereafter referred to as *JN*.
3. Storm Jameson, *The Pot Boils* (London: William Heinemann, 1919) and *The Happy Highways* (London: Constable, 1920).
4. For a useful account of the constituting context of women's writing in the 1930s, see Andy Low, 'Recent Developments in English Studies at the Centre: the English Studies Group, 1978–9', in Stuart Hall *et al.* (eds), *Culture, Media, Language: Working Papers in Cultural Studies, 1972–79* (London: Hutchinson, 1980) pp. 249–56.
5. Stendhal, *The Red and the Black*, introd. Storm Jameson (New York: Collier Books, 1969).
6. *The Mirror in Darkness* series was intended by Jameson to run to five or six novels, but eventually finished at three: *Company Parade* (London: Cassell, 1934, rpt. London: Virago Press, 1982); *Love in Winter* (London: Cassell, 1935, rpt. London: Virago Press, 1984); *None Turn Back* (London: Cassell, 1936, rpt. London: Virago Press, 1984).
7. Storm Jameson, *The Lovely Ship* (London: William Heinemann, 1927); *The Voyage Home* (London: William Heinemann, 1930); *A Richer Dust* (London: William Heinemann, 1931).
8. Storm Jameson, *The Decline of Merry England* (London: Cassell, 1930).
9. Storm Jameson, *The Soul of Man in the Age of Leisure*, rpt. in *The Social Credit Pamphleteer* (London: Stanley Nott, 1935). Other contributors to this collection of pamphlets, published with the imprimatur of A. R. Orage, include Ezra Pound (*Social Credit: An Impact*) and Herbert Read (*Essential Communism*).
10. Storm Jameson, *The End of This War* (London: George Allen and Unwin, for PEN Books, 1941).

11. Storm Jameson, *A Day Off* (London: Nicholson and Watson, 1933), rpt. in *Women Against Men* (London: Virago Press, 1982).
12. Storm Jameson, *No Time like the Present* (London: Cassell, 1933).
13. Storm Jameson, 'Documentary', in *Fact*, no. 4 (1937), cit. Stuart Laing, 'Presenting "Things as They Are": John Sommerfield's May Day and Mass Observation', in Frank Gloversmith (ed.), *Class, Culture and Social Change* (Brighton: Harvester Press, 1980) p. 158.
14. Storm Jameson, *The Novel in Contemporary Life* (Boston, Mass.: The Writer, 1938) pp. 14–15.
15. See the sequence, Storm Jameson, *The Black Laurel* and *Before the Crossing* (London: Macmillan, 1947).
16. Storm Jameson, *In the Second Year* (London: Cassell, 1936).
17. Storm Jameson, *The Single Heart* (London: Ernest Benn, 1932), rpt. in *Women Against Men* (London: Virago Press, 1982).
18. Storm Jameson, *The Green Man* (London: Macmillan, 1952).
19. Storm Jameson, *The Hidden River* (London: Macmillan, 1955) p. 203.
20. On changing attitudes to feminine sexuality in the 1920s and 1930s, see Olive Banks, *Faces of Feminism: A Study of Feminism as a Social Movement* (Oxford: Martin Robertson, 1981) pp. 183–94. Marie Stopes's *Married Love* appeared in 1918, but contraception and abortion were still suspect practices to many feminists, who saw in them the possibility of increased sexual exploitation of women.

Bibliography

Banks, Olive, *Faces of Feminism: A Study of Feminism as a Social Movement* (Oxford: Martin Robertson, 1981).
Beauvoir, Simone de, 'Women and Creativity', trs. Roisin Mallaghan, in Toril Moi (ed.), *French Feminist Thought: A Reader* (Oxford: Basil Blackwell, 1987).
Jameson, Storm, *The Pot Boils* (London: Constable and Co., 1919; rpt. London: Merlin Press Radical Reprints, 1990).
——, *The Happy Highways* (London: William Heinemann, 1920).
——, *The Lovely Ship* (London: William Heinemann, 1927).
——, *The Voyage Home* (London: William Heinemann, 1930).
——, *The Decline of Merry England* (London: Cassell, 1930).
——, *A Richer Dust* (London: William Heinemann, 1931).
——, *The Single Heart* (London: Ernest Benn, 1932), rpt. in *Women Against Men* (London: Virago Press, 1982).
——, *That Was Yesterday* (London: William Heinemann, 1932).
——, *A Day Off* (London: Nicholson and Watson, 1933), rpt. in *Women Against Men* (London: Virago Press, 1982).
——, *No Time like the Present* (London: Cassell, 1933).
——, *Company Parade* (London: Cassell, 1934, rpt. London: Virago Press, 1982).

——, *Love in Winter* (London: Cassell, 1935, rpt. London: Virago Press, 1984).

——, *The Soul of Man in the Age of Leisure*, rpt. in *The Social Credit Pamphleteer* (London: Stanley Nott, 1935).

——, *None Turn Back* (London: Cassell, 1936, rpt. London: Virago Press, 1984).

——, *In the Second Year* (London: Cassell, 1936; rpt. London: Merlin Press Radical Reprints, 1990).

——, *Delicate Monster* (London: Nicholson and Watson, 1937), rpt. in *Women Against Men* (London: Virago Press, 1982).

——, *The Novel in Contemporary Life* (Boston, Mass.: The Writer, 1938).

——, *The End of This War* (London: George Allen and Unwin, for PEN Books, 1941).

——, *Journal of Mary Hervey Russell* (London: Macmillan, 1945).

——, *The Black Laurel* (London: Macmillan, 1947).

——, *Before the Crossing* (London: Macmillan, 1947).

——, *The Green Man* (London: Macmillan, 1952).

——, *The Hidden River* (London: Macmillan, 1955).

——, Introduction to Stendhal, *The Red and the Black* (New York: Collier Books, 1969).

——, *Journey to the North*, 2 vols (London: Collins and Harvill Press, 1969–70, rpt. London: Virago Press, 1984).

Laing, Stuart, 'Presenting "Things as They Are": John Sommerfield's May Day and Mass Observation', in Frank Gloversmith (ed.), *Class, Culture and Social Change* (Brighton: Harvester Press, 1980).

Low, Andy, 'Recent Developments in English Studies at the Centre: the English Studies Group, 1978–9', in Stuart Hall *et al.* (eds), *Culture, Media, Language: Working Papers in Cultural Studies, 1972–79* (London: Hutchinson, 1980).

4 The Negative of a Person: Media, Image and Authenticity in Sylvia Plath's *The Bell Jar*[1]

STAN SMITH

Marilyn Monroe is reported to have said that being photographed gave her a 'womby-tomby feeling'. Characteristically, Norman Mailer interprets this as the expression of a larger identity-crisis in the modern American self. In the photograph, as in death, the subject is expropriated into pure objectivity: the person becomes an image. Yet the image on the movie-screen or in the girlie-magazine continues to go through the motions, a sex-object not released by the death of its original, in a strange post-mortem limbo which is the secular equivalent of Yeats's artifice of eternity: 'I call it death-in-life and life-in-death.' Monroe's own suicide, in this analysis, would seem to be linked intimately with her status as pin-up and movie-star. What I wish to consider here is the link between suicide and the manufacture of graven images in the work of Sylvia Plath, as the symptom of a characteristically American dilemma: a dilemma focused in Monroe's representative and pathetic destiny.

In Sylvia Plath's only novel, *The Bell Jar* (1963), which fictionalises, with dispassionate stringency, the case-history of Plath's adolescent breakdown, the themes of suicide and self-estrangement are continuously linked to the leitmotiv of the photograph, in a curious and significant symbiosis. The photographic image becomes a sign of the self's mortification in a society which everywhere demands submission to imposed stereotypes of behaviour and normality. The photograph becomes, in a sense, as much a *petite mort* as orgasm was for the seventeenth-century poet. In Plath's hands, the conjunction finally implies a political critique of a society where

95

negativity seems the only form of resistance to manipulative conventions of identity and relationship.

The protagonist of *The Bell Jar*, Esther Greenwood, is one of a party of girls from small towns all over the United States who, as winners of a competition run by the magazine *Ladies' Day*, have been invited to New York to participate in the running of the magazine. A final part of their assignment consists of being photographed for the magazine in characteristic poses, with props that express their chosen vocations. Esther, reluctantly admitting the wish to be a poet, is equipped with a rose for her photograph. The prop, in its clichéd commonplaceness, reveals the fraudulence of the celebrity with which each of the girls is momentarily endowed by this attention from the media. In reality, the magazine is indifferent to any real specificity. The girls are merely ciphers, insignificant in themselves, as poetry, Esther's first love, is no more than shorthand for a familiar form of adolescent self-indulgence. At first, unable to emulate the cynicism or naïvety of her companions, Esther is pliant and obliging before the camera, until the photographer's request, 'show us how happy it makes you to write a poem' (p. 106), prompts, not the expected smile, but a collapse into tears. With this first sign of authentic feeling the photographer and the whole flimsy, artificial scene vanish, as if by magic, leaving Esther feeling

limp and betrayed, like the skin shed by a terrible animal. It was a relief to be free of the animal, but it seemed to have taken my spirit with it, and everything else it could lay its paws on.   (p. 107)

This motif, of being merely a surface stretched over some alien, possessing power, recurs throughout Plath's work. But there is also a larger pattern at work here. In the world of the media, all private aspirations and dreams melt down into the homogeneous mass of a statistical average, as the magazine's editor, 'Jay Cee', immediately demonstrates by bringing Esther, to cheer her up, a pile of manuscripts submitted by would-be writers from all over America, flooding in, she says, sixty an hour, over the Fiction Editor's desk. The experience supposedly peculiar to Esther is presented, in what is intended to be a reassurance, as a common ambition. Uniqueness is an illusion: Esther is really no different from any of those other would-be writers, and maturity is to acknowledge this fact. The discrepancy between the actual condition of the character, collapsing

into tears, and the response required of her ('give us a smile')
reproduces that larger discrepancy between reality and image which
is a key theme in the book. The photographic situation reduces real
people to the status of stage props, illustrations of social archetypes,
ultimately, in a recurring image, to the ventriloquist's dummies
whose whole lives are naïve, unthinking or cynical adjustments to
externally regulated norms. Schizophrenia is latent, here, in the
discrepancy between self-identity and identity for others, between
the person and the image marketed by the magazine.

A similar correlation of photograph and inauthentic identity is
offered in Esther's first visit to the psychiatrist. On his desk stands
a silver-framed photograph of his wife and children, half-turned
towards the patient's chair:

> For some reason the photograph made me furious. I didn't see why
> it should be turned half towards me unless Doctor Gordon was
> trying to show me right away that he was married to some glamorous
> woman and I'd better not get any funny ideas. (pp. 135–6)

What Esther observes here – and it is a recurring note throughout the
book – is the artificiality, the artifice, of Doctor Gordon's identity.
Success means fabricating, and believing in, a face to meet the faces
that we meet. He is a public image presented to the world, and
marriage, like the photograph, is a mirror in which he admires his
own image. His narcissism extends even to the choice of a wife, as
we deduce from Esther's casual and cunningly unobtrusive remark
that the woman in the photograph 'could have been Doctor Gordon's
sister'.

The whole reality of *The Bell Jar*, in fact, is a world mediated
through graven images, through photographs, movie films, magazines and newspapers. The novel is littered with copies of
magazines – in homes, in clinics and waiting-rooms, in lounges and
asylums – that propagate the basic imagery of American normality.
The magazine *Ladies' Day* is itself, Esther notes, 'the big women's
magazine that features lush double page spreads of technicolor meals'
(p. 26). The link I've suggested here is initiated in the opening
paragraphs of the novel, which contrast Esther's actual response to
what's happening to her with those responses which will be attributed
to her on the evidence of the derealized, glamorous images the
magazine will distribute:

I was supposed to be having the time of my life. . . . And when
my picture came out in the magazine the twelve of us were
working on – drinking martinis in a skimpy, imitation silver-lamé
bodice stuck to a big fat cloud of white tulle, on some Starlight
Roof, in the company of several anonymous young men with all-
American bone-structures hired or loaned for the occasion –
everybody would think I must be having a real whirl. (p. 2)

That last 'real' has considerable resonance, taking up the 'imitation'
earlier in the sentence, and linking discreetly with the actuality of
'anonymous . . . hired or loaned for the occasion'.

This is only one of many instances in which image-propagation
substitutes for an authentically shared reality. There are, for example, the old numbers of *Time* and *Life* at her boy-friend Buddy
Willard's sanatorium, from which 'the face of Eisenhower beamed
up at me, bald and blank as the face of a foetus in a bottle' (p. 93);
an image significantly inverted at the gynaecological clinic where
Esther later goes to have a contraceptive device fitted and finds
herself leafing through a copy of *Baby Talk*:

The fat, bright faces of babies beamed up at me, page after
page – bald babies, chocolate-coloured babies, Eisenhower-faced
babies. (p. 234)

That almost subliminal link of American president and baby
proposes, though it never explicitly draws, a relation between the
domestic and the political, as if marriage and motherhood were the
essential ideological instruments through which the American way
of life is sustained. Indeed, elsewhere in the novel, Esther speaks
of them as 'like being brainwashed, and afterwards you went about
numb as a slave in some private, totalitarian state' (p. 89). Such
brain-washing is strikingly overt in the *Reader's Digest* article, 'In
Defense of Chastity', which Esther's mother sends her at college.
The deadpan banality of Esther's paraphrase is a skilfully contrived
commentary on the mystificatory special-pleading and final calculat-
ing cynicism that lie behind its high-minded clichés (p. 85).

There are other forms of image-indoctrination: the pop-songs, for
example, quoted occasionally in the novel consistently identify an
'all-American' wholeness with domesticity and parochial quiescence:
'Why, oh why, did I leave Wyoming?' and 'I was born in Kansas, I
was bred in Kansas, and when I marry I'll be wed in Kansas' (p. 16).

In the romantic novels of Philomena Guinea, whose scholarship Esther wins, the same process is at work. They have a primarily ideological function, reinforcing the values and attitudes which privatise and subordinate the individual to the social totality. But as Esther points out, the books earned Philomena Guinea, who confessed to her surrogate daughter that she had been very stupid at college, millions of dollars (p. 42). The correlation, of financial success with moronic conformism, is clear enough.

At times, such a debased art falls into pastiche of itself, becoming a self-parasitic genre which seeks its ratification by reference to an autonomous, counterfeit world of 'conventional' images and 'artificial' expectations. This is apparent in Esther's account of the film at which she begins to feel the effect of food-poisoning from the *Ladies' Day* lunch (the suggestion being that the film too is a form of poisoning). The actresses in the movie do not imitate 'reality'; rather they imitate other, better-known actresses, copies of June Allyson or Elizabeth Taylor, just as the film is merely another manifestation of a worn-out genre, 'a football romance in technicolor'.

The girls perform the ritual actions expected of heroines in a football romance, and, in the ballroom, swoop across the floor in dresses like something out of *Gone with the Wind*. There is no such thing as a 'clean' reflection of reality – only the reproduction of already ideologically structured narratives and characters. Its conventional nature makes the film absolutely predictable, one more American success story and moral fable, reinforcing a simple cultural message which equates marriage with fulfilment. 'Nice' girls get married, and 'sexy' girls end up lonely, abandoned ex-mistresses (p. 43).

Increasingly, Esther's revolt against American values is couched as a rejection of these stereotypes, in which the subordination of the woman in marriage is strangely linked with the power of the camera over its objects. Thus, in an episode with her boy-friend, Buddy Willard, which predicts the later encounter with the *Ladies' Day* photographer, Esther feels a contrast between poetry and the photograph as modes of self-presentation. Esther tries to offer herself authentically to Buddy by reading poetry to him. He is more interested in seeing her naked; but to her the request is depressing and reductive, calling up the impersonal, statistical grading of the posture-picture in which one has to 'stand naked in front of a camera', reduced to an assessable, publicly available image for the college gym files, to be graded A, B, C or D 'depending on how straight you are' (p. 71). The photograph is a primary alienation of the person. One *gives* oneself in poetry, but one is *taken* in a photograph. Buddy Willard's smile, Esther tells us much later, recalling this period, once 'flashed on easily and frequently as a photographer's bulb' (p. 252).

Rejection of the stereotypes peddled by popular culture at times seems possible only through rebellion against the collective American identity itself, as in the skiing episode just after Buddy has proposed marriage to her in classically chauvinist terms ('How would you like to be Mrs Buddy Willard?'). It is a pop-song, with its ironic reminder of Esther's virginity, which prompts her to indignant revolt:

> On every side of me the red and blue and white jacketed skiers tore away down the blinding slope like fugitive bits of an American flag. From the foot of the ski run, the imitation log cabin lodge piped its popular songs into the overhang of silence.
>
> > *Gazing down on the Jungfrau*
> > *From our chalet for two . . .*
>
> One careless, superb gesture, and I would be hurled into motion down the slope towards the small khaki spot in the sidelines, among the spectators, which was Buddy Willard. (p. 99)

Marriage, from this 'Mount Pisgah' height (p. 98), is not the American Promised Land presented by the song, but takes on a chilly desolation as a future already threaded with the filaments of a prearranged destiny. The 'one careless, superb gesture' of revolt is also a near-suicidal flight from that prospect. It is also, in some unexplained way, a breaking free from the statutory conformism represented by the 'American flag', by the duplicitous smiles we make for the camera. But that specious world reconstitutes itself, in all its monochrome monotony, at the bottom of the ski run:

> Buddy's face hung over me, near and huge, like a distracted planet. Other faces showed themselves up in back of his. Behind them, black dots swarmed on a plane of whiteness. Piece by piece, as at the strokes of a dull godmother's wand, the old world sprang back into position. (p. 102)

Earlier in the novel Esther had experienced the indignity of 'shrinking to a small black dot' in the eyes of others (p. 17) and of 'melting into the shadows like the negative of a person I'd never seen before in my life' (p. 10). Here, the condition of being a small black dot is seen as a generic one, while the photographic negative becomes an ambiguous metaphor for that negation of the self which a conformist society requires. Repeatedly, in *The Bell Jar*, authenticity seems to lie only in self-destructive revolt against the levelling anonymity of mass-society, in some negation of the negation that restores freedom to the putative 'real' self lurking behind the 'doubleness' of the image and persona. Yet this 'real' self remains perennially *unrealized*, subsisting only as an aching emptiness and dissatisfaction within the performances of a socially given identity as 'bits of an American flag'.

Revolt against such conventional presentations of self draws equally on the images circulated by the media. After having ECT prescribed for her schizophrenia, Esther becomes preoccupied, for example, with the story of a suicide attempt headlined in the local press. She scrutinises the would-be suicide's face, looking for the meaning of his act:

But the smudgy crags of George Pollucci's features melted away as I peered at them, and resolved themselves into a regular pattern of dark and light and medium grey dots.
The inky black newspaper paragraph didn't tell why Mr Pollucci was on the ledge, or what Sgt Kilmartin did to him when he finally got him in through the window. (p. 144)

If the event itself is endowed with histrionic properties ('spotlighted', 'background'), close scrutiny of its image reveals only the artificiality and limitations of the photograph, as an aesthetic genre arrested in 'attitudes counterfeiting life'. The 'message' dissolves into the medium. The image transcribes only the surface of the event, derealizing it, evacuating its inner content. And that surface dissolves on inspection into its primary constituents, 'dark and light and medium grey dots'. There is nothing 'written' on Pollucci's face; rather, his 'face' is merely a sign, written on the surface of the newspaper. The authentic, 'true' meaning is nowhere in the picture.

After her ECT treatment, Esther returns to the headlines, to find there the story of another suicide, of a 'starlet' whose picture she compares with a snapshot of her own. The only distinguishing difference is the eyes. Hers are open, while those of the dead girl are closed:

> But I knew if the dead girl's eyes were to be thumbed wide, they
> would look out at me with the same dead, black, vacant expression
> as the eyes in the snapshot. (p. 154)

Plath is playing games with the idea of the image here, because, of course, that which is not apparent on the surface of an image does not exist; the 'illusion of depth' leads us to posit eyes beneath the shut lids but, as with the picture of Pollucci, there is no interior, no hidden meaning or hidden self. And this leads Esther herself to summon that 'little chorus of voices' which indict her for being equally 'Factitious, artificial, sham' (p. 155).

Suicide becomes Esther's own paradoxical mode of self-realization, a refusal to be that which the other makes one. But, in fact, she succumbs in her attempt to the very processes against which she revolts, taken up by the media and accommodated to their estranging stereotypes. For the suicide, at once victim and hero of a society which expects conformity and self-sublimation, ratifies by his self-cancellation the right of that society to override his individual wishes and ambitions. Suicide is an institutionalized acknowledgement of inadequacy in face of society's demands. It is a guilty introjection of revolt that is propagated sympathetically by the media because, in its inexplicable, mysterious irrationality, it endorses the rationality of the order against which it protests.

Esther, recovering from her suicide attempt in a mental hospital, finds that her act has converted her into a media celebrity. Here she encounters Joan Gilling, an old rival for Buddy Willard, who has been prompted by the newspaper coverage of Esther's attempt to emulate her. Joan produces a pile of clippings which record in graphic detail the stages of the passion play which have transformed Esther into an 'imitation star'. A 'tarty picture' blown up from the *Ladies' Day* party photograph carries the headline:

SCHOLARSHIP GIRL MISSING. MOTHER WORRIED.
(p. 210)

Even as she tries to defect, Esther is reappropriated by the institutions, defined in terms of media, college, family as a marketable 'image', a news story.

Subsequent headlines reduce her to the generic 'GIRL', as they unfold the lineaments of a conventional melodrama which, at this level of abstraction, takes on mythic proportions. Esther cannot even recognize the image ('I couldn't think who had taken that picture either'), while the last photograph shows her found alive, but totally depersonalized, rolled limply in a blanket, her features invisible, being lifted into an ambulance.

Esther cannot identify her own experience with these alien images. But it is on the basis of such fabricated 'pseudo-events' that Joan has constructed her fantasies, and finally succeeds in killing herself. Clearly these incidents, narrated in such a deliberately offhand way, are making a complex point about the relationship between reality and artifice, between the events of this world and the transmutation they undergo in any reporting of them. For the news item is here seen as a literary genre, a mode for reconstructing reality which endows it with new and fictive elements which in turn may react back upon the world from which they are drawn. The extent to which Esther has freed herself from such conventions is disclosed when Joan and the other woman in the hospital, leafing through a new issue of a fashion magazine, find what they think to be Esther's photograph (pp. 219–20). Esther is dismissive and disowning. The glamour with which she is endowed in their eyes by becoming a magazine image is for her totally extraneous. Likewise the narrating Esther, ten years later, refuses either to confirm or deny, for the reader, that the magazine is *Ladies' Day* or the photograph of her.

I used, above, the term 'pseudo-event' to describe such media-invented stories. The word was usefully coined by Daniel Boorstin in his book *The Image: or What Happened to the American Dream* (1962) to express an America dominated by a public relations ethos in which 'The question "Is it real?" is less important than "Is it newsworthy?" '. Throughout *The Bell Jar*, the photographic image and journalistic report become paradigms of that process by which reality is transfigured into 'pseudo-event', reducing the individual from his or her uniqueness to the status of a commodity circulated through ineluctable systems of exchange. The very flavour of authenticity then becomes no more than a cipher within the production and distribution of a 'news' which has usurped sway over the individuals who 'make it new'. In such a world, nothing is ever in fact new, in any real sense; everything is always simply the repetition of a pre-existent stereotype; personal autonomy is an illusion which can be shed only in self-extinction. But this act too takes on the status of a 'pseudo-event': it is a marketable consummation.

In Plath's novel, the private chronicle thus assumes a generic
dimension which quietly unfolds political depths. When Esther, in
Belsize mental hospital, is summoned by the nurse's call of 'A man
to see you!' (p. 250), she recalls an exactly similar summons in
college (p. 60) which had demonstrated the weakness and dependency of her socio-sexual role as 'a slave in some private totalitarian
state'. The girls in college and the women in Belsize both sit waiting
'under bell jars of a sort' for someone else to call them into being
(p. 251).

She has a similar revelation at Dr Gordon's private hospital, where
the 'uniformity to their faces' (p. 149) of the patients makes them
indistinguishable from the occupants of 'a lounge in a guest house I
visited once on an island off the coast of Maine' (p. 148), of which,
for all its apparent 'character', the hospital living-room is a perfect
'replica'. Uniformity, with the illusion of distinction, is the hallmark
of such a civilization.

Only such an implicitly political dimension to the novel can explain
the apparently casual historical situating, at the height of the Cold
War, of the opening paragraph:

> It was a queer, sultry summer, the summer they electrocuted the
> Rosenbergs, and I didn't know what I was doing in New York.
> I'm stupid about executions. The idea of being electrocuted makes
> me sick, and that's all there was to read about in the papers . . . .
> It had nothing to do with me, but I couldn't help wondering what
> it would be like, being burned alive along all your nerves. . . . I
> kept hearing about the Rosenbergs over the radio and at the
> office until I couldn't get them out of my mind. . . . I knew
> something was wrong with me that summer because all I could
> think about was the Rosenbergs and how stupid I'd been to buy
> all those uncomfortable, expensive clothes, hanging limp as fish
> in my closet and how all the little successes I'd totted up so
> happily at college fizzled to nothing outside the slick marble and
> plate-glass fronts along Madison Avenue. (p. 1)

This apparently gratuitous detail is never explained; but the Rosenbergs recur later, at a crucial moment in the text, just before Esther
breaks down in front of the photographer. Her companion Hilda, a
vacuous 'mannequin' living in a world of 'fashion blurbs, silver and
full of nothing', responds to Esther's authentic horror at the

execution with what seems like a totally conditioned, rote response derived from the media brouhaha: 'It's awful such people should be alive. . . . I'm so glad they're going die' (p. 104). Hilda's voice, we're told, is like that of someone possessed by a dybbuk. Whether the fate of the Rosenbergs invests her subsequent ECT with an extra frisson, or whether, retrospectively, the narrating Esther recalls the execution in unconscious association with her own, more benign treatment, the subliminal link is clear. Esther too, in her rebellion, is a public figure, who has to be restored to quietude and acquiescence. When her mother reports that Doctor Gordon wants her to be transferred for shock treatment to his private hospital:

> I felt a sharp stab of curiosity, as if I had just read a terrible newspaper headline about somebody else. (p. 143)

In one sense, of course, this schizophrenically distanced self *is* another: the estranged being that exists primarily as the object of other people's operations. Yet Hilda's own self-alienation makes it clear that, for Plath, schizophrenia is not merely the condition of the sick, but the characteristic mode of existence of a whole society which can live and think only through manipulated stereotypes of action and feeling. Waking from her first dose of ECT, Esther sees it unequivocally as a punishment for some fundamentally un-American activity, and wonders what terrible thing she has done (p. 152). It's no accident, then, that Esther should envisage losing her 'all-American' virginity to a Russian simultaneous interpreter at the UN. In rejecting a constricted, paranoid definition of what it is to be an American woman – the holy trinity of maidenhead, marriage and motherhood – Esther is defecting, in her mind, from a whole Cold War one-dimensionality, shaped, in the last instance, by the paranoid style of politics of the McCarthy era. The novel, then, speaks to us of two separate moments in postwar American history: of 1953, when feeling 'It had nothing to do with me', Esther Greenwood nevertheless 'couldn't get them out of my mind', when the Rosenbergs became for her, unconsciously, the figure of a larger dilemma; and of that period ten years later when the narrating Esther, apparently cured of her insanity, has entered into the states of marriage and motherhood, and has begun to frame, for herself, the contours of her shaping experience.

The year in which *The Bell Jar* appeared also saw the publication of a text which was shortly to become a classic of the American women's movement: Betty Friedan's *The Feminine Mystique*. Though Plath could hardly have read it, it provides in the main outlines of its analysis a striking parallel to the insights of Plath's novel. Friedan observes:

> The problems and dissatisfactions of their lives, and mine, and the way our education has contributed to them, simply did not fit the image of the modern American woman as she was written about in women's magazines, studied and analysed in classrooms and clinics, praised and damned in a ceaseless barrage of words ever since the end of the Second World War. There was a strange discrepancy between the reality of our lives as women and the image to which we were trying to conform, the image that I came to call the feminine mystique. I wondered if other women faced this schizophrenic split, and what it meant.[2]

Friedan noted that all the women she interviewed were suffering from a profound identity-crisis, whether 'facing or evading the question of who they were'. But these were 'women for whom if the mystique were right there should be no such question and who thus had no name for the problem troubling them'. It's precisely this lack of a language with which to identify and disarm the problem which represents, in Plath's novel, the final triumph of ideology. For ideology seals off the real options that might be available to what Friedan calls 'The Forfeited Self', and offers instead spurious remedies: schizophrenia, madness, suicide. And if these options are not taken, then the self is left where Esther finds herself ten years later, trapped in what one of Friedan's chapter headings called 'Progressive Dehumanization: the Comfortable Concentration Camp'. Living as 'the negative of a person', an image, not a self, is to move in the shadow of death.

Notes

1. This is the revised version of a paper originally delivered at the Warsaw University English Institute Symposium on American Literature and Society, Warsaw University, Poland, May 1980. Page numbers in brackets refer to the Faber edition of *The Bell Jar* (London: Faber and Faber, 1966). *The Bell Jar* was first published by William Heinemann (1963). Another aspect of this argument is covered in my article 'Attitudes

Counterfeiting Life: the Irony of Artifice in Sylvia Plath's *The Bell Jar*', *Critical Quarterly*, vol. 17, no. 3 (Autumn 1975) pp. 247–60. For a discussion of Plath's poetry, see my *Inviolable Voice: History and Twentieth-Century Poetry* (Dublin: Gill and Macmillan; New Jersey: Humanities Press, 1982).

2. Betty Friedan, *The Feminine Mystique* (New York: W. W. Norton, 1963; Harmondsworth, Middx: Penguin, 1986) p. 2.

5 A Question of Inheritance: Canadian Women's Short Stories

CORAL ANN HOWELLS

Canadian women's fiction explores women's relation to their literary and cultural inheritance within a distinctively postcolonial context which both highlights and problematises many of the issues facing the 'determined women' of this collection. The three stories I have chosen – Alice Munro's 'Heirs of the Living Body', Audrey Thomas's 'Crossing the Rubicon' and Margaret Atwood's 'Bluebeard's Egg' – were all written over the past twenty years.[1] They scrutinise 'traditional cultural dependencies', to borrow Robert Kroetsch's phrase.[2] While he used it in a nationalist sense to describe the efforts of the 'best Canadian artists', we may use it in a gendered sense of the 'best Canadian women writers', for it points up the analogy with the colonial mentality through which writers have described women's sense of their own condition.[3] The Canadian novelist Margaret Laurence described it as 'the tendency of women to accept male definitions of ourselves, to be self-deprecating and uncertain and to rage inwardly'.[4] This colonial inheritance is there to be resisted in postcolonial Canadian fiction written by both men and women, though arguably women's awareness is sharpened by their gender sense of marginality and dispossession. So, a question of inheritance becomes a questioning of inheritance in stories that express a very ambivalent relation to tradition and history. As we might expect, these women's stories are about resistance and the need for revision. Though in none of them is tradition fiercely rejected, they are all problematised by their authors' sense of history and their knowledge that they are writing within the very traditions they are determinedly resisting. Consequently they are all stories divided against themselves in an exposure of the limits of fiction and the failure of fiction and real life to coincide.

These three stories of women writing or preparing to write are all responses to the revival of the feminist movement of the 1960s, which coincided in Canada with an upsurge of cultural nationalism.[5] We may perceive a parallel between women's challenge to traditional structures of authority and Canada's questioning of its colonial relations with England and France and also with the United States. Nationalists and feminists alike were trying to create a language through which to express their own experience and to write their versions of history from a different angle. Canadian women are caught in a double bind, writing as Canadians against their European inheritance and forced as women to revise strong patriarchal elements in their Canadian inheritance. 'Heirs of the Living Body' is the only one of these stories which foregrounds Canadianness in its history of Ontario Pioneers, though 'Crossing the Rubicon', with its reference to Montreal, obliquely signals Canada's linguistically divided inheritance and 'Bluebeard's Egg' with its descriptions of the ravines within the Toronto cityscape evokes the wilderness which still dominates Canada's cultural mythology about itself. Certainly these stories are united in their refusal to privilege any one tradition or set of cultural values as authoritative, preferring instead to recognise the multiple, often dissident voices which are interwoven into Canadian women's inheritance.

Though they may all display distinctively Canadian 'field markings' (Atwood's term from birdwatching),[6] these stories demonstrate very different approaches to the question of inheritance, which may in turn be related to the different experiences of the writers themselves. Munro, Thomas and Atwood are all middle-class university-educated women now in their mid-forties and fifties, though the patterns of their domestic and writing lives separate Munro and Thomas quite decisively from Atwood, who is the youngest. Alice Munro sold her first story to the Canadian Broadcasting Commission in 1949 or 1950. Then she married:

> All through the 50s I was living in a dormitory suburb, having babies, and it [writing] wasn't part of the accepted thing for a girl or a woman to do at that time either, but it never occurred to me that I should stop.[7]

Her first short story collection *Dance of the Happy Shades* was not published till 1968, when it won the Governor-General's Award. As she recalls, 'The Victoria paper printed an article that said, "Mother of Three Wins Award." The *Globe and Mail* described me as "a shy housewife" ' (ibid. p. 128). Thomas's experience was not dissimilar. Having grown up in New York State and married in England, she emigrated to Canada in 1959. As a wife and mother she was not taken seriously at the University of British Columbia where she was a graduate student:

> I'll tell you an amazing thing. I was coming along the corridor one day – and I had published *Ten Green Bottles* so this is '67 now – and I met a professor I quite liked . . . I said, 'Oh, I've just published a book.' And he said, 'Is it a children's book?' And I said, 'You wouldn't ask a man that.' And I thought, right, I can't stand this place. That's it.[8]

Atwood's career pattern was different. An unmarried student at the University of Toronto in the early 1960s, she published her first book of poems in 1961. She went on to Harvard graduate school and won the Governor-General's Award in 1966 for her second book of poems, *The Circle Game*. Her first novel *The Edible Woman* was published in 1969 and more poems, novels and criticism in the early 1970s. By the time her daughter was born in the mid-1970s she was already an established writer, so that she did not have to suffer the constraints of female stereotyping in the same ways as Munro and Thomas. Such patterns of experience have consequences in fiction: Munro's stories question the appropriateness of stereotypes but show women camouflaging their resistance, and Thomas's stories are full of the contradictions inherent in women's resistance to tradition. By contrast, Atwood is far more urgent than the others about the need to expose cultural fictions of gender as damaging lies.

The titles of the three stories I have chosen allude to traditions which marginalise women, exclude them, or punish them. 'Heirs of the Living Body' is a reference to the Pauline Christian tradition which has always been notoriously anti-women;[9] 'Crossing the Rubicon' recalls the story of Julius Caesar's act of transgression against Pompey and the Roman Senate as part of the history of Great Men – 'No names of mine' as Adrienne Rich would say; and 'Bluebeard's Egg' is the most sinister of all. Women are there in the fairytale but they are killed for wanting to know more than a husband thinks they should.

It will be noted that the foregoing are all European literary traditions, and we may wonder whether Canadian traditions are any more hospitable to women. Indeed there is one tradition which women have colonised for themselves through their writing and that is, appropriately enough, the wilderness. The wilderness of trackless forests or unending prairie dominated the history of Canadian settlement, and it is noteworthy that since the mid-nineteenth century women's stories of settlement in the wilderness have been told with a different emphasis from men's. Instead of stories of exploration and exploitation, women's stories like Susanna Moodie's *Roughing It In the Bush* (1852) and Catherine Parr Traill's *The Backwoods of Canada* (1836) have tended to focus on the sense of freedom from social conventions that life in the backwoods gave them. Their tales of women's self-discovery established a tradition of women's wilderness writing which has continued to the present day in the work of Margaret Laurence, Alice Munro, Margaret Atwood and Marian Engel. Though living conditions have altered radically, the wilderness is still there in these fictions as an alternative dimension to small town or suburban living. Munro's narrator acknowledges the tradition in 'Heirs of the Living Body' in her resistance to the validity of her uncle's county history where she insists on evading the maps and landmarks that obsessed his vision. It is also there in 'Bluebeard's Egg' in the ravines at the edge of the protagonist's cultivated garden, reminding her of unknown forces which she assiduously tries to shut out.

Munro's, Atwood's and Thomas's stories show the artistic consequences of women's revision of tradition, in forms that differ refreshingly from one another. 'Heirs of the Living Body' looks very like traditional realism, whereas 'Crossing the Rubicon' is a disrupted postmodernist narrative, and 'Bluebeard's Egg' works within a woman's romantic narrative to deconstruct that dangerous fantasy of conventionality. All three are crisscrossed by inter-textual allusions, signalling the traditions within which they are written just as they all attempt to revise them to accommodate more adequately modern women's experience and knowledge. They are all records of partial success, registering dislocation as a feature of these women's lives and of their storytelling. Finally, all are mixtures of genre codes, interweaving history, realism and romance.

Perhaps the most striking example is Munro's 'Heirs of the Living Body' which is really a short story in what is called a 'novel' (*Lives of Girls and Women*) but is structurally a short-story cycle, a very interesting example of mixed genre codes in the collection as a whole. Its title signals that this is a story about heritage and organic continuity, and it is Del Jordan's story about her Canadian heritage,

her family history and her place in it. The custodian of tradition is
a patriarchal figure, Uncle Craig, the clerk of the south-western
Ontario township of Fairmile, the keeper of the family tree and the
chronicler of the county's history since its settlement in the 1860s.
The story Uncle Craig writes focuses on what *men* have done, for
men's work is public and worthy to be recorded (even if, like the
men in Del's own family, they have done 'nothing remarkable'),
while women's work is private and domestic. His history creates a
'solid structure of lives supporting us from the past', an image as
reassuring in its security as his own brick house. However, what is
remarkable about the story Del tells is the revelation of the secret
lives and the secret places that are enclosed within the living body
of social history, for she tells the stories of the women's lives which
exist within this structure. There are the practical jokes and the
hidden rampaging mockery of Del's two maiden aunts who live with
Uncle Craig and who run the farm: 'They respected men's work
beyond anything; they also laughed at it' (p. 32); there are Aunt
Moira's dark female secrets as a 'wrecked survivor of the female
life', and the secret life of her subnormal daughter Mary Agnes, just
as there are the vulnerable moments in Del's mother's life, a 1950s
feminist with advanced attitudes towards possibilities in life for
women and advanced attitudes towards death. Del is the inheritor
of all these women's life stories as she tells her own. The story
begins to look like a mosaic of secret alternative worlds that coexist
under the surface of ordinariness. Everything presents a double
image of itself – even Uncle Craig's solid brick house which has on
the wall a photograph of the original log cabin built on the wilderness
site in the 1860s: 'That picture seemed to have been in another
country, where everything was much lower, muddier, darker than
here' (p. 28).

This doubleness finds its focus in Uncle Craig's death which is the
centre of the narrative. Death transforms the safe house into a maze
with a dead body at its centre, to be avoided at all costs – yet which
cannot be avoided. Del perceives that the mystery of death is the
excess term which cannot be accommodated, the thing within which
is also outside, 'floating around loose, ignored but powerful', the
great disrupter of order and continuity, whatever her mother says
about the beauty of organ transplants as a kind of life after death.
At the funeral Del tries to retreat from death and from family ritual
by going to the old store-room filled with objects from the past; but
she cannot escape being a member of the living body. She cannot

even bite her way out of the family by sinking her teeth into Mary Agnes's arm, for 'freedom is not so easily come by' – and she is forgiven and restored with tea and cake. She even has to accept the gift of her uncle's unfinished county history presented to her by her aunts. She may discard it (which she does) as something 'dead, heavy and useless' and let it rot in the basement, yet later on she herself will tell the local history of her own town. Del discovers that she is Uncle Craig's true heir. Though she refuses to carry on the dead past in her uncle's chosen form, as history, she still carries her memories of the past into the present and writes them down as her uncle had done. The difference is that Del, by writing at all, presents another possibility for women not even envisaged by her uncle but entrusted to her by her aunts. Still committed like her uncle to 'getting everything in and still making it read smooth' (p. 61), Del insists on telling the story in her own way and from her own angle so that it will be a different story. Instead of writing history, she writes fiction, and so though her story is always incomplete, it is for different reasons from Uncle Craig's:

> The hope of accuracy we bring to such tasks is crazy, heartbreak-
> ing. And no list could hold what I wanted; every smell, pothole,
> pain, crack, delusion, held still and held together – radiant, ever-
> lasting.   (p. 249)

The story itself shows the extent of Del's revision of her patriarchal inheritance, for as a female chronicler she writes in the women's stories which her uncle has left out, and as a writer of fiction she tells the dark secrets hidden within the body of official history. Most importantly, her story shows how traditional realist writing can be made to include moments of intense subjectivity and visionary per-ception which challenge the authority of realism, reminding us of the incompleteness and partial truth of all narrative structures.[10]

Audrey Thomas's 'Crossing the Rubicon' is also about women's relation to history, telling the story of women's dissent in a more disrupted form than 'Heirs of the Living Body'. The title signals its inheritance with the reference to Julius Caesar's declaration of war against the established powers of the Roman Senate and his irrevers-ible act of transgression, implicitly compared with that of a modern woman in her attempts at self-assertion against conventional limits. It is a story at odds with the maxims and mottoes of our culture, but also at odds with itself in its exposure of the gap between fiction and real life.

Briefly, the story is about a woman doing several things at once. Because she is a writer, she is trying to write a story which she does not particularly want to write about a woman in Montreal who is going to have lunch with her ex-lover; and because she is the mother of a twelve-year-old girl, she is thinking about the cupcakes her daughter is going to make for the boys at school on Valentine's Day and what this gesture signifies in terms of male/female relationships in the 1980s. There are really two stories here, not a story within a story, for one is not privileged over the other; instead, each disrupts the telling of the other and there are odd points of connection between them. Then there is a third story which we are not told: why telling this story about the woman in Montreal is both important to the narrator and something which she does not want to do. We might be tempted to see the 'I' narrator of the Valentine's Day cupcakes and the 'she' in the Montreal story as doubles, but the absence of the third story problematises the relationship between them. What we get is a disrupted narrative characteristic of Thomas's 'collage technique', which juxtaposes fragments of the narrator's life story with stretches of the Montreal story. Do we read one story as a comment on the other? There are certainly points of similarity but the relationship is unstable throughout, and the ending emphasises the gap between these alternative stories that the woman has been telling.

The narrator's story about cupcakes and Valentine's Day candy hearts with mottoes on is the old female plot about women's romantic fantasies; 'Nothing ever really changes', as she says. Just as her sister and her girlfriend had made food to impress the boys on Valentine's Day in the 1940s and the boys had not been particularly appreciative, so here is her daughter thirty years later still making cupcakes to impress the boys. As if to confirm this fundamental lack of change, the narrator recognises the mottoes on the candy hearts as being the same as those in the 1940s:

'TO EACH HIS OWN', 'WHY NOT SAY YES', 'BE GOOD TO ME', 'LET'S GET TOGETHER', 'KISS ME', 'BE MY SUGAR DADDY', ... 'LOVE ME'.
(p. 157)

The same old romantic plots are encoded on the hearts. As the narrator says, they don't taste quite as nice as they used to:

These have a bitter taste. . . . But the taste is not the important
thing, it's the mottoes.

The old cultural myths seem to have the power to survive social
change.

It ought to be possible now to tell a different version of a love
story which reverses the power dynamics in a sexual relationship.
The narrator does succeed in writing such a story, about the woman
in Montreal who ends a quarrel by crossing a street against the lights
and walking away from 'her ex-lover, her love'. This is her Crossing
of the Rubicon, her irreversible step and her challenge to the established order, and it is all the consequence of her very feminine
demand, 'Tell me that you miss me' – which the man refuses to do.
The end of that story is precariously double-edged; is a crossing of
the Rubicon irreversible when it is only a street? From the other
side the man finally calls out, 'I miss you, you bitch!' And she stops.
But she manages to make her grand gesture of refusal and to wave
goodbye when she remembers the ending of the film 'Cabaret' where
Liza Minnelli waves goodbye with such panache of green fingernails
to Michael York. That film was based on another story, by a
man – Christopher Isherwood's 'Goodbye to Berlin' – though as he
was a homosexual, she reflects, he probably had different attitudes
towards gender stereotypes anyway. At least it reaches a moment
of finality: 'She waves goodbye. And she doesn't look back.' Then
a sudden shift in narrative distance occurs: 'In my story that is. She
doesn't look back in my story' (p. 168). It is the fictionality of the
Montreal story that is emphasised as a gap opens up between its
closure and the narrator's life story, where looking back has been
her principal concern.

So, who is to beware the Ides of March, or indeed of February,
with which this story began? Is it only Julius Caesar or is it the
narrator? Is it her daughter? Is it the 'she' in Montreal? Or is it the
reader? And is telling the story a Crossing of the Rubicon for the
narrator as well as for her protagonist? Irreversible gestures show a
dangerous tendency towards reversals here. There is no possible
resolution in such a double-voiced narrative where a carefully
ordered fictional structure is disrupted by contradictory undercur-
rents of feeling, underlining the difficulties of women trying to write
new versions of old stories in their fictions and in their lives where
the victories are more tentative. Yet strongest of all is our sense of
women's determination not to give up but to be 'still questing, still

moving, still sailing on'. These are, as Thomas says on the dust jacket of *Real Mothers*, 'the women I am particularly interested in'.

If Thomas's story shows how women's revisions of old stories entail a deal of painful unwriting of their own internalised narratives, Atwood's story 'Bluebeard's Egg' takes this dilemma several stages further by focusing on a woman character who does not want to revise traditional male definitions of the feminine and who would prefer to live within the shelter of romantic fantasy. However, the story does not allow her to do so. Sally's modern Toronto fairytale with herself in the role of 'little woman' in her happy marriage to Ed is radically upset when she suspects her husband of having an affair with her best friend – another cliché, though not one that she can accommodate within her precariously balanced structure. Sally's fairytale depends in the best traditional way on the fiction of female innocence, maintaining an enclosed space wherein her husband and her best friend are flattened into stereotypes, reduced like her excellent sauces in a deliberate evasion of complexity which is not at all innocent.

Our interest here is not really in the plot but in the storytelling method, for this is a modern Gothic tale 'set in the present and cast in the realistic code' (p. 156). Told from Sally's point of view, her stories about Ed and her marriage are all versions of the Bluebeard fairytale, for they are based on female fears of male power and knowledge. Ed's silence, which Sally ceaselessly tries to interpret in ways to flatter herself, is very like Bluebeard's secret chamber, or to Sally's Canadian eye like 'the forest, which looks something like the bottom part of their ravine lot, but without the fence' (p. 152). In this story about a woman's self-imprisonment within cultural traditions of femininity, European fairytales form an important part of her inheritance. Sally is taking an evening course on 'Forms of Narrative Fiction', working through the patriarchal tradition of The Epic, The Ballad, and on to Folk Tales and the Oral Tradition, where she is having trouble transposing the Bluebeard story into modern terms for her home assignment. In its exploration of the making of fictions, this story draws attention to the imaginative processes involved in their production and reception by the characters in the story and by its readers too. It is not Sally who dissents from the inherited stereotypes where women are always punished for their curiosity. Indeed, she is puzzled by an earlier version of the Bluebeard story which is one of female resistance to male tyranny and a challenge to the sentimental Perrault version of innocent

female victims. It is within the narrative itself that questions are
raised which Sally would prefer to ignore about the different codes
that characters use and about the kinds of misinterpretations that
may result. Interestingly, when Sally has to revise her fairytale
about her marriage at the end she adopts an ingenious technique of
displacement. Still refusing to see Ed as Bluebeard, she sees him
instead as the egg carried about so carefully by his wives, something
silent and always a symbol of beginnings rather than endings. However, the egg in Sally's version of the tale is double. As she thinks
about it, the egg loses its blandness and takes on a red pulsating life
of its own, becoming the image of her own fears for the future:

> But now she's seeing the egg, which is not small and cold and
> white and inert but larger than a real egg and golden pink, resting
> in a nest of brambles, glowing softly as though there's something
> red and hot inside it. It's almost pulsing; Sally is afraid of it. As
> she looks it darkens: rose-red, crimson. This is something the
> story left out, Sally thinks: the egg is alive, and one day it will
> hatch. But what will come out of it? (p. 166)

Wishing to remain in the world of fairytale romance, Sally finds that
she is caught instead in the Gothic version, one of Bluebeard's
victims.

Atwood's narrative with its undercurrent of female anxiety and its
sudden changes of focus unnerves the reader as well as the protagonist. It urges the necessity for a woman to step outside a duplicitous
fairytale which flatters her self-image and keeps her imprisoned in
a fiction of helpless female innocence. Against her will Sally is being
forced by circumstances to revise the old story, yet her dread of
such a step is written into her new version of 'Bluebeard's Egg'.
Atwood's feminist revision of fairytales has much in common with
Angela Carter's stories in *The Bloody Chamber* (1979), of which
Carter said:

> I'm in the demythologising business . . . I'm interested in
> myths – though I'm much more interested in folklore – just
> because they are extraordinary lies designed to make people
> unfree. . . . [In *The Bloody Chamber*] it turned out to be easier
> to deal with the shifting structures of reality and sexuality by

using sets of shifting structures derived from orally transmitted traditional tales.[11]

In that collection Carter, like Atwood, is intent on exposing the fictions designed to persuade women of their powerlessness:

I am all for putting new wine in old bottles, especially if the pressure of the new wine makes the old bottles explode.[12]

Both these writers use fiction for subtly didactic ends, 'transforming actual fictional forms to both reflect and precipitate changes in the way people feel about themselves'.[13]

The three Canadian stories I treat all recognise the cultural and literary determinations to which women are subject and they all offer versions of women resisting such pressures. In Munro's story a girl's resistance to her inheritance takes the form of revising her uncle's county history as fiction; in Thomas's story a woman manages to encode her resistance to traditional sexual power politics in her written narrative, though not in her life; and in Atwood's story a woman's inherited fairytale is exposed as a dangerous illusion. As carefully contrived narrative structures, these stories are woven from many different codes where voices of tradition and voices of female inheritors engage in unending dialogue; they are filled with multiple voices, not one of which may be taken as exclusively authoritative. The fictional strategies of these stories focus attention on women's revisionism together with the contradictions entailed in writing new versions. They show not only how problematic women's relations to their literary and cultural inheritances are, but also how women's determination challenges the forces of determinism.

Notes

1. Alice Munro, 'Heirs of the Living Body', in *Lives of Girls and Women* (1971; Harmondsworth, Middx: Penguin, 1982); Audrey Thomas, 'Crossing the Rubicon', in *Real Mothers* (Vancouver: Talonbooks, 1982); Margaret Atwood, 'Bluebeard's Egg', in *Bluebeard's Egg* (Toronto: McClelland and Stewart, 1982). All quotations and page references are taken from these editions.
2. R. Kroetsch, 'Death is a Happy Ending', in D. Daymond and L. Monkman (eds), *Canadian Novelists and the Novel* (Ottawa: Borealis, 1981) pp. 244–51.

3. See Margaret Laurence, 'Ivory Tower or Grass Roots? The Novelist as Socio-Political Being', in Daymond and Monkman (eds), op. cit., pp. 251–9; Angela Carter, 'Notes from the Front Line', in Michelene Wandor (ed.), *On Gender and Writing* (London: Pandora, 1983) pp. 69–77; Kirsten Holst Petersen and Anna Rutherford (eds), *A Double Colonization: Colonial and Post-Colonial Women's Writing* (Aarhus, Denmark: Dangaroo, 1986).
4. Laurence, op. cit., p. 258.
5. 1967 was Canada's Centennial Year, marked by Expo 67 in Montreal and by the establishment of a Royal Commission on the Status of Women in Canada. In 1969 the National Arts Centre was opened in Ottawa; in 1970 the National Action Committee on the Status of Women was set up. During the 1970s and 1980s nationalist and feminist efforts have continued to follow roughly parallel courses.
6. Margaret Atwood, *Survival* (Toronto: Anansi, 1972) p. 13.
7. H. Horwood, 'Interview with Alice Munro', in J. Miller (ed.), *The Art of Alice Munro: Saying the Unsayable* (Ontario: University of Waterloo, 1984) pp. 123–35.
8. E. Wachtel, 'An Interview with Audrey Thomas', *Room of One's Own: The Audrey Thomas Issue*, vol. 10, nos 3 and 4 (1986) pp. 7–61.
9. In I Corinthians 12, St Paul uses the analogy of the living body to describe the relationship between members of the Christian Church. Atwood makes the point in *Survival*, ch. 10, that there has been a notable absence of actively sexual female figures in Canadian literature, though she relates this to the equation between women and harsh Canadian nature rather than to religious tradition.
10. For an excellent essay on intertextual encounters in Munro's fiction and of the autobiographical dimensions of this story, see Barbara Godard, 'Heirs of the Living Body: Alice Munro and the Question of a Female Aesthetic', in J. Miller (ed.), op. cit., pp. 43–72.
11. Carter, op. cit., p. 71.
12. Ibid., p. 69.
13. Ibid., p. 76.

Bibliography

Atwood, Margaret, *Survival* (Toronto: Anansi 1972).
——, *Bluebeard's Egg* (Toronto: McClelland and Stewart, 1982).
Daymond, D., and L. Monkman (eds), *Canadian Novelists and the Novel* (Ottawa: Borealis, 1981).
Miller, J. (ed.), *The Art of Alice Munro: Saying the Unsayable* (Ontario: University of Waterloo, 1984).
Munro, Alice, *Lives of Girls and Women* (Harmondsworth, Middx: Penguin, 1982).
Petersen, Kirsten Holst and Anna Rutherford (eds), *A Double Colonization:*

Colonial and Post-Colonial Women's Writing (Aarhus, Denmark: Dangaroo, 1986).

Thomas, Audrey, *Real Mothers* (Vancouver: Talonbooks, 1982).

Wachtel, E., 'An Interview with Audrey Thomas', *Room of One's Own: The Audrey Thomas Issue*, vol. 10, nos 3 and 4 (1986) pp. 7–61.

Wandor, Michelene (ed.), *On Gender and Writing* (London: Pandora, 1983).

6 Whistling like a Woman: the Novels of Alice Walker

JENNIFER BIRKETT

RENEWING THE LANGUAGE

Alice Walker's 'Mississippi Winter IV' opens with the proverbial warning, from parents to daughter, that 'a whistling woman and a crowing hen' are bound to come 'to / no good end'.[1] Ruefully, the daughter concedes they may be right. Yet she has no choice. Whatever proverbs and parents may say, and whatever her own self-doubts, her fate must be to whistle, like a woman, till she reaches wherever her music takes her. A woman in search of a new place must start with a resolute claim for the right to determine her own voice.

For Alice Walker, whistling like a woman is a matter of organising familiar tunes into a fresh harmony. Born into a world overloaded with definitions of the female, a black American woman of the late twentieth century has, for the first time, scope to pick and choose, and in the choosing, the chance to bring into being a new female subjectivity. The struggle for black identity is linguistic as well as political. Through the new coin-word, 'womanist', on which her essay collection *In Search Of Our Mothers' Gardens* (1983) opens, Walker makes her own selection, which becomes a manifesto for radical change. Her keywords in her new language are: *black, wanting, woman, struggle, responsible, connections, survival, wholeness, traditional, love*.

Womanist 1. From *womanish* (Opp. of 'girlish,' i.e. frivolous, irresponsible, not serious.) A black feminist or feminist of colour. From the black folk expression of mothers to female children, 'You acting womanish,' i.e. like a woman. Usually referring to outrageous, audacious, courageous or *willful* behaviour. Wanting to know more and in greater depth than is considered 'good' for one. . . . Responsible. In charge. *Serious*.

2. *Also*: A woman who loves other women, sexually and/or non-sexually. Appreciates and prefers women's culture, women's emotional flexibility (values tears as natural counterbalance of laughter), and women's strength. Sometimes loves individual men, sexually and/or nonsexually. Committed to survival and wholeness of entire people, male *and* female. Not a separatist, except periodically, for health. Traditionally universalist, as in: 'Mama, why are we brown, pink, and yellow, and our cousins are white, beige, and black?' Ans.: 'Well, you know the colored race is just like a flower garden, with every color flower represented.' Traditionally capable, as in: 'Mama, I'm walking to Canada and I'm taking you and a bunch of other slaves with me.' Reply: 'It wouldn't be the first time.'

3. Loves music. Loves dance. Loves the moon. *Loves* the Spirit. Loves love and food and roundness. Loves struggle. *Loves* the Folk. Loves herself. *Regardless*.

4. Womanist is to feminist as purple to lavender.[2]

This is a manifesto studded with contradictions, expressing fresh confidence and old insecurities. The insecurities stem from the limits traditionally inscribed in black womanhood, with which the new speaker struggles in order to achieve her difference: not just the difference expressed by lavender, which invokes separatism (white feminism, lesbian feminism) but the more complex difference of purple, a deeper, stronger totalisation, diverse in its (sexual) orientations, and rooted towards black. Herself a representative of a new type – an educated, relatively well-to-do, middle-class black woman – Walker recognises the disparate strands that merge to produce her identity. The readers from and to whom she speaks include the expanding black middle class, the white liberal bourgeoisie, and the black black proletariat. All have to be incorporated into her fictions, with their own voices. History too has to be taken into account. This manifesto requires the speaker to preserve the past as well as work for change. And politically, there is a Utopian urge to join the collective values of the black community with the liberal individualism of white America.

Utopia is the country of Walker's writing. She herself recognises this in her manifesto, which places a question mark over the feasibility of inventing a new, liberating speech that can still include the old forms. The concepts of 'freedom' and 'escape', which play a crucial part in all Walker's writing, appear here in the child's voice, claiming to have found the way through ('Mama, I'm walking to Canada and I'm taking you and a bunch of other slaves with me'). The statement of desire includes its own negation: 'Canada' can only mean relative freedom; the 'slaves' have not yet lost their label; and the authoritarian 'I' of the old world dominates the utterance. 'Mama' knows better: 'It wouldn't be the first time.' It is the other, ironic voice that rescues Utopian hope from naïve voluntarism. In this manifesto, Utopian dream is linked to realism. The new black woman must begin by asserting herself and her desires, refusing to be overawed by the dead weight of history that stands against her. What she has to say must be set in the context of many voices. Her speech must centre itself on dialogue, in which questioning and answering roles are exchanged, and in which no one speaker has the final answer.

The ground rules of this exchange of voices have been fundamentally changed. The womanist manifesto builds on one particular kind of dialogue: 'the black folk expression of mothers to female children'. Walker's fictions are so many attempts to articulate afresh, within the founding exchange of mothers and daughters, the many voices of women's history.

Beyond the inherited insecurities, Walker looks for a new kind of authority for women. For her, writing is a polemic activity, designed to make practical interventions in the world. Her female fictional voices are sometimes unselfconscious, or even hysterical, but their lack of control is always articulated by their author within a well-analysed context of society or family, and turned thereby into an instrument of change – Meridian's epileptic fits, for example, or the alien voice that speaks through Cely to defy Mr A. For Walker, it is the clear, precise authoritative voice that determines resistance, taking control of its world as it begins to take control of its own language:

> [N]aming our own experience after our own fashion (as well as rejecting whatever does not seem to suit) is the least we can do – and in this society may well be our only tangible sign of personal freedom.[3]

Changes in the balance of power in sexual, racial and class politics require lucid definitions of purpose. In Walker's novels, characters are always moving to increased articulacy; failure to define self and situation accurately is pinpointed as the source of individual and social suffering. Picking her way through determining oppressions of race and gender, Walker marks her path with a rationalist gesture of faith in human intellect, and in the power of language.

RECLAIMING THE TRADITIONS

[B]lack women are searching for a specific language, specific symbols, specific images with which to record their lives, and, even though they can claim a rightful place in the Afro-American tradition and the feminist tradition of women writers, it is also clear that, for purposes of liberation, black women writers will first insist on their own name, their own space.[4]

Alice Walker designates herself primarily as writing with a black voice, in a tradition marginalised by the guardians of 'mainstream' culture, which must be recuperated.[5]

But the black American tradition has to be handled with care, for little if any of it functions in a space free from white influence. This is especially true of its images of the female. Barbara Christian has shown how white and black cultural traditions interpenetrate one another, and in the process set up distorted models of women. In southern white slavery literature, the stereotype of the strong black mammy sustains the idealisation of the white lady: 'Mammy . . . , harmless in her position as a slave . . . is needed as an image, a surrogate, to contain all those fears of the physical female.'[6] Black literature of the same period focuses on the mulatta mistress, illicit crossing point of two cultures, stereotyped as a tragic heroine: read as a source of erotic pleasure by the white reader, and by his black counterpart as living disproof of black inferiority.[7] Neither version considers the pain of displacement experienced by real-life mulattas, rejected by both cultures. Walker makes the point herself in an essay of 1982 ('If the Present Looks Like the Past, What Does the Future Look Like?'), where she attacks particularly William Wells Brown's novel, *Clotelle, or The Coloured Heroine* (1867), which also manages to attribute to the slave all responsibility for the 'immorality' of a liaison imposed by her master.[8] Both stereotypes reappear in a liberating reversal in the more rebellious oral tradition of slave narratives and songs. Here the mammy figure is cunning and powerful, fighting for her children's rights, while the mulatta, no longer idealised, confesses her debasement. But these are still partial versions of the female. Sexual success and strength, femininity and power, never exist, traditionally, in the same person.[9]

Walker's generation attacks the stereotypes. The teenage Meridian, searching for models, finds – with a gasp of comic delight – women who combine sexuality and strength:

> [B]lack women were always imitating Harriet Tubman – escaping to become something unheard of. Outrageous. One of her sister's friends had become, somehow, a sergeant in the army and knew everything there was to know about enemy installations and radar equipment. . . . Two other girls went away married to men and came back married to each other. . . . Then there were simply the good-time girls who came home full of bawdy stories of their exploits in the big city . . . . They commanded attention. They deserved admiration.[10]

Challenging the white stereotype of beauty, and all colourist prejudices in both communities, Walker's heroines include women of every shade of blackness: Meridian, with her 'deep-brown skin' (p. 29); the 'yellow' mulatta Squeak, in *The Color Purple*[11], or, in the same novel, two African black women, the ugly Cely and the fascinating Shug Avery, with her 'long black body with its black plum nipples, look like her mouth' (p. 45). In Walker's short story 'Source', stereotypes of beauty are shown up as changing fashions, exploited by men to divide and rule 'their' women. At the end of the tale, colourist rivalry is abolished by female solidarity: 'They were simply two women, choosing to live as they liked in the world.'[12]

The oral tradition, as Christian points out, is potentially more liberating for women not only in its reversal of the stereotypes but in its crucial shift of focus from the master–slave relationship to the private life of the black community – which meant, essentially, a foregrounding of women's space. There is a close connection between this tradition and the new generations of black women writers, producing demystified, non-stereotyped accounts of individuals in domestic relationships, observed in realistic detail and through their own rhetoric:

The way, for example, that Zora Neale Hurston, Margaret
Walker, Toni Morrison and Alice Walker incorporate the traditional black female activities of rootworking, herbal medicine,
conjure and midwifery into the fabric of their stories is not mere
coincidence, nor is their use of specifically black female language
to express their own and their characters' thoughts accidental.[13]

The anthropologist and novelist Zora Neale Hurston (1901–60),
rescued by Walker from the obscurity into which she fell at the end
of the Harlem Renaissance, is a major connecting link between the
oral traditions of the black community and the writing of Walker
and her contemporaries. Walker writes with admiration of Hurston's
efforts to restore to blacks a sense of their own dignity by restoring
to them their own story traditions, and of her 'sense of black people
as complete, complex *undiminished* human beings'.[14] In Hurston's
heroine Janie (*Their Eyes Were Watching God*, 1937), she appreciates the political implications of a realistic, defiant female model,
strong and sexual, competent in public and private domains.[15] Hurston's emphasis on the private life of the black community seems to
her more fruitful than the charting of familiar conflicts (between
men) in the public spaces where black meets white.[16] Hurston's
Janie prefigures Walker's Cely, and Grange Copeland's wife Mem,
unaware, nine-tenths of the time, of the white culture that ultimately
determines them and primarily experiencing their oppression as
mediated through their intimate relationships with other black men
and women. Walker argues that: 'Twentieth-century black women
writers all seem to be much more interested in the black community,
in intimate relationships, with the white world as a BACKDROP, which
is certainly the appropriate perspective, in my view.'[17] Her aim in
writing is to make black men and women think about conflicts of
gender as well as those of race – the 'real problems in our day-to-
day living',[18] whose solution lies in their own hands.

At the same time, Walker's own experience, a generation after
Hurston's, is one of closer contact with white American culture – in
particular, through the widening educational opportunities which
took her in 1964 to the élite women's college, Sarah Lawrence. Here
especially she came into contact with another kind of
tradition – white feminist writing – which provided a range of very
different formal models to structure her explorations of uncharted
black domestic territory. The idealism of certain writers struck in
her an immediate chord of recognition – Kate Chopin, the Brontës,

Simone de Beauvoir, Doris Lessing.[19] But the author she admires most – for much the same reasons as she admires Hurston – is Flannery O'Connor. O'Connor's witty, objective, economical style has much in common with Walker's own, as have the 'sly, demythifying sentences' which place no burdensome stereotypes on her readers.[20] And O'Connor too had a fresh perspective on the South: 'She knew that the question of race was really only the first question on a long list. This is hard for just about everybody to accept, we've been trying to answer it for so long.'[21]

The white feminist tradition can play only a supporting role in the making of Walker's new language, as her essay 'Beyond the Peacock: the Reconstruction of Flannery O'Connor' incisively points out. The influence of O'Connor and that of Walker's mother – tellers of two very different kinds of tales – are brought together as Walker, in search of her origins, discovers side by side her family shack and O'Connor's ante-bellum mansion, stalked by peacocks. Staying too close to the language of the oppressive culture is dangerous. Peacocks may be 'inspiring', but as Mrs Walker dryly notes: 'they'll eat up every bloom you have, if you don't watch out'.[22]

Yet the supporting role can be a vital one. White female models whose voices respond at least partially to her own are an important source of inspiration for the black woman writer, a counter-tradition to oppose to a literary scene dominated by black men. This is not simply a case of there being little or no room for women on the black publishing scene. Misogyny would appear to play a fundamental part in black men's writing. The archetypal example remains Richard Wright's celebrated hero, Bigger Thomas (*Native Son*, 1940), who comes to self-realisation through the murders of two women, one white and one black. But James Baldwin's *If Beale Street Could Talk* (1974), sketching the ideal black couple, spells out just as explicitly the necessary relationship between man's speech and woman's silence:

> She must watch and guide, but he must lead . . . a woman is tremendously controlled by what the man's imagination makes of her – literally, hour by hour, day by day; so she becomes a woman. But a man exists in his own imagination, and can never be at the mercy of a woman's. (p. 59)

Ralph Ellison's satire, *Invisible Man* (1947), took as one of its targets the presumption that male rhetoric had the right to colonise the female voice, exposing the cynicism of black radical politics that sends a young man to practise his oratory on 'the Woman Question'. But Ellison remained a solitary voice. Eldridge Cleaver's *Soul on Ice* (1968), still perpetuates the radical presumption. In 'The Allegory of the Black Eunuchs', Cleaver (former advocate of the programmatic rape of white women, as a way of destabilising their fathers) offers a convoluted apology for the way black men and white men between them have turned black women into mere symbols of black men's oppression. He then repeats the pattern, inviting the black woman to become a different kind of symbol – 'Mother-Daughter of Africa' – in the black man's rhetoric of his fight for power.

What is being contested now on literary ground is the slow shift in the economic and political situation of black women in the States since the Second World War. Black women are now seeking to write themselves into 'their own name, their own space' because that name and space are, effectively, already theirs. Rochelle Gatlin and Paula Giddings have charted the growing postwar demand for black women to fill the lower-paid ranks of the white-collar workforce, which has meant a widening of their educational opportunities and an increase in their economic independence.[23] Over the same period, black women have been increasingly active in politics, particularly in the Civil Rights Movement, running the bureaucratic machinery, canvassing, demonstrating on the streets and providing some of the most dangerous and significant symbolic gestures: Rosa Parks's refusal to give up her bus seat to whites in Montgomery, Alabama, in 1955, or Viola Liuzzo's death in 1965. Walker's own participation in the Movement (from which she dates her own entry into self-awareness) began at college in Atlanta from 1961, taking part in Saturday morning demonstrations. In the Freedom Summer of 1965, she was canvassing voters in Liberty County, Georgia; in Mississippi in 1966, fighting for black entry into whites-only areas. Her contribution is a representative one.[24]

None of these contributions, or changes, has been adequately recognised. The male leadership of SNCC (Student Nonviolent Coordinating Committee) brushed off the 1964 position paper on women. Black women, already under attack in the Moynihan Report ('The Negro Family: the Case for National Action', 1965) from a Government eager to blame ghetto unrest on the 'role reversal' that was a consequence of many women being the sole family wage-earner, found themselves also the objects of a propaganda campaign by black men to reinforce traditional gender hierarchy. This was intensi-

fied with the spread of the Black Muslim organisation, led by Elijah
Mohammed. Political power for women was out: Shirley Chisholm,
running for President in 1972, was ridiculed by her black male
colleagues.[25] Michele Wallace draws up the balance sheet:

> Though originally it was the white man who was responsible for
> the black woman's grief, a multiplicity of forces act upon her life
> now and the black man is one of the most important. The white
> man is downtown. The black man lives with her. . . .
> She has made it quite clear that she has no intention of starting
> a black woman's liberation movement. One would think she was
> satisfied, yet she is not. The black man has not really kept his
> part of the bargain they made when she agreed to keep her mouth
> shut in the sixties. . . . The black woman's silence is a new silence.
> She knows that. Not so long ago it would have been quite easy
> to find any number of women who would say with certainty, 'A
> nigga man ain't shit.'[26]

Alice Walker writes alongside a number of black women writers
who since the mid-1970s have sought to break the silence – and have
touched a raw nerve. Liberationist traditions which as late as the
1960s still ran side by side – and which her aim is still to hold
together – are now in conflict. A recent reviewer of Steven Spielberg's film of *The Color Purple* noted what he called a new treachery
among black women writers, with their unjustified attacks on black
men:

> [O]ne of the major forces shaping black literature has been the
> commitment to rectify the anti-black stereotypes and propagandis-
> tic images created by non-black writers. The negative stereotypes
> of black men (lazy, servile, shiftless, immoral, brutishly
> aggressive) and black women (easy, mannish, licentious, loud,
> castrating) were not created by black writers and, until recently,
> were almost never reaffirmed by them.[27]

The lack of understanding shown for black women by their male
counterparts, at all levels, poses a major problem: how to write out
the objective fact that white patriarchal values have been adopted
by black men in the context of their subjection, and how to make
black men accept responsibility for the oppression of women, without
at the same time giving hostages to a common white enemy. Uncon-

sidered solidarity is something Walker will not condone. In the women's movement, she sees the means of resisting the double oppressions of race and gender; and in 'One Child of One's Own', she bitterly regrets black women's failure to align themselves with the movement in the 1970s.[28] The loyalty of black women to black men is, she thinks, misplaced; black men must be made to change; and yet, black men are too used to being oppressed to see themselves as oppressors. As a former Methodist, she says, she was conditioned to believe in the possibility of radical transformations: 'I believe in change: change personal and change in society. . . . So Grange Copeland was EXPECTED to change.'[29] The way in which such change can, for Walker, be most vigorously pursued, is through the particular transformations of womanist writing.

CHANGING THE SUBJECT

Alice Walker's novels represent three distinctive efforts to negotiate with an historical inheritance in order to explore new ways of living for both women and men. The first offers a reconstruction of the father; the second, of the mother; and the third, of woman in all her familiar roles (wife, mother, daughter, sister). Rebuilding individuals, within the family, is for Walker the first step in reclaiming the lost community:

> What the black Southern writer inherits as a natural right is a sense of community. Something simple but surprisingly hard, especially these days, to come by.[30]

Walker's first novel, *The Third Life of Grange Copeland* (1970) distinguishes three formative elements in society: family, language and violence.[31] It discusses how the discourse of mother and father shapes the child and how the society in which the family is founded affects this discourse and is affected by it. The family is perceived as the centre of the tangled oppressions of race, gender and class that constitute the Southern hierarchy: the white boss at the top, then the Mother, and last of all, the Father. The father's resentment at his lack of economic and political power produces the violence he turns against his wife and children. Neither black parent plays a proper role in relation to the child, nor to each other. Walker explains in 'From an Interview':

I wanted to explore the relationship between parents and children, specifically between daughters and their fathers (this is most interesting, I've always felt . . .) and I wanted to learn, myself, how it happens that the hatred a child can have for a parent becomes inflexible. And I wanted to explore the relationship between men and women, and why women are always condemned for doing what men do as an expression of their masculinity. (p. 257)

Moving away from the old words – 'blame', 'guilt', 'hate' – the novel looks for a new language of parenting, that will produce a new kind of child.

This is a world in which the men, despite their economic powerlessness, have all the key lines, as husbands, lovers, fathers, sons. The women have to find their own ways of living within the dilemmas experienced by the men. Three couples pass under review between the early 1900s and the 1960s: Grange and his wife, Margaret; Brownfield, his son, and Mem, Brownfield's wife; Ruth, their daughter, and Grange, Ruth's grandfather. The focal point of the narrative, like that of History, moves from Grange's son to Mem's daughter.

Brownfield, the villain of the piece, never stood a chance. His childhood was a swift fall from innocence into humiliation, as he learned from his town cousins first the poverty of his plantation existence, then the associated poverty of his language (what the cousins call a car, he calls an automobile, and country neighbours still call a buggy), and finally, the poverty of his relationship with his parents. His father hardly ever spoke to him; while 'He thought his mother was like their dog in some ways. She didn't have a thing to say that did not in some way show her submission to his father' (p. 5). From this flawed beginning he acquires the attitudes he will reproduce in his own family. From Grange, he learns that all dependants, though burdensome, are a man's property and the mark of his dignity. Margaret's litanies condition him to servility: ' "We ought to be thankful we got a roof over our heads and three meals a day" ' (p. 5). Grange's silence prevents his son from recognising the heroic quality of the father's struggle against futile revolt and his efforts not to turn his self-hatred into scapegoating attacks on wife and children.

In Walker's South, silence is the blacks' first language. Faced with the impossibility of feeding, clothing and sheltering his family,

Grange can only shrug. Brownfield watches Grange and his fellow-workers turn to silent automata on payday, reeking of fear in front of the white man. In his turn, he suppresses his own responses to the white boss's condescension ('ought to stick my feed knife up in him to the gizzard!' (p. 89). His first preoccupation with Mem is to reduce her fluent educated speech to his, not satisfied until it limps into silence, 'flat and ugly, like a tongue broken and trying to mend itself out of desperation' (p. 57). His daughters communicate with him in mumbles and whimpers, concealing their longing for his death. Brownfield's silence only breaks into giggles or demonic laughter, at some fresh humiliation of his wife; or is replaced by acts of violence, culminating in his shooting her dead.

Grange frees himself from silence with his escape to the North. He learns a new language of personal survival: 'stealing had become a useful and ready tool to be used at will, not unlike a second language. He knew tricks and he knew sob stories . . . and he knew cunning and he knew violence' (pp. 148–9). In this perverted tongue he seems to find himself, abandoning a sneering pregnant white woman to drown in an icy lake in a New York park: 'He believed that, against his will, he had stumbled on the necessary act that black men must commit to regain, or to manufacture their manhood, their self-respect. They must kill their oppressors' (p. 153). Walker here deliberately echoes the delusions of Richard Wright's Bigger Thomas. With this new self, constructed in crime, Grange returns to the South, to try to make a life apart from the whites.

In his absence, the women have done well. Josie, his mistress, has her own business (a juke-joint). Her illegitimate daughter, Mem, educated on the money of another absentee father, has acquired the status of a teaching job, and then a different, and less liberating kind of status through marriage with Brownfield. Later in that marriage, Mem's education helps her back into independence, through another job which pays for a better house and fresh aspirations to pass on to her daughters, figured in the glossy images of the store catalogue (smart furniture, electric lights and an inside toilet). But all her literacy – which Brownfield bitterly envies – cannot save her from the uneven relationship between men and women. Briefly, at the end of a gun, she imposes on Brownfield a new language, free from abuse:

'You going to call me Mem, Mrs Copeland, or Mrs Mem R. Copeland. . . . And second, you is going to call our children

Daphne, Ornette and baby Ruth . . . you ain't never going to call me ugly or black or nigger or bitch again. . . .'   (p. 96)

But in the end, it is Brownfield who effectively invokes the phallic violence of the gun, and Mem who can only submit. Black women can make no progress, as long as their men remain unchanged.

In the absence of the reality, the image of a good, powerful male has to be invented. Daphne, who knew Brownfield as a good father, before the marriage turned sour, tells her sisters stories about their 'good daddy'. This is a consoling but dangerous myth, which leads them to forget too quickly the bad times and enables Brownfield to trick and trap his family again. But eventually the girls learn to distinguish between their myth and the reality. Grange steps into the 'good daddy' role after Mem's death. Concealing all his own past, he hands on to Ruth the best he can of her forefathers' traditions. He tells her stories – the Uncle Remus tales, or his own, better stories of clever blacks beating the white master; he teaches her to be at ease with her body, to laugh, spit and dance; he passes on his own hatred of the servile black Church and its hypocrisy; he tells her about black history, from slavery in Africa to present-day exploitation; he opens her mind to other places, beyond the South. The damage he might have done with his hatred of the white man is countered by the independent critical faculties the child has inherited from her mother, and from her own experience. She already speaks a language of her own.

Ruth's survival and her chances of a more open future depend on a very particular convergence of personal and historical factors. Walker, in effect, writes a morality tale, sifting and selecting the ingredients to make Ruth a new world. Ruth's family is purged, to provide support but not shackles. Black school gets better (thanks to Eisenhower's policies), and Grange's lessons make up for those poor teachers who still transmit racist values. There are other, wider transformations, brought home to Ruth by the television screen: the Huntley–Brinkley Report and the lines of marching students behind Martin Luther King. The child begins to reshape the parent. Ruth forces Grange to swallow his prejudices and accept the help of whites aligned with the Civil Rights Movement. At this point, the surrogate father has outlived his usefulness and is ready for final transformation into a myth by which the future can safely live. Grange kills Brownfield, to protect Ruth, and then shoots himself. Ruth sets out on her adult path with a clean slate.

Patriarchal violence is the condition in and through which women enter into speech: a necessary evil, to be abolished as soon as its purpose is served. Sifting from the traditions inherited from Grange – the best he could give – all the cruelty, the limitations and the lies, Ruth prepares herself to write, with her dead mother's help, a new world of her own:

> If she had been shipwrecked on a desert island she would have taken Jane Eyre, a pocket thesaurus she had, all her books about Africa. She would have taken her maps of the continents, everything she owned by Charles Dickens, plenty of paper and a stock of pencils. She would have left on her desk her red-covered Bible, which Grange had lifted from a cart that stood outside a motel room, her big dictionary, which he got for her she knew not how, and which would have been too heavy, and her copy of Miss Vanderbilt's Etiquette, which she ignored as much as she could without making her grandfather feel like a fool for getting it for her. . . . She would have taken her locket picture of Mem, which had been a present from Grange on her fourteenth birthday. (p. 197)

Meridian is focused on the relationship of women to the mother role, and examines the effect this has on a woman's struggle to establish a new balance between herself and her community. Born in 1943, the child of schoolteacher parents with land of their own, in a black community picking up the crumbs of America's wartime boom, Meridian enters the world speaking a relatively fluent and competent language. The narrative equips her from the outset to be a fighter.

Unlike her white counterpart, Marge Piercy's *Vida* (1980), the terrorist on the run from the defeated 1960s, Meridian Hill endures, resting in more deeply-rooted traditions of resistance. Vida's commitment was an intellectual choice; but Meridian's is not only intellectual but physical. She internalises the conflicts of her world with gestures of quiet resistance that engage her whole body in comas and epileptic fits. This is woman physically tuned to the disturbances of the material world and labouring to return it to harmony – a modern version of the African spirit magic tradition resurrected by Walker's mentor, Zora Neale Hurston.

On the other hand, Meridian is recognisably in a white tradition: the Romantic figure of the solitary prophet, made over into the language of the black Church:

'I hate to think of you as always alone.'

'But that is my value,' said Meridian. 'Besides, all the people who are as alone as I am will one day gather at the river. We will watch the evening sun go down. And in the darkness maybe we will know the truth.' (p. 227)

The Romantic image carries new values, for this prophet is no heroic individual but – as the definitions of her name given in the epigraphs suggest – a representative figure, sharing in a collective recovery. More precisely, she becomes a representative mother-figure, revising the traditional female role, and finding new ideals for her generation to live by. Some of these are straight from the 1960s: the search for a new collective subject, founded in rational and egalitarian politics; the optimistic faith in renewal. Others are Walker's own: the recovery of the past; and, most original, the cult of evasion and refusal.

Meridian's 'people', the inheritance she constructs for herself, includes all the victims of oppression – women, children, nations, nature – who are the repressed subjects of the novel. These form the body of a society torn and scattered as Meridian's subjectivity is scattered in her epileptic fits:

I can still see the butchered women and children lying heaped and scattered all along the crooked gulch . . . the nation's hoop is broken and scattered. There is no center any longer, and the sacred tree is dead. (Epigraph, from *Black Elk Speaks*)

Meridian's attempts to share in their recovery are the way-stations on her own journey towards self-healing. What appears a stock Romantic narrative of an individual quest is founded in a sense of the collective. Meridian's story has shifting centres, with the narrative focus constantly moving away from her single figure. She appears first as a Pied Piper, leading a column of black children to challenge an armoured tank crammed with white men. Her adolescence is drawn alongside that of her contemporaries, all struggling with the stereotypes of films and magazines, internalising white moral categories ('Blondes against brunettes and cowboys against Indians, good men against bad, darker men' (p. 70)) and white ambitions, dreaming of 'happy endings' that are not meant for them: 'of women who had everything, of men who ran the world' (p. 70). At school in

Saxon College, Atlanta, she shares the same double pressures of sexual and racial prejudice:

> Meridian and the other students felt they had two enemies: Saxon, which wanted them to become something – ladies – that was already obsolete, and the larger, more deadly enemy, white racist society. It was not unusual for students to break down under the pressures caused by the two. (p. 91)

She shares the struggle of all black daughters against their mothers. Mrs Hill, 'buried alive' (p. 41), like all mothers, seeks in turn to bury her daughter in the graveyard of her own limited ambitions. She is 'Black Motherhood personified' (p. 93), not the nurturing figure of myth but the narrow-minded reality (p. 16), made cruel by her own lack of choices.

Unlike her contemporaries, Meridian manages to put up a resistance to the forces that determine her world. The primary step is to face the tyrannies of the maternal role. The desires of her own body, together with the pressures of social convention, initially force her into the part of wife-and-mother. By an immense (near-Utopian) effort of will, she rejects it. She gives away the child of a premature marriage; she learns the painful benefits of abortion; she accepts the doctor's offer of sterilisation. But her sexuality is still not hers to enjoy freely: society defines it as man's property, if not to reproduce his world, then to serve his pleasure. Truman, her lover, intimidated by her difference, will not accept her unless she agrees to be transformed into familiar sadistic images of desire. Black men's sensuality is, the novel affirms, posited on the humiliation of black women – with an intensity born of racial as well as sexual prejudice. The glamour with which the black man invests white women compounds the contempt he bestows on his black partner. Meridian is rejected by Truman for Lynne, one of the white women who joined the Movement in the Freedom Summers of 1964 and 1965. Lynne in her turn has to struggle with the black man's fantasies. Raped by Truman's friend, the bitter, one-armed Tommy Odds, abandoned by her husband, she presents Meridian with another dilemma: how to relate to white women who, just like black men, are simultaneously oppressor and fellow-victim?[32]

Faced with such insoluble problems and disabling self-images, Meridian's solution is to refuse the context that generates them. She survives by abandoning all claim to her own body. She welcomes

the descent of the policeman's club on Civil Rights marches, hoping
for the annihilation of consciousness which will let her forget the
burden of guilt that stands between her mother's body and her own.
Her epileptic fits are moments of release from the pressures of
reality. These are not simply negative evasions, as the text makes
plain from the beginning. As a child, standing in the coil of the
ancient Indian monument, the Serpent's Tail, Meridian experiences
the bliss of losing self in the spinning forms of the universe, liberated
into a better relationship with the whole bodily world. There are
new relationships to be found between bodies, but black women,
for the time being, have no power to make them. The initiatives for
change lie with white women and black men; all black women can
do, for the moment, is to demonstrate their powerlessness, refuse
to continue to carry burdens they cannot bear.

By refusing all the determining constraints of the personal, and
the domestic, to which black mothers and daughters are heir, Meridian frees herself to enter a new political space. It is in the Civil
Rights Movement that she finds the most effective instrument of
her own redefinition. The Civil Rights Movement, taking over the
language of the white Constitution, fuses the cool language of eight-
eenth-century European claims for human rights with the American
blacks' fierce sense of grievance, to make a new, potent weapon.
Meridian steps carefully through this new terrain, still questioning
the conventional options. She refuses the pressures to violent action
that come from fellow student revolutionaries, and confines herself
to the unglamorous task of raising political consciousness in the
black community by persuasion. Woman's new role in history is to
refuse to participate in a destructive politics as well as a destructive
sexuality, to be determined simply to survive:

> The only new thing now would be the refusal of Christ to accept
> crucifixion. King should have refused. Malcolm, too, should have
> refused. All those characters in all those novels that require death
> to end the book should refuse. All saints should walk away. Do
> their bit, then – just walk away. See Europe, visit Hawaii, become
> agronomists or raise Dalmatians.   (pp. 150–1)

Just surviving is a victory for the whole community (and one won
by mothers throughout the ages). The novel is crammed with images
of endurance and resurgence: the Indians, living beyond the mass-
acre, the Sojourner tree, cut down in a campus revolt but springing

into new blossom, and the Negro Church, whose once servile rituals have, Meridian finds, since the death of Martin Luther King, become a focus for revolutionary solidarity. The past need not be a burial place; it can be a holder of memories that can be called back to renew the present. Woman's traditional role, as guardian of the past, is to give the old tales new birth. In the end, this is how Meridian, like her author, chooses to define her place, determining the direction of the community in the light of its best traditions:

> [P]erhaps it will be my part to walk behind the real revolutionaries – those who know they must spill blood in order to help the poor and the black and therefore go right ahead – and when they stop to wash off the blood and find their throats too choked with the smell of murdered flesh to sing, I will come forward and sing from memory songs they will need once more to hear. For it is the song of the people, transformed by the experience of each generation, that holds them together, and if any part of it is lost the people suffer and are without soul. If I can only do that, my role will not have been a useless one after all. (pp. 206–7)

This is, she says, in a sense an abdication. Meridian shows how effectively a woman can fight to transform the determinisms operating in her world. She also shows an individual woman's limits. Fighting is not always the answer: sometimes, giving in is the solution. When Meridian refuses the strong mother-mammy stereotype, the Trumans and the Lynnes are forced to take at last their own share of responsibility. Truman, learning to be 'intensely maternal' (p. 219), nurses Meridian back to health; the story leaves him and Lynne to work together through their conflicts, as Meridian hurries away into a new arena of her own. What Meridian has invented is a new kind of woman's love, beyond the old possessive hungers of mother and wife:

> [It] sets you free. You are free to be whichever way you like, to be with whoever, of whatever color or sex you like – and what you risk in being truly yourself the way you want to be, is not the loss of me. You are *not* free, however, to think I am a fool. (p. 233)

Leaving the male partner to stand alone, this Mother creates for him the possibility of beginning a new, different relationship with the female.

Steven Spielberg's film version (1985) of *The Color Purple* brought the glamour of the mass media to black women's struggle for liberation. It also took the heart out of Walker's message, substituting mawkish sentimentality, jolly tunes and stereotyped characterisation for what had been, in the novel, a simple but powerful political statement.

Walker's book, though constructed within the forms of popular romance, with simple emotions, melodramatic situations and happy endings, uses these as a vehicle for a forceful analysis and reconstruction of the situation of black women, picking up the keywords of the womanist manifesto. At the centre is Cely, the black mother, speaking within the limited forms her culture assigns to her, and torn by the double role it also assigns: fighting for her children's survival, and destroying them, reproducing in them traditional patterns of servile dependency. In Walker's first novel, all the mothers die – lost generations, for whom their successors can do nothing except understand their limitations. In this book, Cely becomes a liberated and happy woman in her own lifetime, reunited at the end with her children. This is indeed Utopia, more patently fictional than the rest of Walker's work in its coincidences, magical resolutions, escape tricks, redemptions and safe journeys home. Like all Utopias, it is a blueprint for what could be.

The analysis begins with an evocation of Cely's place, set within the limits of Cely's own language and perceptions. The form of the novel re-enacts her entrapment, letters addressed to doubtful or unreliable destinations – a deaf male divinity, who never answers, and a sister escaped to Africa, whose replies are blocked for years by Cely's tyrannical husband. But from the beginning, Walker's own writing contrives to suggest the hope of a happy ending to Cely's enforced silence. The hope lies in the unrecognised qualities of Cely's limited language: the authenticity of her stumbling dialect; the love expressed in the nurturing gestures of traditional female communication (nursing, feeding, clothing); and, most of all, her desire to break her silence, to speak with her own authoritative voice. In Walker's book, the first points come for trying.

Cely's crippling sense of her own inadequacy has its origins outside her own head. First and foremost, there is the Southern black patriarchy and its compensatory sexuality that kills its wives, and sells and rapes its daughters; and whose values are reinforced by its Church:

> I used to git mad at my mammy cause she put a lot of work on me. Then I see how sick she is. Couldn't stay mad at her. Couldn't be mad at my daddy cause he my daddy. Bible say, Honor father and mother no matter what. Then after while every time I got mad, or start to feel mad, I got sick. Felt like throwing up. Terrible feeling. Then I start to feel nothing at all.   (p. 39)

The origins of the black man's treatment of black women lie in white patriarchy and white capitalism. This book is written from Cely's perspective, and white oppression is not something she experiences with the same frequency as she does black domestic violence. Nevertheless, Walker signals how the white community draws tight limits round the lives of black women. Sofia is beaten and thrown into prison for refusing to be the white mayor's maid and for returning the mayor's slap in the face. As history moves on, her boys are sent off to fight the Second World War, while the mayor's son runs his father's cotton gin, making profits from soldiers' uniforms. Cely's sister Nettie is caught in the war, coming home on a ship blown up by German mines. At this point, even Cely recognises that 'colored don't count to those people' (p. 236).

Resistance begins at the bottom line. Survival is Cely's priority:

> I think bout Nettie, dead. She fight, she run away. What good it do? I don't fight, I stay where I'm told. But I'm alive.   (p. 21)

To survive, any instrument will do. Hence her appeal to God, in the only guise she knows ('that old white man'). Only when Nettie's letters start coming through can she unhook from this dependency:

> [T]he God I been praying and writing to is a man. And act just like all the other mens I know. Trifling, forgitful and lowdown. (p. 164)

The divine patriarch has blocked her own view of the world:

> I been so busy trying to think about him I never truly notice nothing God make. Not a blade of corn (how it do that?) not the color purple (where it come from?). Not the little wildflowers.

Nothing. . . . [I]t is like Shug say, You have to git man off your eyeball, before you can see anything a'tall.   (p. 168)

From Shug Avery, her husband's former mistress, she learns to value the body she had previously learned to hate. Cely's articulacy develops as her repressed sexuality is released. Before she can speak with confidence, she has to learn to feel. Her 'father' raped her; her husband's indifference humiliates her. But Shug introduces her to the pleasure of her own body, teaching her to look 'down there', at her 'own pussy', her 'button', her 'titties'. 'Shug don't actually say making love. She say something nasty. She say fuck' (p. 96). Shug gives her new experiences and new words. In bed with Shug, she is able to speak for the first time about her rape.

With this new knowledge of herself, Cely can reach out for wider connections. Shug gives her this too, releasing Nettie's letters from Mr A's hiding place. Cely can start writing to Nettie, in place of God. She begins to communicate with Mr A – first through the knife she jabs into his hand, then to curse him, and finally, when Shug leaves with her new lover, for companionship ('He ain't Shug, but he begin to be somebody I can talk to' (p. 233). When he starts making shirts to go with her pants, she even manages to address him with his own full name.

Cely's resistance is only possible because of the other women who surround her. Shug is the most important – black and strong as the mammy stereotype, but also sexually aggressive and economically independent, the jazz-singer who knows Duke Ellington and Sophie Tucker, and in turn, 'Everybody know her name' (p. 95). To Cely's amazement:

> Shug talk and act sometimes like a man. Men say stuff like that to women, Girl, you look like a good time. Women always talk about hair and health. How many babies living or dead, or got teef. Not bout how some woman they hugging on look like a good time.   (p. 72)

A radically new mother- and sister-figure, she snatches both Cely and Harpo's mulatta girl-friend Squeak out of mute dependence, into economic as well as moral and linguistic self-sufficiency.

Sofia, Harpo's wife, is a daughter who gives lessons to her mother. Grown naturally into unquestioning self-confidence among a gang of sisters, she is horrified when Harpo tries to beat her, imitating his father, and even more horrified when Cely tries to make her accept the beatings. Interestingly, it is Sofia, inveterate hater of white folks, who draws Eleanor Jane, the mayor's daughter, into the community that gathers in the closing pages of Walker's book. Sofia's honesty, like Meridian's, will never let her pretend affection for her white sisters; but that very refusal of pretence makes it possible for Eleanor Jane and herself to associate on a basis of mutual respect.

In Walker's fiction, change is manufactured out of other people, other times and other places. The alternative place in *The Color Purple* is Africa – or rather, the myth of Africa, which plays a major part in Cely's resistance. To Cely, Africa of itself means little. For her, it is overwhelmingly the place where Nettie is; as such, it becomes the land of lost desire, holding the hope of her self-restoration. For Nettie it has its larger, traditional symbolic value as the place of origins, the locus of the lost pride of the black black community. It is, however, a learned myth, taught to her by her missionary protectors. It supports her through her first steps towards recovery of her self-respect, but much of it, she finds, has to be discarded when she meets the reality. The Olinka Paradise is flawed, overrun, like everywhere else, by white capitalism; and, just as in America, the mothers of the tribe collude with the patriarchs in the exploitation of their daughters. Nettie's struggles in Mother Africa are those of Cely in the Mother Country, and she is glad to come 'home'.

What Walker says most clearly in *The Color Purple*, is that there is no abiding home to inherit: women have to make their world. Cely's yard, where all the characters are finally united, is, like the garden of Voltaire's *Candide*, a flawed Utopia. Cely's children are scarred by tribal tattoos, as she is scarred by her memories. Shug prefers her male lovers, and Cely is left to make do with the simple companionship of Mr A. Making coloured pants, like cultivating a garden, is a low-key answer to the evil of the universe. But making the best of the material to hand is what surviving means; and Cely has, at least, survived into a world in which men and women have changed a little, for the better. Day-to-day struggle with the inherited language of patriarchal culture is what Walker draws in this novel, as in the others, reforming the images to suggest better configurations to live by, conscious always of the dead weight of a past that cannot be fully exorcised, except in fantasy.

Notes

1. Alice Walker, 'Mississippi Winter IV', in *Horses Make a Landscape Look More Beautiful* (New York: Harcourt Brace Jovanovich, 1984; London: Women's Press, 1985) p. 22.
2. Alice Walker, *In Search of our Mothers' Gardens: Womanist Prose* (New York: Harcourt Brace Jovanovich, 1983; London: Women's Press, 1984). All essays by Alice Walker referred to in the present work are collected in this volume (hereafter abbreviated to *MG*), unless otherwise stated. All page references to Alice Walker's work are to the editions published by The Women's Press.
3. Alice Walker, 'Gifts of Power: the Writings of Rebecca Jackson' (1981), *MG*, p. 82.
4. Mary Helen Washington (ed.), *Any Woman's Blues* (London: Virago Press, 1986) p. xvi (rpt. of *Midnight Birds*, New York: Anchor Books, 1980).
5. See, for example, Alice Walker's essays, 'The Unglamorous but Worthwhile Duties of the Black Revolutionary Artist, or of the Black Writer Who Simply Works and Writes' (1971), *MG*, pp. 130–8; 'Saving the Life That Is Your Own: the Importance of Models in the Artist's Life' (1976), *MG*, pp. 3–14; 'One Child of One's Own: a Meaningful Digression Within the Work(s)' (1979), *MG*, pp. 371–6. See also Paul Lauter's 'Race and Gender in the American Literary Canon', in Judith Newton and Deborah Rosenfelt (eds), *Feminist Criticism and Social Change: Sex, Class and Race in Literature and Culture* (New York and London: Methuen, 1985) pp. 19–44.
6. Barbara Christian, *Black Feminist Criticism: Perspectives on Black Women Writers* (New York and Oxford: Pergamon Press, 1985) p. 2.
7. Ibid., pp. 3–4.
8. *MG*, pp. 290–316.
9. Christian, op. cit., p. 5.
10. Alice Walker, *Meridian* (New York: Harcourt Brace Jovanovich, 1976; London: Women's Press, 1982) pp. 105–6.
11. Alice Walker, *The Color Purple* (New York: Harcourt Brace Jovanovich; London: Women's Press, 1983) p. 99.
12. Alice Walker, 'Source', in *You Can't Keep a Good Woman Down* (New York: Harcourt Brace Jovanovich; London: Women's Press, 1982) p. 165.
13. Barbara Smith, 'Toward a Black Feminist Criticism', in Newton and Rosenfelt (eds), op. cit., pp. 8–9.
14. Alice Walker, 'Zora Neale Hurston: a Cautionary Tale and a Partisan View' (1979), *MG*, p. 85.
15. Alice Walker, 'If the Present Looks Like the Past, What Does the Future Look Like?' (1982), *MG*, pp. 301–6.
16. Alice Walker, 'A Talk: Convocation 1972' (1972), *MG*, p. 35.
17. Interview with Alice Walker, in Claudia Tate (ed.), *Black Women Writers at Work* (Harpenden, Herts: Oldcastle Books, 1985) p. 181. Walker's claim is true for her own work, but cannot accurately be

generalised; see for example Toni Morrison's more complex perceptions in *Tar Baby* (1981) of the limits white power sets to black
sexuality: ' "While you making up your story of what this one thinks
and this one feels, you have left out the white bosses. What do they
feel about it? It's not important who this one loves and this one hates
and what bowtie do or what machete-hair don't do if you don't figure
on the white ones and what they thinking about it all." He tapped her
on the chest bone and left her sitting there with a half-finished plot
on her tongue' (London: Triad Grafton Books, 1983) p. 111.

18. Alice Walker, in Tate (ed.), op. cit.
19. Alice Walker, 'From an Interview' (1973) *MG*, p. 251.
20. Alice Walker, 'Beyond the Peacock: the Reconstruction of Flannery
O'Connor' (1975), *MG*, p. 52.
21. Walker, 'From an Interview', *MG*, p. 259.
22. Walker, 'Beyond the Peacock', *MG*, p. 59.
23. See Rochelle Gatlin, *American Women Since 1945* (London: Macmillan, 1987) and Paula Giddings, *When and Where I Enter: The Impact
of Black Women on Race and Sex in America* (Toronto and New York:
Bantam Books, 1985).
24. Alice Walker, 'The Civil Rights Movement: What Good Was It?'
(1967), *MG*, pp. 119–29; 'Choosing to Stay at Home: Ten Years After
the March on Washington' (1973), *MG*, pp. 158–70.
25. See Giddings, op. cit., ch. 17, 'The Women's Movement and Black
Discontent' (on the Black Muslims, see pp. 317–18) and ch. 18, 'Strong
Women and Strutting Men: the Moynihan Report'.
26. Michele Wallace, *Black Macho and the Myth of the Superwoman* (New
York: Dial Press, 1978; London: John Calder, 1979) pp. 14–15.
27. Mel Watkins, 'Sexism, Racism and Black Women Writers', *New York
Times Book Review*, 15 June 1986, p. 36.
28. Walker, 'One Child of One's Own', *MG*, pp. 376–9. See also, 'Looking
to the Side, and Back' (1979), *MG*, pp. 316–18.
29. Walker, 'From an Interview', *MG*, pp. 252–3.
30. Alice Walker, 'The Black Writer and the Southern Experience' (1970),
MG, p. 17.
31. Alice Walker, *The Third Life of Grange Copeland* (New York: Harcourt Brace Jovanovich, 1970; London: Women's Press, 1985).
32. For another version of the Lynne sequence, see 'Advancing Luna and
Ida B. Wells', in *You Can't Keep a Good Woman Down*. For other
attempts by Walker to deal with black men's erotic versions of black
and white women see 'Coming Apart' and 'Porn', in the same collection. See Giddings, op. cit., pp. 300–3 and 307–11, for an account of
the conflicts between black and white women in the late 1960s and
early 1970s.

Bibliography

Baldwin, James, *If Beale Street Could Talk* (New York: Dial Press, 1974).

Christian, Barbara, *Black Feminist Criticism: Perspectives on Black Women Writers* (New York and Oxford: Pergamon Press, 1985).

Cleaver, Eldridge, 'The Allegory of the Black Eunuchs' in *Soul on Ice* (New York: McGraw-Hill, 1968).

Ellison, Ralph, *Invisible Man* (New York: Random House, 1952).

Gates, Henry Louis Jr, *Black Literature and Literary Theory* (New York and London: Methuen, 1984).

Gatlin, Rochelle, *American Women since 1945* (London: Macmillan, 1987).

Giddings, Paula, *When and Where I Enter: The Impact of Black Women on Race and Sex in America* (Toronto and New York: Bantam Books, 1985).

Hemenway, Robert E., *Zora Neale Hurston: A Literary Biography* (London: Camden Press, 1986).

Hurston, Zora Neale, *Their Eyes Were Watching God* (New York: J. B. Lippincott, 1937).

Lauter, Paul, 'Race and Gender in the American Literary Canon', in Judith Newton and Deborah Rosenfelt (eds), *Feminist Criticism and Social Change* (New York and London: Methuen, 1985) pp. 19–44.

Morrison, Toni, *Tar Baby* (London: Triad Grafton Books, 1983).

Smith, Barbara, 'Toward a Black Feminist Criticism', in Newton and Rosenfelt (eds), op. cit., pp. 3–18.

Tate, Claudia (ed.), *Black Women Writers at Work* (Harpenden, Herts: Oldcastle Books, 1985).

Walker, Alice, *The Third Life of Grange Copeland* (New York: Harcourt Brace Jovanovich, 1970; London: Women's Press, 1985).

——, *Meridian* (New York: Harcourt Brace Jovanovich, 1976; London: Women's Press, 1982).

——, *The Color Purple* (New York: Harcourt Brace Jovanovich; London: Women's Press, 1983).

——, *You Can't Keep a Good Woman Down* (New York: Harcourt Brace Jovanovich; London: Women's Press, 1982).

——, *In Search of Our Mothers' Gardens: Womanist Prose* (New York: Harcourt Brace Jovanovich, 1983; London: Women's Press, 1984).

——, *Horses Make a Landscape Look More Beautiful* (New York: Harcourt Brace Jovanovich, 1984; London: Women's Press, 1985).

Wallace, Michele, *Black Macho and the Myth of the Superwoman* (New York: Dial Press, 1978; London: John Calder, 1979).

Washington, Mary Helen (ed.), *Any Woman's Blues* (London: Virago Press, 1986) (rpt. of *Midnight Birds*, New York: Anchor Books, 1980).

Watkins, Mel, 'Sexism, Racism and Black Women Writers', *New York Times Book Review*, 15 June 1986, p. 1 and pp. 35–7.

Wright, Richard, *Native Son* (New York, Harper, 1940).

7 Beyond Paper Heroines: Maxie Wander's *Guten Morgen, du Schöne* and its Reception in the GDR

PATRICIA HARBORD

I

In 1977 a book was published in the GDR which generated an unusual level of excitement amongst the country's large reading public, and particularly amongst women. For several years afterwards, this book was the subject of continuing animated discussion. It appeared at a time when many literary texts in the GDR, especially those by female writers, were questioning their society's accepted notions about femininity, and were casting doubt on the validity of current discourses on women. However, this particular book challenged established ways of writing about women more radically than any other GDR publication before or since. It was received with enthusiasm by the prominent GDR women writers Irmtraud Morgner and Christa Wolf who praised it for its openness, welcoming it in much the same spirit as Soviet intellectuals have welcomed the rise of *glasnost* in the culture of the Soviet Union in recent years.[1] The new publication was like a signpost pointing towards new, richer and more subtle ways of representing subjectivity in general, and female subjectivity in particular, within the bounds of a Marxist–Leninist aesthetic. This book was *Guten Morgen, du Schöne* (*Good Morning, My Lovely*), a collection of interviews with women of a variety of ages, origins and occupations. The interviews were recorded, and then transcribed and edited by the interviewer Maxie Wander. They became the basis for a well-attended stage version which by 1985 had been performed in 35 theatres throughout the GDR. The book also aroused much interest in the Federal Republic

146

and by 1985 it had been published in Czechoslovakia, Denmark, Holland and Italy, as well as in West Germany.[2]

This essay looks at how *Guten Morgen, du Schöne* relates to socialist-realist traditions of the documentary representation of women. It also discusses the book's reception by readers and critics in the GDR, especially those who are concerned with the interaction of gender and identity in their society. I write from the perspective of a Western feminist aware of some twenty years of work within the women's movement towards overcoming some of the contradictions between socialism and feminism, work aimed at bringing the cause of women's liberation in from the periphery of socialist politics to take up a key position at their centre.

After the GDR's inception in 1949 a rather different political process was initiated within the Republic's variety of 'actually existing socialism', with the introduction of a series of measures which made its legislation more favourable to working women than that of any other country in the world.[3] This might suggest that the numerous problems besetting those in the West who have attempted to combine feminism and socialism had been resolved in the GDR. Yet since the mid-1970s, women there have been voicing their aspirations for a new phase of emancipation which goes far beyond legislation in favour of 'the socialist wife and mother'. Like many of their contemporaries within Western women's movements, they believe the question of the relationship between gender and social identity has been neglected too long by socialist orthodoxy. Both *Guten Morgen, du Schöne* itself and the manner of its reception in the GDR raise the question of how GDR women who are concerned about this issue see themselves in relation to Western feminism. My essay examines how, departing from a very different basis from that of the women's movements of the West, they have envisaged a way forward out of their situation, towards a socialism able to address the contradictions of industrialised societies which categorise and value human attributes according to social perceptions of 'feminine' or 'masculine' characteristics.

II

The discourse of *Guten Morgen, du Schöne* has been compared to that of Western feminist consciousness-raising groups. As Susan Bassnett has pointed out, the comparison extends beyond the way

language is used in both instances, into the social relationships
between women that are formed through this use of language, into
'the kind of conversations that lie behind the monologues, and the
process whereby Maxie Wander obviously managed to create a
relationship with other women that would allow such openness'.[4]
Alongside the striking similarities, there are, of course, contrasts
between two phenomena arising in such different political circumstances. The context of discussions, not usually recorded or published, between groups of Western women who would generally
consider themselves to be part of a grassroots women's movement,
is not the same as the context of interviews which are edited versions
of one-to-one conversations between Maxie Wander and nineteen
individual women, arranged with a view to publication, and situated
in the GDR where the rejection of what is described as 'bourgeois'
or 'capitalist' feminism has been widespread.[5] However, the essence
both of consciousness-raising and of *Guten Morgen, du Schöne* is
the speaking of the individual biography, making public and important that which had until the moment of speech been consigned to
the realms of the private and/or of the unspoken. This act, the
making political of the personal, is one which has been central to
post-1960s Western feminism. In an article on the significance of
spoken and written biography in the Western women's movement
of the last two decades, the West German sociologist and feminist
Ilse Brehmer recalls one of the movement's earliest campaigns, in
which women publicly accused themselves of having infringed the
restrictive abortion legislation then in force. 'What women were
doing at that point was taking a very intimate factual detail of their
own biography, one which was punishable by law, and making it
public.'[6]

Wander's interviewing style was to give the women she talked to
the opportunity to speak their biographies for themselves; in her
foreword to *Guten Morgen, du Schöne* she writes: 'I'm interested in
how women experience their own personal history, how they imagine
their personal history to themselves. . . . Perhaps this book only
came about because of my desire to listen.'[7] The West German
feminist historian Erika Adolphy recommends a very similar
approach to interviewing. Writing on the interpretation of women's
biographical data by social historians and sociologists, Adolphy criticises the extent to which 'dominant his-toriography' generalises,
and reduces detail to statistics, in order to reach conclusions about
women's lives.[8] Adolphy argues in favour of oral history:

Oral history enables us to take a look at the underside of history. People who, until now, have been regarded by the writers of history as objects, people indeed who have not learnt to see themselves other than as objects, are asked about the stories of their lives, and asked to include all their experiences, their wishes, their creative potential, their suffering and the strength of their resistance.[9]

Oral history can help to produce 'new sources . . . which are on the side of the narrator'. Adolphy emphasises the importance of language in this process, because 'in the interview situation normative hegemonic language isn't nearly as all-pervasive [as in written sources]'.[10] As an alternative to dominant models of biographically-based research using normative concepts and statistics, Adolphy suggests the use of interview techniques which focus on particular aspects of the individual biography. 'By considering particular aspects in this way the tension between the individual biography and social processes can be revealed.' However, she emphasises that these techniques should be used not only for the benefit of the interviewer, but also for the benefit of its subject, the person interviewed, who should be involved in the revelation of the tension just described. The correspondences and discrepancies which come to light between subjective behavioural ideals on the one hand and socially determined role possibilities on the other can, Adolphy believes, allow the individual to adopt a critical distance to her (or his) own biography and to social norms. 'Coming to a new understanding of one's own biography would thus mean . . . a confrontation with history.'[11]

The potential for the women interviewed by Wander to confront history in such a way is high given the biographical material of the interviews. Whether or not this potential is fulfilled can be considered by examining a particular historical development which had significant effects on the social behaviour of women in the GDR. One development which stands out in this respect from the pages of *Guten Morgen, du Schöne* is the liberalisation of access to abortion and contraception. Under paragraph 218 of the *Strafgesetzbuch* (Penal Code), abortion was an offence during the Weimar Republic as well as in the postwar Federal Republic until 1974, when it was permitted under certain restricted circumstances. During the Weimar Republic, the KPD (German Communist Party) mounted a vehement campaign against paragraph 218, using slogans such as

'Dein Körper gehört Dir!' ('Your body belongs to you!')[12], and in the SED (German Socialist Unity Party), whose monopoly of power in the GDR is only now being dismantled, older members would have recalled this campaign. Yet abortion was restricted in the GDR until 1972 when the VIII Party Congress of the SED instituted free abortion on demand up to the end of the third month of pregnancy.[13] Within a few years, deaths due to abortion fell to almost a tenth of their previous level.[14] It is evident from Wander's interviews that contraception and sexuality in general remained taboo subjects for many mothers and their daughters in the GDR during the 1950s and into the 1960s, despite liberal legislation on single mothers and their children, who since 1950 had enjoyed the same rights as married mothers and their children, as well as positive discrimination in the form of special measures. Indeed, Charlotte Worgitzky's novel *Meine ungeborenen Kinder* (*My Unborn Children*), published in the GDR in 1982, suggests that taboos on the discussion of abortion persisted even into the 1980s.

The availability or otherwise of contraception and abortion – and also of any reliable information about sex – is a recurring theme in *Guten Morgen, du Schöne*. It is particularly the older women, growing up when these subjects were not talked about, and going through their childbearing years while contraception was inadequate and abortion illegal, who speak of these factors as having made a difference.

Karoline is 47 in the year of her interview.[15] Seventeen when the war ended, she trained as a hairdresser, married, and had five children at a time when young women in the GDR were encouraged to aspire to a career, while remaining largely responsible for the care of the family and at the same time being denied effective control over their reproductive systems. 'Reading our literature here at that time, or listening to the radio, I would think: Why can't I succeed in doing what these marvellous women achieve with such ease? Why does it have to be me who's such a failure? In fact more or less all my strength was being used up on the most basic tasks' (p. 226). Karoline is sharply aware of the position to which she was reduced by the deficiencies of birth-control and the illegality of abortion:

> I got this fitted and that fitted, asked for contraceptives, but we only had to look at each other and it had already happened. When I said: Doctor, it can't go on like this, another child every year, he said: Even if it was your eighteenth, my answer would

still be no. That's how it used to be, we were animals. Not human
beings, who could make decisions about their own lives. In 1966
Andreas came along as well, then came the contraceptive pill,
that was a life-saver for me.   (p. 225)

Relieved of the burden of repeated pregnancies, Karoline fights to
achieve self-fulfilment, and when interviewed by Wander she has
become a personnel manager (*Kaderleiterin*) in the Youth Welfare
Department – a job which she finds demanding, but evidently also
enjoys.

Erika, interviewed at the age of 41, was more fortunate than
Karoline. She travelled about with, and later married, a musician,
and managed, by illegally terminating unwanted pregnancies, to have
children only by choice (pp. 174–5). In sexual matters she had been
patronised by her avuncular, possessive husband and ill-informed by
her hypocritical mother who had one set of moral standards for her
daughter and quite another for herself. Erika's control of her own
fertility was thus achieved against considerable odds.

Unlike the older women in the book, most of the younger ones
seem to have escaped experiencing their fertility as a problematic
issue which uncontrollably structures their lives. However Ute, a
skilled worker interviewed at the age of 24 and born in 1951 into a
family of workers, had much the same difficulties as women twenty
years her senior. Just two years before the liberalisation of abortion
legislation in the GDR, Ute found herself an unwilling single mother
at the age of nineteen, an event which she blames on a lack of access
to contraception or abortion, and on deficient sex education:

They explained it to us theoretically at school, from a Marxist–
Leninist standpoint, about how people have to behave responsibly.
But what that really means in practical terms, nobody told us that,
did they? How can anybody still be so thick at eighteen, eh? If
there'd been the pill then, or abortion on demand, well, Jens [her
son] wouldn't be around now, that's for sure.   (p. 84)

For each of these women, the telling of her life-story involves the
recognition of the extent to which a combination of restrictions
imposed by the State and of taboos in force in her social environment
have limited her control of her capacity to bear children and thus
altered the course of her life. Karoline's vehement complaint that
women were treated as 'animals' is an implicit condemnation of the

policies by which women were exhorted to fulfil the dual role of workers and family caretakers, but exposed at the same time to the strains of unplanned motherhood and the dangers of illegal termination. No doubt the women already had some awareness of the extent of the limitations imposed on them; but in talking to Wander (and, by implication, to her future readers), they confirm the validity of their experience and (re-)define their perspective on it. Furthermore, in a society where events in the individual biography such as abortion are thought of as being 'private' matters, and thus as being outside the terms of public discourse, the very act of speaking out publicly about such a 'private' event is one which challenges the status quo.

The behaviour of the women who talk about their experience of abortion in *Guten Morgen, du Schöne* can be compared to that of the Western women referred to above who publicised their illegal recourse to abortion. The stance of the women in *Guten Morgen, du Schöne*, speaking to Wander approximately three years after the institution of free abortion on demand in the GDR, is less evidently defiant than that of the Western women, who incriminated themselves in the context of political campaigns to change restrictive abortion legislation. But both groups of women are involved in initiating public discussion of the issue, and a re-examination of social attitudes to it. They are also offering to other women who have had abortions the opportunity of perceiving this experience, not as a private and personal source of guilt or unhappiness, but as part of a shared history. The awareness of a shared history of oppression has been an important feature of all liberation movements, including the women's liberation movement in the West. Although there was until the recent political changes virtually no grassroots women's movement in the GDR, individual women there have for some years been pointing to the need for the growth of such an awareness. The GDR Germanist Eva Kaufmann, for instance, commented in 1982 that 'sufferings which had been perceived as entirely personal must now be seen in an objective light and understood to be sufferings in common'.[16] The possible role of *Guten Morgen, du Schöne* in such a transformation of consciousness is a question I consider later in this essay.

In the instance of attitudes to reproductive rights, then, Wander's approach to the interviews would indeed seem to have the effect which Adolphy, in her article on oral history, argues a good interview should have. In their attitudes to the issue of reproductive rights the

women discussed above are in fact identifying points of conflict
between their personal ideals and social developments as they tell
their stories, effecting, as Adolphy suggests 'a confrontation with
history' – one which ultimately involves not only the women themselves, but also the readers of *Guten Morgen, du Schöne.*
However, confronting history through the individual biography
and breaking free of social norms may not always be as straightforward an undertaking as Adolphy implies in her article. For
instance, one area in which this liberating confrontation has failed
to occur for the women in Wander's book is that of their perception
of the way they relate to their daughters. The women interviewed
have much to say about their relationships to their own mothers –
unsurprisingly, for these relationships are one context in which the
conflicts referred to by Adolphy between personal aspirations and
social expectations have been played out. Yet the narration of these
conflicts lived through earlier in their lives does not appear to have
encouraged the women to reflect in turn on their relationships to
their daughters, or on whether it might be possible to offer this new
generation of women a better experience of the mother–daughter
relationship than the interviewees themselves remember having had.
Relationships to sons are considered briefly by several of the women.
However, of the seven women in the book with female children,
Christl, Margot and Karoline hardly mention their daughters; Lena
actively dislikes her unfortunate daughter because she resembles
Lena's despised second husband, the girl's father (p. 198); Erika
longed for, and gave birth to, a son who was just like the husband
she adored, and then to a daughter who is described merely as 'a
bundle of nerves' (p. 177); and Katja talks of enjoying her small
daughter's company but says nothing about her upbringing (pp.
133–58). Only one of the women interviewed, Rosi, reveals having
any specific aims in bringing up her daughter; she tries to encourage
her to be true to herself whatever pressures are put on her (p. 9),
and to have a 'healthy' and open attitude to her sexuality (p. 15).
The women's relative silence on the subject of the experience of
mothering daughters, and their display of negative attitudes towards
some of the girls, tempers the mood of hope for the future prevalent
elsewhere in the book.

III

In the previous section, I examined perspectives of the interviews in *Guten Morgen, du Schöne* on history: in this one I shall discuss the history of the interviews, as a literary form. *Guten Morgen, du Schöne* has antecedents in a journalistic form which has long been popular amongst socialist writers, that of the character sketch or *Porträt*, a form of reportage. Wander's interviews both acknowledge and challenge this ancestry.

According to John Willett, reportage owed its popularity as a genre in Weimar Germany to the writings in the mid-1920s of journalist and KPD member Egon Erwin Kisch. At that time it was already a favourite journalistic technique in the Soviet Union. Reportage or factography, the practice of 'letting the facts speak for themselves'[17] came to the fore again in the GDR of the early 1950s, as writers developed ways to document 'the establishment of a new society and the model human behaviour patterns which evolved within it'.[18] However, it has been accepted among GDR literary historians that there was a tendency to depict the subjects of reportage in a manner which displayed too much 'schematism and uniformity' and presented a black-and-white moral universe.[19]

The genre of reportage continued to influence the literature of the GDR in the years after the Bitterfeld Conferences on literature and culture. The V Party Conference of the SED in 1958 established cultural goals such as 'overcoming the separation of art and life, the alienation of the artist from the people'.[20] This call was taken up by the first Bitterfeld Conference, held in 1959, at which both professional writers and worker-writers resolved that a socialist cultural revolution should be initiated in literature. Professional writers, whose work was held to be insufficiently influenced by revolutionary change in the productive sphere, were to be encouraged to go into the factories to work with a brigade and study socialist productive relations on the spot. Workers, on the other hand, were to be encouraged (with the help of slogans such as 'Reach for the pen, mate!') to document from their own perspective struggles and progress in production.[21] Documentary writing was of course an important feature of this two-pronged campaign.

The writer Sarah Kirsch (best known as a lyric poet) refers to this campaign when discussing influences on her book *Die Pantherfrau* (*The Panther-Woman*):

After Bitterfeld, 'Novels from Production' became a widespread concept. As this side of things had been more or less passed over until then, it wasn't such a bad idea for professional writers to spend some time within the productive sphere. I did so myself, twice, once in an LPG [Agricultural Production Collective, i.e., a collective farm], and once in a big factory. . . . In the end some aspects of those themes – the world of production, what life's like for a worker – would turn up now and then in my short stories, and came through in *Die Pantherfrau* as well.[22]

Die Pantherfrau is a collection of interviews with five women, subtitled 'Five Unadorned Stories From a Cassette Recorder' and produced in much the same way as *Guten Morgen, du Schöne*, but appearing four years earlier, in 1973. However, unlike Wander's book, *Die Pantherfrau* was commissioned (by the publishers Aufbau for Women's Year, according to Kirsch).[23] The poet identifies the relentlessly optimistic tone of GDR journalism, and the continued schematism and uniformity (persisting long after the 1950s) in reports portraying individuals, as motivating factors in producing *Die Pantherfrau*. It is clear from remarks which Kirsch makes during a RIAS radio discussion with schoolchildren in West Berlin[24] that she intended *Die Pantherfrau* to be more honest and more interesting than traditional GDR reportage:

> People used to write a lot of character sketches in the GDR . . . which were rather boring. Where the people they were portraying came off pretty well. Where they were really great blokes and made suggestions at work about how productivity could be improved and where everything was very rosy, but just a bit far removed from reality.[25]

Later in the discussion, she concurs that *Die Pantherfrau* is 'to some extent a criticism of socialist realism'.[26]

However, if Kirsch did indeed intend the book as a criticism of the false heroism of the GDR *Porträt* (or character sketch) in the past, she did not realise this intention to any significant extent. All of the women she interviewed, with the possible exception of Beate Sch. in the interview 'Relay Swimming', are presented so that they appear to conform to an implausible extent with socialist ideals of womanhood – just like the 'superwomen' who so discouraged Wander's Karoline. Two of the women interviewed (Beate Sch., and

Frau Beyer in 'Twins') talk a little about their personal lives as well
as about their careers. However, the other three interviews (with
Frau Coldam – 'The Panther Woman', Frau Häntzsche – 'Years of
Agitation', and Hannelore – 'A Bath-Tub Full of Whipped Cream')
are concerned with little more than the women's success in their
various fields of work. The Hero of the Workplace has merely been
replaced by the Heroine of the Workplace.

By contrast, the discourse of *Guten Morgen, du Schöne* allows a
style of self-representation which does not always flatter the women
interviewed but which permits their lives beyond the workplace
to be discussed and leaves room for inconsistencies, doubts and
contradictions to be voiced. These emerging ambiguities call the
heroic mode itself into question.

The interview with Karoline (in *Guten Morgen, du Schöne*) already
referred to above is one which particularly challenges the heroic
mode. Although there are hints that the women Kirsch interviews
have experienced difficulties in integrating their successful careers
with the demands of their personal lives, such questions are never
discussed in *Die Pantherfrau*, but only intimated. While Karoline
resembles in many ways several of the women in *Die Pantherfrau*,
having come from an impoverished background and built a successful
career for herself, she does not conceal the struggle which this cost
her – a life-or-death struggle at times, as it emerges in her interview.
For three years Karoline, exhausted by the effort of bringing up her
five children with only financial support from her husband, was
seriously ill. During her illness her husband had an affair. When
Karoline recovered she decided that it was time to shift the balance
of power in their relationship more in her own favour. First, she
took a lover herself (to her husband's consternation); but she realised
that this was not enough: 'I said to myself: Pull yourself together,
Karoline, forget about fooling around, you've got to become independent, so that at last you can say: "If it doesn't suit you, you can
go" ' (p. 229). In the end she gained independence and self-confidence not through her lover, but through her new career in youth
welfare. Her struggle to change her relationship with her husband
was eventually successful; he began to take more responsibility for
the family, and to acknowledge that he needed Karoline. She
remarks: 'My life with "Tubby" is great now, it's grounded on a
basis of equality. I paid dearly for that basis. . . . Now he's come
to realise just what I'm worth to him' (p. 229). Although Karoline's
story has a happy ending, the insistence on the effort which she

expended to achieve this ending prevents her from sounding like the superwomen of the typical character sketch. Karoline herself says of the images of women presented in GDR media and literature: 'Later I came to realise that reality's quite different and the positive heroines are only made of paper' (p. 226).

If the interview with Karoline challenges the heroic mode of the GDR character sketch, then the interview with Ruth (pp. 51–71) effectively subverts it. Ruth, who is 22 when interviewed, serves drinks in a bar and lives on her own with her five-year-old son. While Karoline has resolved the conflict between her dual role as a working woman and as the emotional nurturer of her family, Ruth's life is full of conflicts which are a perpetual site of anxiety and self-doubt: 'I think that what's tearing me apart inside is that I'm living at a time when it's already possible for women to achieve all sorts of things, but I'm a coward. . . . Between the possibilities and my fear, there's this crazy rift which opens up, and it's destroying me' (p. 51). Ruth cannot reconcile her perception of the realities of her life with her perception of the ideals of femininity in her society. She is confused and unhappy because she cannot live up to these ideals: she describes feelings of alienation from her body, for instance, particularly from her breasts. 'Sometimes – sometimes I seem unreal to myself. . . . The stupid pill hasn't made me any different. Perhaps I would become a proper woman, if I had proper breasts' (p. 53). Motherhood, too, fills her with a sense of inadequacy: 'I know I do everything wrong. I'm not even fit to be a mother. And not even an animal does that wrong, does it?' (p. 61).

A single mother with a relatively unskilled job, depressed and uncertain of herself and undergoing psychotherapy, is hardly a suitable candidate for the post of stereotypical socialist heroine – especially when she makes no overtly political statements, and is critical of social values which emphasise conformity and success, leaving her feeling isolated and marginalised. While the discourse of the traditional GDR character sketch, criticised by Kirsch but still apparent in *Die Pantherfrau*, denies and suppresses contradictions, within the more open discourse of *Guten Morgen, du Schöne*, the unresolved contradictions of Ruth's existence can stand as they are. Ruth can be read as a fragmented subject, and her interview as resisting closure, phenomena more appropriate to a modernist aesthetic than to a socialist realist one, which prefers the contradictions of the subject to reach closure by resolving themselves within the text.

Kirsch herself admits the importance of reading between the lines in *Die Pantherfrau*, because it is not only what the women she interviewed are prepared to talk about that matters, but also what they try to avoid mentioning.[27] She concedes that this is a shortcoming of her book, and pays tribute to Wander's interviews:

> In the GDR people aren't used to talking about themselves and to making direct statements about how they live their lives, what they think. I have to admit that Maxie Wander was really much more successful in that respect. . . . In Maxie Wander's character sketches of women you really do notice that things have developed a lot in that direction: the women are much more open with her and reflect much more deeply on their personal and their social situation.[28]

The contrast between the superficiality of the interviews in *Die Pantherfrau* and the depth of those in *Guten Morgen, du Schöne* indicates the extent to which Wander's book opened up a public space within which it immediately became appropriate to discuss issues previously considered personal. It overcame the strength of GDR taboos in this area and supplied a way of using language which suddenly made such discussion possible. Many people in the GDR talk of having experienced an extraordinary revelation on reading *Guten Morgen, du Schöne*, and the following remarks by Regina Griebel, who produced the stage version of the book for the GDR's 'Deutsches Theater', are a written account of the effect of the interviews on some of the first people to read them:

> We were introduced to the book in the spring of 1977. We passed it around rapidly amongst ourselves. The very first encounter with these 19 women, with their various experiences which are so very different from one another, was the same in one important respect: it was an encounter with the assertion of the right to be happy [*Glücksanspruch*] – an assertion which has been made since time immemorial but which then became suddenly, unmistakeably specific and immediate to the here and now. This assertion of the right to be happy is a thread which runs through each of the individual stories in this collection and weaves a relationship between them and with the reader as well, who, by making comparisons with personal experience, reaches a fuller self-awareness. One's own individual story is revealed to one as an adven-

ture, an adventure which matters. This experience is so thrilling that it has to be communicated immediately to someone else. There were phone calls late at night, there were conversations in the intervals between rehearsals. We talked, moved and encouraged by the honesty of these life-stories – we talked about ourselves, about what we had discovered, or what we could, ought to, discover together. There was a great deal of mutual trust in this use of . . . the grammatical form of possibility and of the first person plural.[29]

I suggested above that although there are similarities between *Guten Morgen, du Schöne* and Western feminist consciousness-raising (in terms of their discourse and the relationships between women governed by that discourse), the context in which the interviews were produced differed in various ways from the context of consciousness-raising in the Western women's movement. I would add here that the parallels between *Guten Morgen, du Schöne* and Western consciousness-raising are most evident not in the production of Wander's book but in its reception by some GDR readers; these parallels are striking in Griebel's account above of the book's significance to her friends and colleagues. In that account, the reading of the interviews brings about a sudden change in self-awareness in the reader; the encounter with the assertion of the right to personal happiness is a moment of revelatory force. The individual biography, previously disregarded or perceived as trivial, is now seen to be of interest and to 'matter'. The experience of reading, and the excitement of discussion in pairs and in groups, leads first to personal 'discoveries' and then to a sense of the further discoveries which could be made collectively, 'together'. Here the personal, emerging precipitously from the domain of the unspoken into the public arena, is on the verge of becoming political.

IV

Despite the parallels which I have described above between the impact of *Guten Morgen, du Schöne* in the GDR and the discourse and practice of consciousness-raising in the Western women's movement, the reception of Wander's book in the GDR has displayed an eagerness to distance the text from Western feminism. What is more, it has not been the guardians of orthodox socialist ideology who have shown themselves eager to establish this distance, as one might expect; instead, it has been some of the few GDR women who are relatively sympathetic towards Western feminism. Indeed, the text itself provides a foothold for anti-feminism, when one of the women interviewed – the strong-minded and independent Rosi, who hopes to encourage her daughter to have a positive attitude to her sexuality – expresses her disapproval of feminists[30] in these terms:

> I could behave like some feminists, who let loose like savages, because they've been given the chance; who complain about their husbands because they don't do the washing up for them or wash the children's shitty nappies. They just run amok, they'll never come to an understanding with their husbands. . . . Without love all these experiments in emancipation will just remain a grind. What use is it to women if they emancipate themselves *in opposition to* their partners? (p. 19)

The writer Christa Wolf,[31] in a review which later became the preface to the West German edition of *Guten Morgen, du Schöne*, assures us of the women Wander interviewed: 'These women do not see themselves as the opponents of men – unlike certain women's groups in capitalist countries, who are often accused of fanatically hating men.'[32] For Wander herself, Wolf's assurance was not enough, perhaps because it is made before some more admiring comments on the Western women's movement. Writing to the West German publishers of *Guten Morgen, du Schöne* about the preface to their edition of the book, Wander – evidently disturbed by the marketing of feminism in the capitalist West – favours an alternative to the review by Wolf: 'If there has to be a preface, then rather one by Gerti Tetzner, who will keep the book right out of the rest of the feminist merry-go-round!'[33]

The negative attitudes of most women in the GDR towards the women's movement in capitalist countries may at first seem puzzling. They can be ascribed to various factors. The most obvious is the position of the former political orthodoxy, which is exemplified in the following extract from a GDR sociological textbook, *Wie emanzipiert sind Frauen in der DDR?* (*How emancipated are women in the GDR?* [Kuhrig/Speigner, 1977]). It is coloured by the view frequently taken by orthodox socialists of the 'woman question' as a secondary contradiction, which must not be allowed to interfere with the more important business of class struggle. The numerous

political stances adopted by women in the West in relation to socialism and to feminism are here reduced to two caricatures – autonomous feminists, it is implied, are strident man-haters with no concern for the cause of the working class, and may be neatly opposed
to enlightened female socialists who gladly work hand-in-hand with
their helpful male comrades:

> The solution of the 'Woman Question' is inseparably linked to
> the working class's fulfilment of its historic mission. This solution
> cannot be achieved through the battle of the sexes, through the
> struggle of women against men – as is noisily proclaimed by the
> representatives of the feminist-oriented women's movement – but
> only in the struggle of women and men together for social pro-
> gress, for the elimination of social relations under which human
> beings are enslaved and oppressed beings.[34]

The image which GDR women like Rosi have of feminist activity
as amounting to time-wasting, shrill domestic quarrels with men
who won't 'help' with the housework may have been influenced by
orthodox ideologues such as Kuhrig and Speigner. However, this
image of feminism is also remarkably similar to that often projected
by the Western electronic mass media. Until recently, most people
in the GDR were unable to obtain Western publications, but did
have unlimited access to West German television and radio. They
have thus been exposed to the way the women's movement is represented on the airwaves, and yet cut off from the mass of written
debate produced by the movement itself, and so vital to it. The
majority of the GDR's inhabitants have been able to experience
Western feminism only at several removes, and so have only ever
formed a very partial impression of a movement which has frequently
emphasised the central importance of direct personal experience.

The various factors which have encouraged GDR women to
deplore Western feminism have been an unfortunate hindrance to
mutual understanding and dialogue between the two. Those women
who have had the will and the opportunity to disregard these factors
have sometimes formed a better impression of the women's movement in capitalist countries than have their compatriots. Writers
such as Christa Wolf, Irmtraud Morgner and Maxie Wander have
undoubtedly had much contact with feminists in the West, and have
been able to read Western publications widely.[35] Wolf is perhaps
the writer who is most well-disposed towards feminism. In her review

of *Guten Morgen, du Schöne*, she discusses the deficiencies she sees in the Western women's movement, but finds them understandable given the conditions of industrial capitalism, adding:

> And yet: what solidarity they show to one another, what an effort they put into perceiving their own situation, what spontaneity and inventiveness they display in the projects they undertake to help themselves, what imagination, what variety. I cannot conclude that we in the GDR might have nothing whatsoever to learn from them.[36]

Furthermore, despite such attempts to dissociate Wander's book from Western feminism, the GDR women writers who have spoken out in support of it have also used it in support of their own ideas about the politics of gender identity in the GDR and the role that women, and writing about women, can play there. At the same time, they have been writing mostly within a framework of Marxism and Marxist aesthetics keeping itself largely inside the limited boundaries of what has until recently been considered acceptable and fit for publication in the GDR. The writer Irmtraud Morgner[37] has worked to develop a Marxist theory of culture which takes account of the factor of gender in GDR social relations without disregarding the factor of class – though perhaps 'theory' is a term which suggests too much coherence to be applied to the ideas which emerge through oblique and cryptic references in Morgner's novels, short stories, articles and interviews, and which are generally given a provocative and polemical twist to suit the politics of the situation and the moment. One of Morgner's most 'theoretical' pieces is a speech which she gave to the VIII Writer's Congress of the GDR, in which *Guten Morgen, du Schöne* and Morgner's ideas on cultural hegemony are presented as a mutual justification of one another. Morgner supports Wander's interviews in particular and the practice of interviewing 'ordinary' people in general. She argues that oppression in pre-socialist society has left a cultural legacy of discourse from which members of social groups which were historically at the bottom of the power-structure have been excluded. This exclusion has affected women in just the same way as the workers and peasants at whom GDR cultural policies are more traditionally aimed, and all of these groups, who have been the objects of dominant discourse, must be encouraged to become its subjects:

An exploratory mode is generally recognised as being appropriate when the people one is dealing with are females, as it is generally felt that so far, very little has been found out about them as objects, and almost nothing at all has been discovered about them as subjects. But this state of affairs applies not only to the female sex. It applies to all unimportant, ordinary people, who have been the objects of history, and so to the workers as well, and to the peasants.[38]

Morgner criticises her country's cultural establishment for having failed to provide such encouragement. She believes that it should be the function of contemporary socialist literature to give previously oppressed groups of people a voice – as *Guten Morgen, du Schöne* has done.

In her cunningly argued speech, Morgner uses Wander's interviews as a point of departure from which to develop several more of her own favourite themes. For instance, Morgner (who has been a single parent herself for many years) claims that because of the creative tension which she believes arises between intellectual work and their burden of domestic tasks, women working intellectually in the GDR are exempt from the problems of the division of labour (those problems which so exercised the V Party Congress of the SED and the Bitterfeld Conferences on Culture).

Like Morgner, Wolf considers the interviews with women in *Guten Morgen, du Schöne* an important contribution to the process of 'human beings' becoming subjects.[39] And, like Morgner, she believes women can develop into subjectivity partly through finding a voice, although she sees those who have been dispossessed of the right to exist as subjects as a more marginalised group than Morgner's women, workers and peasants:

That which the dominant consciousness [*Selbstverständnis*] is unaware of, the unspoken, the unspeakable, is always to be found amongst the underprivileged, the figures on the margins, those who have been deemed ineligible to speak for themselves and declared outcasts; wherever poverty and degradation do not permit a subject which would have the ability to speak ever to come into being in the first place; amongst those who perform the most menial and mindless of labours; in prisons, in barracks, in homes for children, for adolescents, for the old, in hospitals and in mental asylums. And of course, for a very long time: amongst women, who remained virtually voiceless.[40]

Thanks to the transformation of conditions for women in the GDR since the war, Wolf asserts, the women in Wander's interviews can begin to speak of 'experiences which affect [them], not generally, as human beings of the female sex, but personally, as individuals'.[41]

In Wolf's view, then, women in a socialist society can develop away from their roots of common oppression into individual subjects. By implication, collective action by women in such circumstances should no longer be necessary; on the other hand, they still share their collective history of oppression, which gives them a continuing group identity within socialist society which is different to that of men. In this line of argument Wolf's retrospective stance diverts attention away from the controversial question of separatist political activity by women in socialist societies; at the same time (as in her novel *Kassandra*, 1983) women's history – as it has been recorded or may be reconstructed – is used as a complex lever to apply pressure indirectly on present-day circumstances.

The term 'subject' in Wolf's review of *Guten Morgen, du Schöne* is used to denote a consciousness which, having escaped the uniformity of a de-humanizing oppression, has been able to afford to develop an individual identity, to acquire self-awareness and the power of self-expression. Christa Wolf's work has always been concerned with the creation within GDR literature of a space for the expression of the subjective, and has surveyed the social landscape from the personal and individual perspective. Wander, as I have described, created a similar space by encouraging the women she interviewed to talk subjectively about the personal aspects of their lives. This emphasis suggests another lineage may be established for *Guten Morgen, du Schöne* besides that which can be traced through the history of the *Porträt* and which has already been discussed above. Wolf, whose work on German women writers of the Romantic period has retrieved them from obscurity in the German-speaking world, sees a link between women of that period and GDR women such as those in Wander's interviews: both groups of women can be described as living through a time of high political aspirations and rapid social change, and experiencing a state of flux in the role of women in their society. She suggests that there is also a link between the forms of self-expression chosen by both groups, commenting that the Romantic women 'often express themselves in diaries and letters, in poetry, in travel writing, the most personal and subjective forms of literature, . . . within which the woman writing can move more freely, and also more convivially, than within the structures of the novel and the drama'.[42] Because women have previously been denied a voice in literature and in society, Wolf argues, they will turn more readily to less formal literary techniques which allow them to communicate personal experience in a direct way.

Educated women of the Romantic period were outsiders amongst their male associates – artists and writers who were themselves outsiders. They pursued creative activities for no purpose other than personal development and pleasure, but at great personal cost, suffering the mental and physical consequences of their alienation from 'a society relentlessly committed to efficiency'.[43] The GDR of the 1970s, too, Wolf believes, 'like all present-day communities, imposes – and to some extent must impose – many constraints upon its members'.[44] One such constraint is the pressure to achieve, which has until now been applied to women there in much the same way as to men. She quotes two of the older women in *Guten Morgen, du Schöne* who have been successful in their careers: Margot – 'When you spend a long time training yourself to achieve, you destroy something important in your personality. . . . When I'm not working I'm alien to myself' (p. 205), and Lena – 'no one who is as divided in themselves as I am can be happy' (p. 193). Many of the GDR's working women, Wolf observes, are not satisfied with this kind of equality: 'The possibility which our society gave them: of doing what men do, brought them, as was to be anticipated, to the question: Just what *is it* that men do? And is that what I really want?'[45] Wolf sets the negative values of 'utilitarian thinking, pragmatism, [and] . . . logical reasoning' – which she sees as the values of a male-dominated world – against the positive values of 'common sense, sensuous enjoyment, and the longing for happiness'.[46]

Yet, despite the restrictions which GDR society has imposed on its members, the interviews in *Guten Morgen, du Schöne* demonstrate (Wolf argues) that this society has awakened in women the desire to fulfil personal aspirations and pursue pleasure. She suggests that because of the responsibility society has traditionally given them for the private sphere, women tend to be more sharply aware of the contradictions between efficiency, relentlessness and competition on the one hand and affectivity, pleasure and co-operation on the other. She sees this legacy of historically feminine attributes as a repository of hope in an increasingly technological, industrialised world, caught in the escalation of a nuclear arms-race. This is a major theme in both Wolf's *Kassandra* and Morgner's *Amanda*, while Wander writes in a letter to Wolf that she feels it increasingly important to 'become a human being, as a design model in opposition to the brand of beings who build bombs!'.[47] Women are at present, by virtue of their inheritance, better equipped than men to formulate the current aspirations of humanity, Wolf asserts. In her opinion the interviews give the reader the opportunity to sense the potential of a future 'community, whose laws would be mutual sympathy, self-esteem, trust and friendliness – characteristics of sisterliness, which it seems to me is to be encountered in greater abundance than brotherliness [fraternity]'.[48]

V

I have suggested above that *Guten Morgen, du Schöne* was a challenging book in the GDR of the late 1970s – yet it was not so challenging that it placed itself outside the political boundaries of what was acceptable for publication there at that time. Wander, like Morgner and Wolf, successfully negotiates various political problems relating to the status of women in the GDR under orthodox socialism. For instance, it has long been conventional for writers there to emphasise women's gains since the institution of socialism. Yet while Wander, Morgner and Wolf stress the considerable improvements in the status of women in the GDR against the backdrop of countless years of suffering and oppression, they nevertheless represent conditions in the GDR of the 1970s and 1980s as part of a long process which has only just started – taking a historical overview which cannot easily be faulted by Marxist–Leninist ideologues. With this dual perspective which takes in both past and future, these writers avoid becoming mere apologists for the situation of the moment. In Wander's interviews the long-term vision of a better future for women can be seen to materialise in initial and still modest terms within the span of individual lives, each life a separate, micro-historical process. Yet, while some of those interviewed are old enough to have memories of the hard times women had under Fascism, or even earlier, the accounts of those women who speak out about their pre-1972 experience of abortion (which I discussed above) reveal that the suffering and oppression of women did not automatically end with the institution of socialism. The GDR's record regarding the status of women may have been comparatively good, but in the 1970s and 1980s these three writers believed that a considerable change of consciousness would be necessary if the situation were to be improved any further.

Besides the political problem just described, Wander, like Wolf and Morgner, also contends with a related, but aesthetic problem. These writers believe that to overcome the present consequences of their history, women must start by becoming aware of that history as a shared one and identifying with it, and must also glimpse how much better their future might be in a changed world. The written word can offer women both this sense of history and this intimation of a better future. However, Wander, Morgner and Wolf have lived through the attempts of their socialist society to provide similar literary encouragement to workers and peasants, and are well aware of the pitfalls of such a project. These pitfalls have not always been avoided by feminist writers in the West. For instance, Verena Stefan's novel *Häutungen* (1975) (*Shedding*) was rapturously received by some West German feminists. It had achieved its fourteenth reprint in the FRG by 1979.[49] Yet the book portrays its female characters as two-dimensional earth-mother figures and objects of reverence in the way that discourse on women has commonly done, despite Stefan's project to introduce a new way of thinking and writing.[50] On the other hand, feminist writing in the West has often suffered from what Toril Moi described as '[the assumption] that feminists must at all costs be angry all the time'.[51] On the whole, Wander, Morgner and Wolf succeed in finding their own narrow paths between anger on behalf of the female sex and idolatry of it. They have each devised ways of offering women the awareness of a shared history and the intimation of a better future, without making their female protagonists into superwomen, or writing in a perpetual self-righteous rage that leaves no room for any other emotion. To borrow Christa Wolf's remark – I cannot conclude that we in the West might have nothing whatsoever to learn from them.

Since the political changes of 1989–90 and the appearance of an autonomous women's movement in the GDR, it will now be easier for women from both sides of the former political divide to learn from each other. It remains to be seen how writing by women there will respond to this freer climate, and whether women in the West can work to help prevent the unique and valuable voices of GDR women from being swallowed up by political developments.

This essay is dedicated to the memory of Ann Duncan, Fellow of Newnham College, Cambridge, whom I liked for her courage and honesty and who taught me a great deal. She died in March 1989.

Notes

Page references in the text given in brackets refer to Maxie Wander, *Guten Morgen, du Schöne: Frauen in der DDR. Protokolle* (Berlin/GDR: Der Morgen, 1977).

1. Irmtraud Morgner, 'Rede auf dem VIII Schriftstellerkongreβ', *Neue Deutsche Literatur*, vol. 26, no. 8 (1978) pp. 31–2; Christa Wolf, 'Berührung', *Neue Deutsche Literatur*, vol. 26, no. 2 (1978) pp. 54–5.
2. Regina Griebel, sleeve notes to *Guten Morgen, du Schöne: Sechs Frauenporträts nach dem Buch von Maxie Wander* (Berlin/GDR: VEB Deutsche Schallplatten, 1985).
3. These measures have been amply documented elsewhere – see especially Susan Bassnett, *Feminist Experiences: The Women's Movement in Four Cultures* (London: Allen and Unwin, 1986) pp. 56–9; G. E. Edwards, *GDR Society and Social Institutions: Facts and Figures* (London: Macmillan, 1985) pp. 1–112. For the situation up to the mid-1970s, see Herta Kuhrig and Wulfram Speigner (eds), *Wie emanzipiert sind Frauen in der DDR?* (Cologne: Pahl-Rugenstein, 1979). To summarise the situation briefly, the percentage of women between the ages of 15 and 60 in employment or training in the GDR had risen steadily, to reach 88 per cent by 1985, the highest percentage in the world. The number of GDR women in part-time employment dropped from 35 per cent in 1971 to 28 per cent in 1982. Behind these figures lies a considerable system of support facilities and material benefits for women and for families, which are still available at the time of writing, despite political changes. These include extensive provision of free crèche, kindergarten and after-school care places. State financial support for women who have children is generous, as are periods of maternity leave (with initial payment of net average earnings). Special provision is made for single mothers and for large families. Many women are entitled to one day's paid leave a month as a day for carrying out household tasks. Further facilities useful to women, such as birth-control clinics, are extensively available. Abortion on demand was introduced in 1972, and there is a system of no-fault divorce. Women also benefit from positive discrimination in vocational training and further education. However, it has been pointed out that one overall effect of most of the provisions just described is to reinforce women's role as housekeepers and child-carers at the expense of encouraging change in male behaviour patterns; see, for example, Kathy Vanovitch, 'Innovation and Convention: Women in the GDR', *GDR Monitor*, no. 2 (Winter 1979–80) pp. 18–19.

4. Bassnett, op. cit., p. 73.
5. Ibid., p. 60.
6. Ilse Brehmer, 'Historische Genese: Frauenbewegung und die Erforschung des weiblichen Lebenslaufs', in *Beiträge 7 zur feministischen Theorie und Praxis* (Munich: Verlag Frauenoffensive, 1981) p. 10. All translations from German in this essay are my own.
7. Maxie Wander, *Guten Morgen, du Schöne: Frauen in der DDR. Protokolle* (Berlin/GDR: Der Morgen, 1977) p. 8.
8. Erika Adolphy, 'Einige Gedanken zu der Frage: Was ist eigentlich eine normale Frauenbiographie?', in *Beiträge 7 zur feministischen Theorie und Praxis*, p. 9.
9. Ibid.
10. Ibid.
11. Ibid., p. 8.
12. Petra Schneider, *Weg mit dem §218: Die Massenbewegung gegen das Abtreibungsverbot in der Weimarer Republik* (Berlin/FRG: Oberbaumverlag, 1975) p. 64.
13. Kuhrig and Speigner (eds), op. cit., pp. 348–9.
14. Ibid., p. 355.
15. The women interviewed are referred to in *Guten Morgen, du Schöne* by forenames only, which are not their real names.
16. Quoted in cover notes to Charlotte Worgitzky, *Meine ungeborenen Kinder* (Berlin/GDR: Der Morgen, 1982).
17. John Willett, *The New Sobriety: Art and Politics in the Weimar Period* (London: Thames and Hudson, 1978) p. 107.
18. Horst Haase, Hans-Juergen Geerdts *et al.*, *Geschichte der Literatur der Deutschen Demokratischen Republik* (Berlin/GDR: Volk und Wissen, 1977) p. 248.
19. Ibid., pp. 248–9.
20. Cit. Wolfgang Emmerich, *Kleine Literaturgeschichte der DDR* (Darmstadt and Neuwied/FRG: Luchterhand, 1981) p. 87.
21. Ibid., pp. 86–9.
22. Sarah Kirsch, *Erklärung einiger Dinge: Dokumente und Bilder* (Reinbek bei Hamburg/FRG: Rowohlt, 1981) p. 68.
23. Ibid., p. 28.
24. Kirsch emigrated from the GDR to West Berlin in 1979 in the wake of the Wolf Biermann affair.
25. Kirsch, op. cit., p. 27.
26. Ibid., p. 29.
27. Ibid., p. 26.
28. Ibid., p. 76.
29. Griebel, op. cit. 'Grammatical form of possibility' refers to the form used in the German '*könnten*', '*müßten*' (could, ought to).
30. She calls them '*Frauenrechtlerinnen*' (that is, women who support women's rights) – a term used to refer to suffragettes.
31. Christa Wolf is probably the GDR writer best known in the West, and much of her writing has been translated into English. Since the early 1960s she has published many novels, short stories and essays. One of

170   *Determined Women*

her most recent novels, *Kassandra* (1983) is a re-telling of the story of
the Trojan War from the point of view of the unheeded prophetess.

32. Wolf, 'Berührung', p. 60.

33. Fred Wander (ed.), *Maxie Wander: Leben wär' eine prima Alternative: Tagebuchaufzeichnungen und Briefe* (Darmstadt and Neuwied/FRG: Luchterhand, 1980) p. 222.

34. Kuhrig and Speigner (eds), op. cit., p. 14.

35. It is largely impossible to determine which particular feminist texts a GDR writer may have read, as GDR writers have not usually documented such sources in the past.

36. Wolf, 'Berührung', p. 60.

37. Morgner's publications include *Leben und Abenteuer der Trobadora Beatriz nach Zeugnissen ihrer Spielfrau Laura* (1974) (Life and Adventures of Beatriz the Trobadora as Witnessed by her Minstrel Laura) and *Amanda* (1983). In these two rumbustious novels Morgner charts the exploits of various characters, including a female troubadour who escapes sexual discrimination in her chosen field in twelfth-century France and emigrates to the twentieth-century GDR; her minstrel Laura, a graduate in German who works in the GDR as a train-driver and as single parent to a small son (and who, in the second novel, acquires the *Doppelgängerin* Amanda, a witch); and a serpent with seven-mile wings. The novels' female protagonists constantly illuminate and subvert the sexist workings of society in the GDR and various other locations, often by supernatural means or with the help of various *dei ex machina*.

38. Morgner, 'Rede auf dem VIII Schriftstellerkongreβ', p. 30.

39. Wolf, 'Berührung', p. 58.

40. Ibid., p. 57.

41. Ibid., p. 58.

42. Ibid., p. 57.

43. Ibid., p. 58.

44. Ibid., p. 61.

45. Ibid., p. 60.

46. Ibid., p. 62.

47. Wander (ed.), op. cit., p. 196 (letter of 4 August 1977).

48. Wolf, 'Berührung', p. 53. These foundations for a Utopia are undoubtedly the basis of the fictional community in the caves at Skamandros to which Kassandra retreats in Wolf's novel of 1983.

49. Heinz Puknus, *Neue Literatur der Frauen* (Munich: Beck, 1980) p. 208.

50. Verena Stefan, *Häutungen* (Munich: Verlag Frauenoffensive, 1975) p. 4.

51. Toril Moi, *Sexual/Textual Politics: Feminist Literary Theory* (London and New York: Methuen, 1985) pp. 39–40.

Bibliography

Where this may not be obvious, I have made clear whether texts in German are published in West Germany (FRG) or in the GDR. Most of the GDR texts given below also exist in West German editions.

Adolphy, Erika, 'Einige Gedanken zu der Frage: Was ist eigentlich eine normale Frauenbiographie?', in *Beiträge 7 zur feministischen Theorie und Praxis* (Munich: Verlag Frauenoffensive, 1981).

Bassnett, Susan, *Feminist Experiences: The Women's Movement in Four Cultures* (London: Allen and Unwin, 1986).

Brehmer, Ilse, 'Historische Genese: Frauenbewegung und die Erforschung des weiblichen Lebenslaufs', in *Beiträge 7 zur feministischen Theorie und Praxis* (Munich: Verlag Frauenoffensive, 1981).

Edwards, G. E., *GDR Society and Social Institutions: Facts and Figures* (London: Macmillan, 1985).

Emmerich, Wolfgang, *Kleine Literaturgeschichte der DDR* (Darmstadt and Neuwied/FRG: Luchterhand, 1981).

Griebel, Regina, Sleeve notes to *Guten Morgen, du Schöne. Sechs Frauenporträts nach dem Buch von Maxie Wander* (Berlin/GDR: VEB Deutsche Schallplatten [*Litera*, Stereo 8 65 371–2] 1985).

Haase, Horst, Hans-Juergen Geerdts *et al.*, *Geschichte der Literatur der Deutschen Demokratischen Republik* (Berlin/GDR: Volk und Wissen, 1977).

Kirsch, Sarah, *Die Pantherfrau: Fünf Frauen in der DDR* (Reinbek bei Hamburg/FRG: Rowohlt, 1973). (Originally published as *Die Pantherfrau: Fünf unfrisierte Erzählungen aus dem Kassetten-Recorder* (Berlin and Weimar/DDR: Aufbau, 1973.))

——, *Erklärung einiger Dinge: Dokumente und Bilder* (Reinbek bei Hamburg/FRG: Rowohlt, 1981).

Kuhrig, Herta and Wulfram Speigner (eds), *Wie emanzipiert sind Frauen in der DDR?* (Cologne: Pahl-Rugenstein, 1979; printed on licence from Leipzig/GDR: Verlag für die Frau).

Moi, Toril, *Sexual/Textual Politics: Feminist Literary Theory* (London and New York: Methuen, 1985).

Morgner, Irmtraud, *Leben und Abenteuer der Trobadora Beatriz nach Zeugnissen ihrer Spielfrau Laura* (Berlin/GDR: Aufbau, 1974).

——, 'Rede auf dem VIII Schriftstellerkongreß', *Neue Deutsche Literatur*, vol. 26, no. 8 (1978) pp. 27–32.

——, *Amanda: Ein Hexenroman* (Berlin/GDR: Aufbau, 1983).

Puknus, Heinz, *Neue Literatur der Frauen* (Munich: Beck, 1980).

Schneider, Petra, *Weg mit dem §218: Die Massenbewegung gegen das Abtreibungsverbot in der Weimarer Republik* (Berlin/FRG: Oberbaumverlag, 1975).

Stefan, Verena, *Häutungen* (Munich: Verlag Frauenoffensive, 1975). English translation published as *Shedding* (London: Women's Press, 1979).

Vanovitch, Kathy, 'Innovation and Convention: Women in the GDR', *GDR Monitor*, no. 2 (Winter 1979–80) pp. 15–22.

Wander, Fred (ed.), *Maxie Wander: Leben wär' eine prima Alternative: Tagebuchaufzeichungen und Briefe* (Darmstadt and Neuwied/FRG: Luchterhand, 1980). This is an edited version of the GDR edition: *Maxie Wander: Tagebücher und Briefe* (Berlin: Der Morgen, 1979).

Wander, Maxie, *Guten Morgen, du Schöne: Frauen in der DDR. Protokolle* (Berlin/GDR: Der Morgen, 1977). Published in the FRG under the same title (Darmstadt and Neuwied: Luchterhand, 1978).

Willett, John, *The New Sobriety: Art and Politics in the Weimar Period* (London: Thames and Hudson, 1978).

Wolf, Christa, 'Berührung', *Neue Deutsche Literatur*, vol. 26, no. 2 (1978) pp. 53–62. An edited version of this article under the same title forms the preface to the West German edition of *Guten Morgen, du Schöne* (see Wander, Maxie, above).

——, *Kassandra* (Berlin and Weimar/GDR: Aufbau, 1983). English translation published as *Cassandra* (London: Virago, 1984).

Worgitzky, Charlotte, *Meine ungeborenen Kinder* (Berlin/GDR: Der Morgen, 1982).

8 Sexism in French: a Case Study

ROBIN ADAMSON

Women are determined by many things in their environment, but perhaps this determining is most subtle when it is achieved by language. The effects of conditioning through language may not immediately be obvious; but research by linguists, psychologists and sociologists indicates that understanding the determining effects of language is fundamental to understanding other kinds of cultural determinations.

The relatively late development of feminist studies of language might be ascribed to various causes. Language, at first glance, might seem to be one feature of life that, in most western societies at least, is undifferentiated with regard to women and men. Then there is the fact that linguistics, which like other fields of learning has traditionally been dominated by men, possessed no tools to make the kind of analysis which could show how men's use of language reinforced their dominant position. A third factor in English-speaking countries was the apparent absence of a clearly-defined system of grammatical gender. It is now however recognised that:

> Whether or not we can in fact escape from the structuring imposed by language is one of the major questions facing feminist and non-feminist thinkers today.[1]

The use of the word 'thinkers' here is particularly important, since much of the new thinking on the role of language comes not from linguists but from psychologists and psychiatrists working in a post-Freudian and – especially in France – post-Lacanian perspective:

> Because all the practices that make up a social totality take place in language, it becomes possible to consider language as the place in which the social individual is constructed.[2]

173

In some ways this makes the task of the feminist linguist harder, since her subject matter has to a certain extent been appropriated by other thinkers whose knowledge of linguistics is arguably limited. Hence the need for a book like Deborah Cameron's *Feminism and Linguistic Theory* which addressed the problems faced by feminists trying to develop a linguistic theory:

> Impelled . . . not only by outside influences but more importantly by feminist practice itself, feminists have begun to develop a linguistic theory. They have started to explore the disciplines which look useful, particularly sociolinguistics . . . and semiology . . . . [F]eminists have much to gain by turning to linguistic theory, provided they understand, and have some method of assessing, conflicting views. . . . Many women feel incapable of making this sort of judgement.[3]

In France, where the influence of psychoanalysis in intellectual spheres is greater than in the English-speaking world, writers such as Benoîte Groult, Hélène Cixous, Luce Irigaray and Julia Kristeva (and there are many others) exemplify this close relationship between psychoanalysis and linguistics.[4] There is some controversy among linguists over the linguistic judgements of the psychoanalytical school, especially as they relate to linguistic structure and the structuring of the individual by language. These differences apart, there is nevertheless a considerable area of shared ground. Although there are important divergences between schools, the various writers on feminism and language

> all subscribe to some degree of determinism, to the idea that men control language and (especially) to the notion that women are alienated from it to a degree men are not. They stress the basic inauthenticity of women's language at present, the difficulties women have in talking about their experience, or sexuality. They trace back to this linguistic disadvantage important elements of women's subjection . . . .[5]

Luce Irigaray, one of the most controversial and influential products of the Lacanian school of psychoanalysis in France, states the position forcefully:

> I do not believe that language is universal, or neutral with regard to the difference of the sexes. . . . A language which presents

itself as universal, and which is in fact produced by men only, is this not what maintains the alienation and exploitation of women in and by society?[6]

The analysis of sexist language in writing about cars and car advertising that follows is an attempt to assess the extent to which language is dominated by male stereotypes of women, and to show how two features of grammar – gender and agreement – facilitate this process. This case study concentrates on French since it is a language with only two genders, masculine and feminine. This creates a starker contrast than other languages such as German where there are more than two genders, or a language like English where gender is 'natural' rather than grammatical. The choice of French also accentuates the importance of grammatical agreement – a feature only occasionally observable in English. We take as our focal point the language of car advertising and articles about cars: not only because sexism is so rampant in that area, but also because of the iconic status of the car in our society. The car industry sets out to manipulate not female but male consumers – on their own admission advertising *men*, when preparing their copy, are working on figures that show that more than 90 per cent of their consumers are male. Here is one area of consumer society where women are not corseted into the stereotype of the perfect housewife or the devoted mother. They are not addressed as consumers. Instead, advertisers evoke the stereotype of the eternally desirable female: particularly in France, the (feminine) car is seen as the object of male desire, creating a desperate wish to possess it, to enhance status by being seen to be the owner of such a desirable object. Woman as car – or car-as-woman – there are sufficient metaphors here to satisfy any literary critic.

Such metaphors throw into particularly sharp focus the influence of gender and its determining power in a language such as French.[7] It is to the issue of gender that we now turn.

GENDER

In English we have what is technically referred to as 'natural gender'. This is supposed to correspond to the natural order. Thus persons or animals which in nature are female have feminine gender, male persons or animals masculine gender, and anything which has no natural gender is neutral or 'common' gender in English ('it'). The 'naturalness' of the gender system in English is more apparent than real, particularly if you happen to be female. If you are a man it may seem perfectly natural to you that man 'embraces' woman (robust laughter), that *he* 'includes' *she*, that whenever both women and men are being referred to, all agreements are masculine. It can be argued however, as Dale Spender says, that:

> For the female half of the population there is [in English] even greater confusion than that caused by grammatical gender, because they have constantly been informed by grammarians that English possesses natural gender and there is an expectation that sex and gender should correspond.[8]

This point of view is not restricted to militant feminists. A recent and highly prestigious grammar of English by four men (*A Comprehensive Grammar of the English Language*) speaks of the issues raised by 'those campaigning against sexual bias in language', and goes on to conclude that:

> What is clear is that the feminist movement in language has made many language users aware of problems of sexual bias which were overlooked by previous generations.[9]

In other languages the situation with regard to gender is different from that in English. German, although it also has three genders, differs from English in that its gender system is grammatical, not natural: in other words the genders are decided according to grammatical conventions rather than the natural order. This gives rise to various gender attributions which are surprising to the English speaker – for example, the word for a girl is neuter (*das Mädchen*). In French the situation is even more 'unnatural' since all words must be either feminine or masculine. Thus a sentry is always feminine (*la sentinelle*) while a teacher is always masculine (*le professeur*). The question of gender has been studied by numerous grammarians and linguists, most of whom, being male, refuse to see that there is a question of sexism at all. They confidently assert that gender is simply a technical grammatical term to describe the ways in which nouns influence other words; just a useful scientific way of describing the ways in which words such as adjectives and pronouns change to show grammatical agreement with nouns. This would be easier to accept if gender could be shown to be distributed completely randomly – if there were in fact nothing 'natural' about it at all and the terms *feminine* and *masculine* were not used. If nouns could belong by grammatical convention to Gender 1 or 2 or 3, just as they belong to declensions or as verbs belong to conjugations in languages which have these grammatical features, it would be easier for us to accept the 'scientific' argument.

Because grammarians chose to use the words *feminine, masculine, neuter* to classify nouns, there has been an inevitable link established between sex and gender in the minds of all who use language. To deny this is to refuse to recognise the simplest and most fundamental classification system used by scientists and lay people alike: the division of the whole human race into two classes – female and male. Furthermore, such a bi-partite classification is always hierarchical: it is not by accident that the pair is usually referred to as male first and female second. Hélène Cixous is convinced that the first mentioned term is always seen as in some sense superior to the second:

> Wherever an ordering intervenes, a law organises the thinkable by (dual, irreconcilable; or mitigable, dialectal) oppositions. And all the couples of oppositions are *couples*. Does this mean something? Is the fact that logocentrism subjects thought – all of the concepts, the codes, the values – to a two-term system, related to 'the' couple man/woman?[10]

For Simone de Beauvoir the fundamental opposition is clearly 'irreconcilable', set up in such terms that the female cannot be defined except passively, as the Other whose reality depends on its difference from the One. The hierarchical superiority of the One is never in doubt.[11]

This view is supported by linguistic evidence in both French and English where so many of the words used to describe women – dame, tart, sheila – have, at least for male users, a pejorative or at least a reductive and diminishing sense, while the words used for men – bloke, guy, chap – carry positive and admiring overtones. In French, the *Dictionnaire Larousse des synonymes* lists ten slang words for women, all referring to women of suspect morals. The synonyms for *homme* (man) are found under 'person', a fact that seems to indicate that persons are male. The terms used – thirteen slang terms – carry a sense of swagger and pride quite absent from the words given for women.

As Marina Yaguello points out, there is also evidence in French of a different kind of gender focusing.[12] The correspondence between gender and size (masculine = large, important; feminine = small, less impressive) in pairs of near-synonyms cannot, she suggests, be dismissed as coincidence:

la maison (house)	*le manoir* (manor house)
la masure (shack)	*le castel* (castle)
la chaumière (cottage)	*le château* (castle)
la cabane (hut)	

The effect of gender systems on our thought patterns is further enhanced by the immense potential for figurative, and particularly metaphorical, use of language which is one of the defining features of all natural languages. The recent revival of interest among linguists in rhetoric has revealed that it's not only poets who use metaphor, synecdoche and litotes. Such figures are present in the most ordinary conversations between people of every kind; indeed, there is no such thing as 'simple' natural language. Such is the human capacity for metaphorical and comparative modes of thought and expression that the attaching of the label *feminine* in one area of human activity – grammar – will automatically carry with it attributes attached to that label in other areas. The German philologist Grimm confidently affirmed:

The masculine means the earlier, larger, firmer, more inflexible, swift, active, mobile, productive; the feminine the later, smaller, smoother, the more still, suffering, receptive.[13]

This automatic assumption that ideas associated with a word in one context will apply to it in all contexts is a categoric denial of the 'objectivity' of scientific thought. It is typical of the muddled thinking of male linguists on grammatical gender.

The muddles are emphasised when we move from one country to another, as translators and sociologists have long been aware. The French find it hard to understand that the sea (*la* mer), so obviously feminine in character, can be masculine in Italian; they are equally puzzled by the fact that Death (*la* Mort) is masculine in some other languages, in Swedish for example. Work on translating folktales in particular has been made difficult, if not impossible, by changes in gender from one language to another. A character may be female in the original and suffer a sex change in the translation from one language to another. For example, the character Death, which is feminine in Russian, becomes masculine in German; Sin, a female character in German, becomes masculine in French. Such metamorphoses cause problems that go far beyond grammatical gender.[14] However, human beings are capable of accepting many inconsistencies, and in spite of a rational conviction that gender is simply a grammatical accident, speakers of languages in which gender is very strongly marked are convinced (subconsciously, at least) that *feminine* is female and *masculine* male.

In the same way as people accept inconsistencies in the gender of human beings (the feminine sentry in French, for example: *la sentinelle*) they attempt to rationalise other obvious inconsistencies in the gender system. They often cope with the irrational attribution of gender to inanimate objects, such as the car, by discovering appropriately male or female qualities in those objects. So it is that in French the car, which is feminine, is described as curvy, bewitching, alluring, seductive. Some models of car, though, are masculine: hatchbacks, station wagons. These are perceived as tough, strong, reliable. As we shall see, their curves never rate a mention.

AGREEMENT

As we have seen, grammatical gender is the term used by grammarians to describe what happens when nouns are used in conjunction with other words: that is, describe the linguistic phenomenon of noun agreement. In French, if we want to describe the noun for the car (*l'automobile*; *f*) by using an adjective, that adjective must be feminine: *l'auto verte*. Even if the adjective occurs at some distance from the noun in the sentence, it must 'agree', that is, show the grammatical property defined as *feminine*: *L'auto de mon père est verte*.

In any sentence there may be several reminders that the noun is *feminine*: *L'auto verte est petite et laide*. If we refer to the car in another sentence, instead of repeating the noun we may choose to use a pronoun: **Elle** *est petite et laide:* **Elle** *appartient à mon père*. In this way a network is created, and the marks of gender help us to understand that subsequent references are to the car, and not to my father, for example. Such pronouns have an important role to play in establishing cohesion and in limiting the possibility of ambiguity.

In English we have to use other ways of ensuring that what we say is clear.

But after all, there are only two genders in French. What happens if we are talking about more than one *feminine* person or thing? if we are discussing both my mother and the car for example? In that case the sentences: *Elle est petite et laide: Elle appartient à mon père* are potentially shocking or at least surprising. So, when we join the system of gender to the pronoun system, we need to be especially careful if we want to be unambiguous. At first glance, this may seem to be a weakness in languages which have grammatical gender. On the other hand, we do not always want to be unambiguously clear in what we say. Humour in all languages is largely based on deliberately fostered ambiguities, and a quick glance through a book of French jokes shows that many of them are simply ambiguities based on pronouns whose referents are unclear. Of course, this does not always work to the disadvantage of women – while jokes where 'she' may refer either to a mother-in-law or a rubbish bin (*feminine* in French) are possible, we can also raise a laugh by using '*il*' (the French *masculine* subject pronoun) to refer either to the husband or the dog.

What interests us here is that the use of the pronoun allows us to put a distance between the first mention of a person or an object and subsequent references to her/him/it. The greater the distance, the weaker the grammatical link between the two becomes. If we use pronouns to distance ourselves from the first mention of a *feminine* object such as a car, the objective reality of the car is weakened and its feminine-ness strengthened. This grammatical feature, the combination of a bi-partite gender system and the pronoun system, allows advertisers of cars and men writing about them in French to write and speak of the car as a female. Once it has been referred to as *elle*, it is simply incorporated into the vast category 'female', and it seems that anything that can be said about a woman can be said about it.

THE SITUATION OF WOMEN IN FRANCE

If we are to be able to judge the degree of sexist bias found in car advertisements in France, we need to know something about the position of women there and about male attitudes to them.

Different societies approach the male/female opposition in different ways, but there is a limited number of ways of resolving the implied confrontation. Observers of the situation in France perceive French society as being predominantly male dominated, with tendencies towards political egalitarianism (*Liberté, Egalité, Fraternité* – the French language contains no word for sisterhood) complicated by marked tendencies to idealise the female and to consider her superior to men in certain restricted domains:

> There is no more constantly vilified object than the stupid, inert *con* [cunt], there is no more constantly adored object than the elegant, decorative woman. There is the coexistence too of a strong tradition of centralised government . . . which reinforces the old Roman worship of the pater familias, and an equally strong revolutionary tradition which allows women to join in a common struggle for the civil and political rights of 'mankind', and then represses them.[15]

This is a complex situation. The two extreme positions are highly developed in France and women tend to situate themselves within one of these dominant tendencies rather than attempt to make sense of the contradictory messages they are receiving about their role.

If they accept the dominance of men (which has given rise within the French tradition to *l'esprit gaulois*, a lusty strain of vulgar humour denigrating women), they see themselves as passive, submissive, receptive, powerless to fight against the prevailing ideology – woman as 'an insatiable cunt'.[16] If, on the other hand, they accept the idealisation of women which may be a development from the worship of the Virgin – woman as 'the charming, gracious, virgin mother of God'[17] – they accept a role outside the power structure. In return for being worshipped and admired, they consent to being owned, to being elegant adjuncts to males, carefully packaged inessential objects. Their status is high, yet they have their only access to power through seduction and highly developed charm. The view of women as elegant adjuncts to males is extremely pervasive in France, even in the 1990s, and is widely recognised in many other cultures. For many men, even in other countries, it is axiomatic that a Frenchwoman is more elegant, more beautifully dressed, more seductive, a better lover than other women.

The men who most readily accept the idea of women as desirable, decorative objects are also, without realising it, themselves conditioned by that view. If woman is seen as a coveted possession, a valuable adjunct to male power and influence, a beautiful artefact the possession of which enhances a man's status, men will have great difficulty in considering women as people, in accepting their status as equal human beings. Even if, in some spheres, French men are now prepared to consider that women have been disadvantaged, they are still prisoners of the worship syndrome.

French feminism, in responding to the situation of women in France, has developed somewhat differently from British or American feminism. The explanation given by Marks and de Courtivron .in the introduction to their book on *New French Feminisms*[18] suggests that although women in France have been confused by the various messages they have been receiving from men about their nature and their role in society, they have a long tradition of independent activity in the written and spoken word. The new French feminisms are rooted in these linguistic activities and take as their focus for attack the language of men:

> Nowhere else have groups of women come together with the express purpose of criticising and reshaping the official male language and, through it, male manners and male power.[19]

The crucial role of language is also recognised by Canadian feminists, some of whom are particularly interested in the problem of gender. In a country where all official documents must be available in both French and English, many difficulties arise. Both French and Canadian feminists have suggested that the fact that there are in French no feminine equivalents for 'engineer', 'surgeon', 'magistrate' and other traditionally male professions may actually dissuade women from thinking of taking them up.[20]

Women speakers of French have tried to attack male dominance in society through an approach to their language which emphasises the ways in which that language conditions all those who speak it. We turn now to the language used by (male) French speakers to describe and to sell cars which, like women, are seen by some of them as just another decorative adjunct to male power, another elegant enhancer of male status.

CASE STUDY: THE CAR AND SEXISM IN FRANCE

You don't have to peruse many magazines or listen to many radio or television advertisements for cars in France to realise that for many Frenchmen, owning a car, particularly an expensive and obviously luxurious one, is similar to possessing a beautiful woman. The enhanced status, the aesthetic pleasure, the thrills of superb performance, of total obedience, these are the fantasies a car can fulfil better than most women. To obtain the raw material for this study, I collected several different kinds of evidence. I collected advertisements for cars from all kinds of general interest magazines over several months at the beginning of 1987. Pretending an interest in purchasing a car, I obtained copies of the advertising brochures produced by many French car manufacturers – particularly for their more up-market models. I also purchased at least one copy at various dates of all the nine French magazines currently devoted to ordinary cars (this meant neglecting a considerable number dealing with other kinds of motorised transport, notably motorbikes). In addition, I purchased copies for June 1987 of six of these car magazines.[21]

In these I analysed all the advertisements, concentrating on the ones for cars, and I also studied all the articles written about cars. Women are almost entirely absent from these magazines, other than in their metaphorical presence as cars or their almost nude presence in advertisements. One manufacturer of car seats relies very heavily on topless females to sell his product. In this section of the study I was dealing exclusively with material written by men, for men. You have only to try to elbow your way through the males in front of the car section in any shop selling magazines, in Britain or in France, to realise that females are not welcome.

Then I took a series of ten copies of *Le Figaro Magazine* from early 1987 and analysed all the car advertisements in them. Here the advertisements will be seen by at least as many women as men, since this is a sort of French equivalent of the *Telegraph* – or perhaps *The Sunday Times* – magazine. I also studied the copies of the French *Cosmopolitan* for this period and found that, although each issue of the *Fig. Mag.* carried several advertisements for cars, *Cosmo* concentrated on other aspects of the consumer society. This probably reflects the fact that French advertising agencies have not yet caught up with the fact that women also buy cars, although there are a number of other indications that the writers in French *Cosmo* are

writing for readers who are less liberated than their British counterparts.

Next I examined (but refrained from buying) all the French magazines in the *Playboy* section. *Playgirl* was nowhere to be seen,
although the English version of *Playboy* was widely available. (Who
needs language?) But these offerings contained no car advertisements at all! Perhaps when you have pictures of the real thing
you don't need to fantasize about your car? Other general glossy
magazines for up-market readers tended to concentrate on advertisements for the usual status markers: expensive drinks (sometimes
exotically foreign), watches, foreign travel, time-share, beauty products, designer-name clothes and sports wear, men's toiletries.

Finally, I taped all the car advertisements on the radio station
France-Inter (vaguely like Radio 4, with elements of Radios 1 and
2) for one day in June. The addition to the text of the advertisements
of a male voice with sexy overtones can make even the most apparently innocuous words sound misogynist.

The description that follows does not separate findings about the
car magazines from findings about more general magazines, mainly
because the car advertisements were usually identical. Similarly the
themes exploited in the car magazines were the same as those in
general magazines.

Sexist language 1: Themes

Close study of all the advertisements and articles reveals that where
the car is a metaphor for woman, a number of themes recur, not all
of them predictable. Most of the comments would be perceived by
men as complimentary. They are positive statements about how the
car in question compares with an ideal of woman. Taken together,
they give us a clear picture of at least one of the female stereotypes
currently prevalent in France.

What is she like, this ideal female? The advertisements and the
articles give us a clear picture of her appearance and her character.
To take her appearance first: among the most frequent words found
in writing about cars (and this includes advertisements) are *belle*
(beautiful – feminine), *ligne* (line, or more usually figure), *élégante*
(f) or the noun *élégance*. As far as appearance is concerned these
are the most highly prized attributes. Beauty is frequently referred
to: Beauty and the Beast – the Beast is the driver who will be
transformed once he owns Beauty; Beauty as a stripper; Beautiful

enough to eat; Beautiful shape; Beautifully equipped. The following headline is very revealing:

SOIS BELLE ET TAIS-TOI!

Look beautiful and shut up! Just to be beautiful is enough. There is certainly no need for her to be articulate.

Elegance is a quality that confers class, a mark of refinement and good taste which is extended to the purchaser. She (the car) has an elegant figure; a cat-like elegance; refinement and the insolence that comes from awareness of class; the power which elegance confers; the nervous elegance of a racehorse. Her figure (*ligne*) is aesthetically pleasing, with alluring curves; it is fluid, harmonious and distinguished. The fact that she is seen as a woman is emphasised by references to her hips, her thighs, her waist, her curves and by invitations to run your hand over her:

ENHARDISSEZ-VOUS ET CARESSEZ SA CROUPE

Don't be shy. Stroke her bottom. There are also references to her *postérieur* for which English has borrowed the French word *derrière*.

Her appearance (*look*) is vital to the creation of the impression of beauty and elegance. The borrowing of the English word is a clear indication that we are in a domain where fashion is all important: the English word *look* carries in French (much more than it does in English) overtones of youth, exoticism, high fashion and glossy allure.

In addition to these physical attributes, she must be seductive – seductiveness is mentioned even more often than beauty. Its importance is shown by the fact that it occurs more frequently than any other characteristic in writing about car-as-woman. The car is the eternal temptress whose wiles men cannot resist:

PEUT-ÊTRE A-T-ELLE

ÉTÉ CRÉÉE

POUR ÉPROUVER

VOTRE SAGESSE

Perhaps she was created to test your self control. Sometimes she bypasses the temptation stage and even goes so far as to rape (*violer*) the clients but usually she tempts and seduces by her great *charme*. This essential ingredient is composed of a variety of elements: it is sensual, insolent, highly strung; certainly not the hidden violet kind of charm. Through her charm (which is enhanced by her *équipement*) and her *personnalité* – strong, individual, determined – she can provoke love at first sight (*le coup de coeur*), arouse furious passion, give her driver a wonderful sensation of physical one-ness with her, a feeling they belong together, convince him they were made for each other. This experience of physical pleasure is frequently highlighted and the word *plaisir* clearly means, in this context, sexual pleasure:

L'ACCESSION AU PLAISIR

As well as beauty, seductiveness, charm and personality she must have *tempérament*. This adds an essential element of paradox to her charm. She tends to be young, headstrong, wild, *sauvage*. She is appealing yet demanding, exclusive, all together. All this adds up to 'star' quality – the French often use this English word to give added Hollywood overtones and glamour to the idea of a star.

This portrait is recognisable as a typical adolescent male fantasy of the feminine. It is also recognisable as a model which is bound to inspire in women a conviction of failure and a feeling of inadequacy. Nothing is ever said, in this type of writing, about the male paragon who would deserve the dream companion the writers describe. All you have to do is be male. Well, not quite all. You also have to be wealthy. It is very noticeable that as the cars become more expensive and luxurious, the language becomes more sexist.

Zippy little models suitable for housewives and families in a modest income bracket are not so often feminised – but their presentation is sexist nevertheless. These lower-priced models may be driven by women and they correspond to the cheerful busy little housewife, performing a multitude of tasks with good-humoured efficiency. The parallel between the smaller cars and this completely different stereotype of women is emphasised by the kinds of tasks the advertisers mention: taking your *son* to school, doing the shopping or, for slightly more liberated women, delivering that important document to your (male) boss. These two different types of car mirror almost exactly the familiar male double standard: the mistress: decorative, elegant, sexy; the wife: capable, busy, efficient. Ideally, if one is male, one has both.

Then there are the cars for he-men, adventurers, sportsmen: Land Rovers, four-wheel drives, country-style hatchbacks. These frequently turn out to be masculine in French: *le cabriolet (sportif)*, *le roadster*, for example. These it seems have virile virtues: strength, reliability, power, toughness. Women are totally excluded from most of these male domains.

So it is clear that if women's self-images are determined by male attitudes to them, men's self-images are also being determined – by other men and also by women eager to accept female stereotyping. From the articles, and especially from the advertisements for these three types of car, comes a frighteningly clear portrait of the male car-buyer: ostentatiously wealthy, upwardly mobile, dominant, aggressive, possessive, fashion conscious and self-confident. He is as far removed from most human males as the beautiful, sexy, elegant, classy female car he covets is from real women.

Sexist language 2: Reinforcing the image

The sexist language in writing about cars does not always make the car the clear equivalent of the woman, but, as in any type of writing, once we are aware of the more dominant metaphors this shapes our thinking so that we perceive more subtle uses of figurative language. The dominant figurative climate encourages us to interpret other metaphors in a new way, to perceive them as parts of an interrelated set of metaphorical notions which are characteristic of the type of text we are reading. Once the consciousness-raising process has begun, all sorts of other images and metaphors suddenly assume a less innocuous character and come together to reinforce one another in what now seems an inevitable way.

Looking again at the various kinds of language used in the articles and advertisements, some now appear of greater importance than at first glance. In several advertisements the car is personified and the words of the possible buyer are in the familiar patronising tone men think is appropriate for woman-as-decorative-object. The familiar *tu* form of address is used, and the advertisement is a French equivalent of 'Come here you beautiful thing, you'.

Metaphors drawn from the family are frequent. This is in curious contrast to the extra-marital relationships evoked by much of the writing, but serves to reinforce other stereotypes of women. A new car is 'born'; she is 'the latest arrival', 'the little sister', the 'god-daughter', the 'cousin (*f*), or 'the twin (*f*)' of a previous model. She has certain 'inherited' or 'family' qualities, or she is the 'best-endowed (girl)' of her *génération*. Sometimes the 'pregnancy' has been long or the 'birth' difficult. Extending this family metaphor is the metaphor of *mariage*. When companies (especially automobile companies) merge, they may 'marry' or even 'make it legal'. Their relationships are described in the way we might describe a marriage: getting on well, a happy union. Of course, metaphors such as these are also used in talking about other kinds of take-over or merger in the business world. Here the fact that the context is so clearly marked by sexist language gives them a special importance.

Into this complex picture of interrelated figures of speech are inserted a number of blatantly racist misogynist remarks: the kind of thing that passes for humour in the pub after work. The following examples of headlines in articles on cars are typical:

À NOUS LES PETITES ANGLAISES!

English girls this way!

LES FRANÇAIS PRÉFÈRENT LES BLANCHES . . .

Frenchmen prefer white women . . . A revealing way of headlining an article about national preferences for colour in cars.

LA MARÉE JAUNE
LES PETITES NIPPONES

. . . une belle geisha dans son kimono

The yellow flood. The little Japs. A beautiful geisha girl in her kimono. These are just a few of the ways of expressing a misogynist xenophobia which is also extended to *les Américaines* and *les Allemandes*.

Sexist language 3: The image of men

Our analysis so far gives a slightly one-sided view of the situation. Although the stereotyping of women is quite explicit, car-as-woman is not the only sexist metaphor used. In car magazines we also find a series of less linguistically obvious metaphors based on qualities usually associated with men.

The most common slang term used for men is *les mecs*, an abbreviation for *les mécaniques* – 'muscles'. Mechanical power is a metaphor for male sexual prowess; control of the machine is equated with control of others; quick responses and flexible strength are prerogatives of male youth. But more than one figure of speech is involved, for together with the 'feminine' and 'masculine' metaphors there is widespread use of synecdoche: the owner for the owned – or in other words, the implication that if you buy this car you will somehow acquire its *masculine* attributes, you too will be powerful, young, in control. So the implication of possessing the desirable object – car/woman – is a complex figure of speech. The male acquires the admired and desired feminine object; he simultaneously acquires its *masculine* attributes, becomes strong, dynamic, magnetic; he is then implicitly promised the admiration of all elegant, sexy, decorative females for the masculine qualities implicit in his ownership: power, wealth, youth, machismo.

The sexist language used about cars is often only a small part of an advertisement or an article. Much of the writing is factual and straightforward, dealing with technical details and performance statistics, although once sensitized to the prevalent sexism, one inevitably interprets a word like 'performance' as a *double-entendre*.

The car advertisements, since they set out to persuade men to buy a car, have a greater tendency to use figurative language than the articles, but the prevalent sexism is reinforced by the way in which strength, power and speed are emphasised in writing about cars and also by other parts of the magazine. For example, a heartily masculine atmosphere is created by the range of advertisements car magazines carry for car parts and accessories. Car seats have already been mentioned in this connection. In the ambience of rampant sexism which characterizes these magazines, even the advertisements for things like oils and tyres seem to contribute to the reinforcing of stereotypes. One brand of car oil is currently using simulated Personal Advertisements (habitually far more explicit in France than in Britain) as a sales pitch:

Very attractive engine seeks serious oil with wide experience.

Experienced engine seeks stable oil capable of giving him security, to share long journeys.

Up-to-date engine seeks refined and faultless oil for a hectic life.

Oil is feminine in French, engine masculine. Another oil promises to let your car 'flex its muscles', and a brand of tyres is described as having 'broad shoulders'. These advertisements are accompanied by pictures of bronzed, muscular giants, stripped to the waist.

The two different male stereotypes in advertising mean that men too are receiving conflicting messages, especially from the advertising world.

First, there is the he-man. Other advertisements, that have nothing to do with cars, also contribute to the building up of this male stereotype. The image of strength and toughness is reinforced by advertisements for certain brands of cigarettes which picture a hearty, he-man smoker; for beer, seen as a male drink; for razors to remove that luxuriant growth that separates the men from the boys; for sporting magazines and outboard motors.

On the other hand, the suave, wealthy, refined man of taste is reflected in some of the other advertisements carried in car magazines and also, as I found, in glossy magazines of all kinds: expensive drinks, male toiletries (especially perfume), cigars, designer clothes, foreign travel, luxurious time-share.

Men as well as women are being manipulated and determined by advertising. The confusion caused by conflicting stereotypes reflected in advertising affects us all.

Sexist language is obviously only one part of the problem confronting women in this area of the consumer culture. In advertisements for cars they are exploited in the attempt to persuade male consumers to buy but, as we have seen, very rarely credited with consumer status. This is to some extent changing in Britain as evidenced in recent TV commercials for some cars where high-powered working women are featured. Even here the tone is somewhat wry, and the success of the advertisements depends on an implied comparison between the successful woman executive and the usual female stereotypes.

The same car advertisements are heard and seen by both women and men on the radio, on television and in general-interest magazines like *Le Figaro Magazine* (or in Britain *The Sunday Times* or *The Observer* magazines). The fact that *The Observer Magazine* can publish a two-page car advertisement and picture with the slogan:

BEHIND A SUCCESSFUL MAN
YOU'LL FIND
AN ELEGANT LADY

simply shows how common the sexism is and how powerless women are to do anything about it. The power of the (male-dominated) press is enormous and its ability to mould thought and attitudes is unquestioned, but women have perhaps been too ready to accept uncritically the distorting stereotypes of themselves so often to be found in newspapers and magazines and on television. Until they are employed at the high levels where editorial policy is decided, they have virtually no power to change what is published. The forces at work are overt but women are unable (some are even perhaps unwilling) to resist or oppose them.

The difficulty with writing about cars (as opposed to car advertisements) is that it is an almost exclusively male preserve. A few French magazines regularly publish, at the end of an article, comments by women about the car they have been testing: 'Quand elle roule pour nous' ('When she does the driving'), *L'Automobile Magazine*; 'Le point de vue de Madame' ('The woman's point of view'), *L'Auto-journal*. These comments, in spite of the titles, avoid the usual sexist tone of writing about cars and, more encouragingly, do not fall into the trap of reverse sexism – car-as-man. They also manage to avoid being cutely feminine, and refrain from discussing only the colour of the upholstery or the space available for baby carry-cots. But who reads them?

Car magazines belong in a world from which women, although constantly present as metaphors and stereotypes, are in fact excluded. Since they have virtually no input into these magazines, they are powerless to prevent the dissemination of the blatant sexist stereotyping through language which such magazines encourage. The publishers of car magazines have no need to consider the possible reaction of women and they have presumably found that their male readers do not protest at their constant feeding of male fantasies.

On the other hand, most women are completely unaware of the way in which they are portrayed in these magazines. This makes the sexism even more pernicious. In such areas women cannot resist or refuse the determining forces since they have no access to decision-making either as publishers or as readers. This is male dominance at its most powerful. Car magazines, like many other male preserves, are, for women, a no-go area where their rights are simply irrelevant. With forces like these at work, women need to be very determined indeed to refuse the roles in which society casts them; but until they gain access to all the areas from which their conditioning has traditionally excluded them, their power to shape their own lives will be constantly undermined.

The power of language and its effect on our consciousness, its ability to shape the way we think and the way we see ourselves goes far beyond the car industry. Nevertheless, this example gives some indication of the extent to which language can act to reinforce stereotyping and to condition our view of ourselves and the world. It is not only in the advertising world that this happens. Both English and French are languages of male-dominated societies; both enshrine a male view of the world and consequently, wherever they are used, whether in the most apparently insignificant conversation or in the powerfully manipulative media, they serve to reinforce and normalise male domination. Unless women and men, recognising their vulnerability to all that is implicit in the language they unthinkingly use, consciously create a climate in which linguistic change is encouraged, unless there is an attempt to exploit the determining power of language to defeat sexism, other attempts to do so may be condemned to failure.

My thanks to François Blanc for his invaluable help and contacts with advertising agencies in Paris.

Notes

1. Elaine Marks and Isabelle de Courtivron (eds), *New French Feminisms* (Brighton: Harvester Press, 1980) p. 4.
2. R. Coward and J. Ellis, *Language and Materialism* (London: Routledge and Kegan Paul, 1977) p. 1, cit. Deborah Cameron, *Feminism and Linguistic Theory* (London: Macmillan, 1985) p. 119.
3. Cameron, op. cit., pp. 6–7.
4. Benoîte Groult, *Ainsi soit-elle* (Paris: Grasset, 1975) and *Le Féminisme au masculin* (Paris: Denoël/Gonthier, 1977); Hélène Cixous, *La Jeune Née* (Paris: UGE, 1975) and *Chant du corps interdit, le nom d'Oedipe* (Paris: des femmes, 1978); Luce Irigaray, *Speculum de l'autre femme* (Paris: Minuit, 1974) and *Ce sexe qui n'en est pas un* (Paris: Minuit,

1977); Julia Kristeva, *Des Chinoises* (Paris: des femmes, 1974) and *Polylogue* (Paris: coll. Tel Quel, 1977).
5. Cameron, op. cit., p. 133.
6. Cit. Cameron, op. cit., p. 128.
7. A theory of metaphor as the basis for the determining power of language over women is given in Marina Yaguello, *Les Mots et les femmes* (Paris: Payot, 1987) pt ii, ch. 1, 'Genre et sexe: La Métaphore sexuelle'.
8. Dale Spender, *Man Made Language* (London: Routledge and Kegan Paul, 1980) p. 161.
9. Randolph Quirk, Sidney Greenbaum, Geoffrey Leech and Jan Svartvik, *A Comprehensive Grammar of the English Language* (London: Longman, 1985) p. 343.
10. Hélène Cixous in Marks and de Courtivron (eds), op. cit., p. 91.
11. Marks and de Courtivron (eds), op. cit., p. 45.
12. Yaguello, op. cit., pp. 74–6.
13. Cit. Cameron, op. cit., p. 65.
14. Yaguello, op. cit., pp. 95–6. She is here quoting from Roman Jakobson, 'Aspects linguistiques de la traduction', in *Essais de linguistique générale* (Paris: Editions de Minuit; vol. i, 1963, vol. ii, 1973), first pub. as 'On Linguistic Aspects of Translation', in *On Translation* (Cambridge, Mass.: Harvard University Press, 1959), pp. 232–9.
15. Marks and de Courtivron (eds), op. cit., p. 5.
16. Ibid.
17. Ibid.
18. Ibid., pp. 3–9.
19. Ibid., p. 6.
20. For Canada, see, for example, A. Paquot and H. Dupuis, 'Aspects linguistiques, socio-linguistiques et économiques de la planification langagière: le cas de la féminisation des titres de profession dans les pays francophones', *Terminologie et traduction*, no. 2 (1986) pp. 51–8. For France, see for example *Le Dossier du Monde*, December 1987.
21. The six asterisked magazines are those also bought in June: **L'Action automobile et touristique*; *Auto-hebdo*; **L'Auto-journal*; **Automobile magazine*; **Automobiles classiques*; **Automoto*; *Echappement*; **Le Fanauto*; *Le Moniteur automobile*.

Bibliography

Beauvoir, Simone de, *Le Deuxième Sexe* (Paris: Gallimard, 1949); trs. H. M. Parshley, *The Second Sex*, (Harmondsworth, Middx: Penguin, 1972).
Cameron, Deborah, *Feminism and Linguistic Theory* (London: Macmillan, 1985).
Coll, Philippe, 'Le Dossier *Stratégies*; La Communication automobile', in *Stratégies*, no. 535 (3–9 November 1986) pp. 27–34.
Le Monde, Dossier: *Images de femmes*, June 1987.

194   *Determined Women*

tftMarks, Elaine and Isabelle de Courtivron (eds), *New French Feminisms* (Brighton: Harvester Press, 1980).

Paquot, A. and H. Dupuis, 'Aspects linguistiques, socio-linguistiques et économiques de la planification langagière: le cas de la féminisation des titres de profession dans les pays francophones', *Terminologie et traduction*, no. 2 (1986) pp. 51–8.

Phillips, D. I., 'Quelques problèmes de genre – en anglais', *Terminologie et traduction*, no. 2 (1986) pp. 83–5.

Spender, Dale, *Man Made Language* (London: Routledge and Kegan Paul, 1980).

Yaguello, Marina, *Les Mots et les femmes* (Paris: Payot, 1987).

9 The Castration of Cassandra[1]

HELGA GEYER-RYAN

A little while ago, the following short item appeared in the British press. A family from Hull was on holiday at a seaside resort. The husband set about building a deep tunnel into the dunes. When he had got so far that he had completely disappeared inside the hole, his wife began to warn him of a possible accident. The man did not listen, of course, but carried on burrowing all the more determinedly, as his honour obliged him to do. Just as you would expect, the hole collapsed at a certain point and the man was suffocated.

The incident provides a perfect example of what I would call the Cassandra syndrome. It is certainly not restricted to Britain. It is ubiquitous in the Western world, and it has a classical history. Cassandra, the prophetess whom no one believed, is carried prisoner by Agamemnon to Mycenae. There she is put to death – ironically, as a symbol of the same male power which had seized her as its prize. Clytemnestra, Agamemnon's wife, who killed them both, is unable to see this irony. She is herself blinded by hatred for the patriarchal power structure, which had first claimed the life of her daughter Iphigenia, then placed her for ten years in the vulnerable position of royal wife without a husband, and had finally returned in the form of an estranged husband bringing a barbarian into her home as his concubine.

In Mycenae Cassandra is finally silenced, but not because of what she says, which the Achaeans do not believe and no longer even understand. The complete absence of understanding and response is the final point in the process of silencing to which she has always been subjected. What is also destroyed at this point is the language of her body, which signals the same message as her speech: mutilation and silencing by male violence. In the Mycenaean context Cassandra's body is no longer her own. It has become merely a sign of Agamemnon's phallic power.

But this is not yet the full story. In addition to the tragedy there is the satirical version. It is well known that mockery follows close on the heels of affliction, not least in the case of women. The Sicilian vase-painter Assteas, who lived in the fourth century BC, could not resist the opportunity to replace Cassandra's expropriated voice with the equivalent of a male speech-bubble. A clay fragment found in Buccino parodies the famous scene in which Ajax rapes the Trojan princess and priestess of Athene in the goddess's shrine, after the conquest of Troy. To do this, Ajax must first tear Cassandra away from the statue of Athene to which she is clinging in search of protection. In Assteas's version it is Ajax who seeks protection from the goddess and Cassandra who is trying to steal him away. The parody demonstrates a cornerstone of male fantasy, namely that a woman would like nothing better than to be raped. In other words, our Sicilian artist supplements sex scenario number one – overpowering the woman without further ado – with the much more flattering sex scenario number two, in which the woman declares that to be overpowered by the man is her deepest desire. It is not just from the word of de Sade that this lethal strategy is familiar. The silencing of Cassandra, which might otherwise be interpreted as the stigma of the violence she has suffered, is translated into the humorous discourse of the macho male.

Scenarios one and two are the most basic backdrops to the expropriation of female speech, and the Cassandra figure is the archetypal illustration of this, where the silencing of woman is bound up with the mutilation of her body. But Cassandra is not the only one. The phenomenon is reiterated in the figures of Philomela, Echo and Xanthippe, who similarly portray the destruction of female speech on various levels of communication by the symbolic and physical violence of men. The images we have of these women are important because they have come down to us unquestioned and sacrosanct as part of our cultural tradition. They represent social patterns of perception by which we organise our allocations of power and gender, body and voice. It is only when we deconstruct these allocations and dismantle their logic of violence that we are able to bring the dead voices back to life.

There is a proverb which says 'Speech is silver, but silence is golden'. This is the very essence of logocentrism. For if we are silent, the purity of our thoughts is unsullied by the swarms of signifiers. But it is also the very essence of phallocentrism. For if we are consciously silent, we still have the power to speak and, at the same time, the power to control access to speech through the ethics of silence. Observances of silence are power strategies.

When Bakhtin describes speech as always 'in an alien mouth, in alien contexts, in the service of alien intentions'[2] and recommends that 'it must be taken from there and made one's own'[3] or when Lyotard says 'to speak is to fight . . . and speech acts fall within the domain of a general agonistics',[4] what they are saying is that women must win back the speech which has been systematically *expelled* or *exorcised* from their bodies since antiquity.

PHILOMELA

The figure of Philomela provides a bloody and therefore even more graphic example of the violence that men practise on women's bodies and words. Tereus, king of Thrace and husband of the Athenian princess Procne, falls in love with Procne's sister, Philomela. He is especially enamoured of her beautiful voice. Instead of bringing her straight to his wife when she comes to visit, he hides her in a hut on the way and rapes her. To stop her telling anyone what has happened, he simply cuts out her tongue. Philomela weaves a message into a robe for her sister. Procne sets the mute woman free, and in revenge slays Itys, the son she bore Tereus, who bears a strong resemblance to his father. She cooks the boy and then serves him up to Tereus to eat.

In an essay written in 1924, J. Flügel describes the close connection between tongue and phallus, speech and sexual power.

> The unconscious equations, speech = sexual power, dumbness = castration or impotence, are clearly shown in the numerous customs connected with the cutting out of tongues. Excision of the tongue would appear to have been practised occasionally as a form of punishment at the same time as there were practised other punishments easily recognizable as castration displacements, such as blinding and the cutting off of hands (as well as castration itself).[5]

These interrelationships rooted in violence, in which silencing means taking away the *right* to speak, as well as the ability, and implies the castration and enforced impotence of women, are illustrated in the story of Philomela. Flügel points to a strong tradition of enforced silence, which principally applies to women. 'A woman's greatest virtue is her silence', says a Sicilian proverb. 'Nothing is as unnatural as a woman who likes to talk', says a Scottish one. 'Only silence makes women truly charming', writes Sophocles in *Ajax*; and German popular wisdom tells us that 'Women who whistle and hens that crow should have their necks wrung without further ado'. Current studies in linguistic pragmatics and feminist linguistics confirm the universal validity of Flügel's findings.

Flügel underlines the fact that Philomela is indeed castrated in the process of mutilation – and this I think is the most exemplary demonstration of the interrelation between silencing and castration – by drawing attention to the punishment of Tereus upon whom the castration is repeated. His son is slain – the son being the symbol of the father's phallic power. The resemblance between father and son is given special emphasis. The son is dismembered: fantasies of dismemberment are also fantasies of castration.

Flügel comes to the conclusion that 'The whole story seems thus to constitute . . . a series of variations on the general theme of castration.[6] He reminds us of *Titus Andronicus* where, in a similar way, Lavinia, after being raped, has her tongue cut out and her hands chopped off. In addition, the dismembered bodies of her sons are served up to the queen of the Goths, Tamora. These observations also clearly reveal the techniques of *damnatio memoriae*,[7] where the defacement of the statues of disgraced rulers constitutes a castration ritual which is intended not so much to wipe the persons concerned from the public memory as to divest them of their power.

Ovid, who tells the story of Philomela in the sixth book of the *Metamorphoses*, mentions yet another symptomatic detail. According to his version, Tereus raped Philomela several more times and with particular pleasure after he had cut out her tongue. It is this bloody consolidation of power over the silent, helpless body of the other – in this case and almost always the woman's body – which increases Tereus's sexual excitement.

The *Metamorphoses* are full of incidents of rape, mainly perpetrated against virgins, priestesses and fugitives. The obstacles increase the level of violence used; but they also increase that outrageously inflated self-esteem which forms the basis of sexual pleasure for those who have power over others.

When Flügel says, 'a violent sexual assault on a woman may easily be associated unconsciously with the idea of her castration (in the last resort the castration of the mother)',[8] it can be concluded that the ever-present threat of rape hanging over women in patriarchal societies and the speech controls to which they are no less continually subjected are part of a desire to castrate the female which can be seen as the wish to destroy her autonomous individuality and sexuality. Language and sexuality, tongue and gender are the points of intersection between psyche and soma. That is why they are the preferred settings in the drama of the battle of the sexes. Within that drama, the Philomela story is one more variation on the fundamental conflict: the clash of female and male power in the patriarchy.

In Philomela's case, the material conditions of her speech, the speech organs, are mutilated. Compared with other practices used to silence women, this is somewhat ineffective. As it is, Philomela merely requires a different set of signifiers to intimate what has been done to her. She manages to outwit the logocentrist Tereus by using a system of notation which itself is markedly female: her weaving, or *text*, which is the original sense of the word. In a violent context where the spoken word is in the control of the powers-that-be, subversion comes through text, the written word.

Tereus falls victim to his own ideology. He forgets that the woman he thinks he has reduced to nothing more than a sign, a sign of *his* sexuality, is herself a creator of signs, an author. Tereus's view of reality is inadequate because it is distorted by his own self-centred will to power. His view of women is wrong, as is his evaluation of the relationship between speech and reference. The logocentrist viewpoint (the confirmation of the truth and authenticity of what is said by the presence of the speaker) always contains an element of physical violence. The violence lies in a presence in which space is seized, penetrated and incorporated, in short usurped, in speech acts.

ECHO

In the story of the nymph Echo we encounter another episode of female mutilation by male power. In the *Metamorphoses* again there is an account of the destruction of Echo's voice by jealous Hera, the goddess of patriarchal marriage. From then on, Echo can only imitate what others say before her. She falls in love with Narcissus, who loves only himself, and when this egomaniac *par excellence* rejects her, refusing to return the image of her ego by feeling desire for her himself, her body turns to stone.

In *Daphnis and Chloe*, Longus offers a more radical variation on the theme of woman withering into silence and the confirmation of male power.[9] Pan, rejected by Echo, is angry at the nymph 'because he envies her her singing and may not enjoy her beauty', as Longus puts it. In other words, he is required to respect her as a subjective being – she will not sleep with him – but as a subjective being himself, he must immediately envy her, since her transformed status makes her a competitor, a threat to his ego. So he has her torn to pieces by crazed shepherds, upon which echoes rise from the scattered members of her body. Pan completes and surpasses the task of annihilating the female, begun by Hera and Narcissus in the name of male supremacy.

XANTHIPPE

Xanthippe's speech too is handed down by tradition in a fragmented form. There is no record of her body. The pictorial tradition does not normally extend to the physical aspect of the bodies of wives and mothers. The only type of female body which is put on display is the sexualized body, which falls within the sphere of influence of the phallus. It is the body which still denotes resistance, which has not yet given up its mystery, which gives a narcissistic boost to the male ego in the act of discovery and appropriation.

Xanthippe's body is already the battlefield of what men have imputed to it in writing and has disappeared amid these scrawlings. Only her voice comes down to us, her shrill voice. In her book *Thinking about Women*, Mary Ellmann describes a rhetorical trick of male criticism of texts by women: whatever these men do not like about the texts they describe as 'shrill', especially when they sense signs of female rebellion behind it.[10] It is precisely because this reproach, when levelled against the written medium, has a comic effect, that one recognizes it all the more readily when it is levelled against the spoken word. Here the purely acoustic difference between the female and male speech organs is conflated with the content of the utterance, and by overemphasising the expressive form in this way, what is actually expressed, the content, is completely obscured.

From the male point of view, Xanthippe and Socrates are the epitome of the classic arguing couple. He is the great sophist and maieutic philosoper, she the shrew, the opinionated, quarrelsome hysteric. This negative evaluation of female argumentation is one of the most effective means of cutting off the speech of women. The real target here is the phenomenon of *contradiction*. Whenever we

encounter hierarchies of power, subordination and codes of obedience, we find that contradiction from the lower ranks is excluded.
In the process of contradiction an individual will assumes that it has
equal rights and is free. Children, pupils, servants, soldiers, prisoners, slaves, members of the lower orders, petty officials, employees
and women: they are not to argue, for they are not to contradict.

Xanthippe is a woman who contradicted her husband, one of the
greatest talkers of western civilisation. The means by which her voice
is silenced in the collective memory is more subtle than the brute
force employed by mythical figures. It is a means more appropriate
to the refined customs of a culture centred upon language and its
trustees, the philosophers, philologists, psychologists, hermeneutic-
ists, theoreticians and historians.

The main focus of Xanthippe's speech is shifted away from the
arena of criticism and rationality (which is reserved for men) into
the sphere of psychological pathology – the traditional stamping
ground of female figures. The female critic becomes a grouse, the
woman who sticks to her guns is labelled insane. This strategy of
reducing what is said to the way it is said, the process of restricting
a referential utterance to the expressive dimension, has remained
the most effective method of castrating female speech to this day.

CASSANDRA

What has been said about Xanthippe is even truer of Cassandra.
For in this case a female figure establishes her linguistic sphere not
in private life but in public. Apollo had bestowed the gift of prophecy
upon the Trojan princess on the condition that she sleep with him.
Cassandra would thus have been promoted to the status of a public
figure, a seer. According to an older version of the myth, however,
both Cassandra and her twin brother Helenos were born with this
power. The later version asserts that Cassandra must earn by high-
class prostitution that which is given to Helenos as a man for nothing.
Women who want to get on in their professional lives are not
unfamiliar with this phenomenon.

The Trojan woman refuses to pay this price, so Apollo punishes
her. But he does not simply take away the gift of prophecy. Far
worse than this, he robs her of the power to convince others, leaving
his victim forever torn between subjective and objective reality. This
is the classic picture of hysteria and insanity, which are both meant

to signify the split between the logic of the patient's personal world and the logic of her social environment.

Apollo here represents the male usurpation of the public sphere, which is denied to woman. She is held to embody the private sphere, and therefore is excluded from the public world. Indeed, public life is such *because* women are removed from it. Women do not simply *exist within* the private sphere; they *are* the private sphere. To move from there into the public sphere would not only constitute a blurring of demarcation lines but would also make it impossible to distinguish the division between reality and sign. Women would become more fully alive. It would be a return from their representational status as the private sphere to the presence of public life.

Women who displace these demarcation lines are deemed insane. Cassandra's speech, which uncharacteristically deals with affairs of state and war, in short with men's affairs, is made to appear nonsensical. Xanthippe brings aspects of public speech, that which is reserved for men who enjoy certain rights, into the private sphere: logic, argument, dialogue. Cassandra imbues the public code of heroism, warmongering and depradation with private motives: peaceableness, fear of violence and death, anti-heroism. For, as Helene Foley writes in 'Sex and State in Ancient Greece', 'left to himself the male will destroy his domestic life in the name of military glory'.[11]

Cassandra's ambiguous position between two spheres makes her sensitive to transgressions. In Troy, these are the intrusions of the outside upon the inside, of foreign bodies filled with brutality upon the internal sphere of women and children. The seer gives an accurate warning against the return of once banished Paris to Troy, against the arrival of Helen from Sparta and against bringing the Wooden Horse inside the walls of Troy. Later in Mycenae, she alone knows that her transition from outside to inside, her entry into the fortress of Agamemnon, spells death for her.

The offence Cassandra has committed as a *female* seer is to undermine the male discourse of power with a woman's voice and with her life-saving critique of the deadly narcissism that lies behind the ideologies of honour and fame. As Phyllis Chesler writes, 'it is clear that for a woman to be healthy she must adjust to and accept the behavioral norms for her sex, even though these kinds of behavior are generally regarded as less socially desirable. . . . The ethic of mental health is masculine in our culture'.[12]

By being deemed insane, Cassandra is robbed of the most import- ant component of her speech as a communicative act: its performative force. This combination of speech deprivation and psychological anguish is well expressed in the German word *Ent-Mündigung*, which corresponds to the English legal term, incapacitation. In Xanthippe's case, there is merely an attempt to shift the focus of her speech on to the means of its expression in order to obscure the content of what she says. It is precisely the deliberate occlusion of this content which serves as proof of its unimpaired validity. In the case of Cassandra, on the other hand, the content itself becomes the evidence of insanity. Thus there is no longer a differential aspect within the speech act from which it can be made clear that the loss of the criteria of validity results from a violent distortion from outside.

The linguistic dehumanisation of the prophetess is accompanied by the control and domination of her body. It is not only possible to plot the stages of her degeneration temporally through her successive connections with Apollo, Ajax and Agamemnon. The dramatic monologue *Alexandra* (= *Cassandra*) by the Alexandrian poet Lycophron, dating from the third century BC, presents us with an arrangement in which the destructions of Cassandra are gathered in a synchronic plane. She is shut in a cave, in the dark. Her body has as good as disappeared, rendered motionless and invisible. Only her voice can still be heard. She prophesies the destruction of Troy, the suffering of the Greeks, the conflicts which will rage between Asia and Europe before settlement is reached. This monologue is heard by no one. Only Priam himself has been secretly informed by the guard of what his daughter predicts, and thus reveals the duplicity of political power in the field of ideology.

The graphic split within Cassandra, between voice and body, and between wisdom and madness, is reproduced by cultural tradition even today. The Cassandra figure crops up in two separate areas, either as a voice in text or as a body in pictures. But it is a voice and an image within the bounds of male appropriation and control. The voice is fragmented, the body shot through with sexuality to appeal to male eyes and hands. Thus Cassandra is entered into the traditional register of female representation. Full female voices, such as those of the Sphinx, the Sirens and Sappho, or a sight which repels male sexuality, such as that of Medusa, are banished by the dominant cultural discourse into the shadowy realm of the abnormal and inhuman. The fact that the woman in the world of patriarchy is never a full voice, indeed not a voice at all but always a sexualized body – Helen of Troy is a prime example – is apparent in the following paradox. In the textual tradition Cassandra is dominant principally as a voice. So much so that even today men use this pseudonym. Journalists and feature-writers have adopted the name in anticipation of their supposedly wise predictions proving unpopular. Yet in the pictorial tradition of antiquity, Cassandra is shown more often than not in the proto-pornographic scene when she is raped by Ajax in the temple of Athene.

Of all the depictions which have come down to us, only eight show Cassandra giving prophecies, eight depict the scene with the Wooden Horse, twenty-three portray the confrontation with Paris. Seventeen show Apollo taking away her power to convince others and four represent her being killed by Clytemnestra. But there is a total of one hundred and five showing her being raped by Ajax.[13] The publishers Luchterhand are an example of the fact that not much has changed since then. Although in the popular wisdom of our time Cassandra is known almost exclusively as a voice – everyone knows that a Cassandra is a prophet of doom and gloom, but who knows who Ajax is? – the rape scene was chosen as the cover picture for Christa Wolf's text *Voraussetzungen einer Erzählung: Kassandra*.[14] Furthermore, of the one hundred and five pictures available, it is the most explicit. Juliette Davreux highlights the pornographic function:

> As we know, it is very rare in the art of the sixth or the fifth centuries BC for women to appear unclothed . . . Cassandra's nakedness is significant: it indicates that the scene taking place in Athene's temple has all the characteristics of an erotic spectacle.[15]

Since the middle of the nineteenth century, however, women have been claiming Cassandra for themselves. Unlike men, who tend to associate themselves with the exclusive tradition of the prophets or apocryphal truth, women expose the practices of subordination which are linked to the name. In this way, two things are achieved. Women place their own disadvantaged and oppressed situation within the context of a history dating back to early antiquity. At the same time, they bring about this historical revelation by making the silenced mouths and bodies speak again. In so doing they are following the historical dynamics described by Walter Benjamin:

> There is a secret agreement between past generations and the present one. We have been awaited on earth. As with every

generation preceding us, we are given a slight messianic power which the past has a right to.[16]

In 1852 Florence Nightingale, herself a famous victim of misogynist propaganda ('the angel in the house' or 'the lady with the lamp'), wrote a searing manifesto against the Victorian treatment of women as infantile beings. She ominously entitled it *Cassandra*.[17] She showed it to her friends John Stuart Mill and Benjamin Jowett (the latter then Regius Professor of Greek at Oxford and from 1870 Master of Balliol College), to find out what they thought of it. Both men advised against publication. The manuscript remained unpublished.

Only the revolt of women in the twentieth century against the silence imposed on them for thousands of years, and the accompanying new knowledge which strives to overcome the old androcentric superstitions is finally throwing light upon the dark continent of female pasts. Benjamin talks of the angel of history.[18] In the face of the historical catastrophe known as progress, which piles ruins upon ruins and throws them down at his feet, the angel would like to stop, wake the dead, and rebuild what has been smashed. It is just this sort of reconstruction that Christa Wolf has undertaken in her ground-breaking novel, *Kassandra*. In this twentieth-century poet's restoration of the bronze-age prophetess's tongue and voice, we have the first successful attempt in the history of the Cassandra myth to gather the fragmented pieces of her body and her speech together and make her whole again.

Notes

1. This essay is an expanded version of a paper delivered at an international symposium on 'Silence' in Palermo, April 1987.
2. Mikhail M. Bakhtin, *The Dialogic Imagination: Four Essays*, ed. Michael Holquist (Austin, Tx.: University of Texas Press, 1981) p. 294.
3. Ibid.
4. Jean-François Lyotard, *La Condition postmoderne: Rapport sur le savoir* (Paris: Minuit, 1979); trs. Geoff Bennington and Brian Massumi, *The Postmodern Condition: A Report on Knowledge* (Manchester: Manchester University Press, 1984) p. 10.
5. J. C. Flügel, 'A Note on the Phallic Significance of the Tongue and of Speech', *International Journal of Psychoanalysis*, vol. 6, no. 2 (1925) p. 209.

206   *Determined Women*

6. Ibid., p. 215.
7. See Thomas Pékary, *Des römische Kaiserbildnis in Staat, Kult und Gesellschaft* (Berlin: Gebr. Mann, 1985) ch. 9, 'Damnatio memoriae und spontane Statuenvernichtung'.
8. Flügel, op. cit., p. 215.
9. Longus, *Daphnis and Chloë*, Book 3, ch. 23.
10. Mary Ellmann, *Thinking about Women* (New York: Harcourt Brace Jovanovich, 1968) pp. 149–50.
11. Helene Foley, 'Sex and State in Ancient Greece', *Diacritics*, vol. 5 (1975) p. 36.
12. Phyllis Chesler, *Women and Madness* (New York: Avon Books, 1973) pp. 68–9.
13. Juliette Davreux, *La Légende de la Prophétesse Cassandre d'après les textes et les monuments* (Paris: Droz, 1942), 'IIᶜ Partie: La Tradition artistique', pp. 102–223.
14. Christa Wolf's work on Cassandra consists of two different books: her novel *Kassandra*; and *Voraussetzungen einer Erzählung: Kassandra*, a meta-narrative about the details on various levels of experience which informed the production of the novel. Both are published by Luchterhand, Darmstadt und Neuwied, 1983.
15. Davreux, op. cit., pp. 140–1.
16. Walter Benjamin, 'Über den Begriff der Geschichte', in *Gesammelte Schriften*, vol. I (2) (Frankfurt-am-Main: Suhrkamp, 1982); the translation is taken from Walter Benjamin, *Illuminations* (London: Fontana, 1973) p. 256.
17. Florence Nightingale, *Cassandra*, in Ray Strachey (ed.), *The Cause* (London: Virago Press, 1978) Appendix I, pp, 395–418. The work had previously appeared in Florence Nightingale's book *Suggestions for Thought in Searchers after Religious Truth*, pt II, 'Practical Deductions', privately printed in 1859.
18. Benjamin, 'Über den Begriff der Geschichte', pp. 697–8; *Illuminations*, pp. 259–60.

Bibliography

Bakhtin, Mikhail M., *The Dialogic Imagination: Four Essays*, ed. Michael Holquist (Austin, Tx.: University of Texas Press, 1981).
Benjamin, Walter, 'Über den Begriff der Geschichte', in *Gesammelte Schriften*, vol. I (2) (Frankfurt-am-Main: Suhrkamp, 1982).
——, *Illuminations* (London: Fontana, 1973).
Chesler, Phyllis, *Women and Madness* (New York: Avon Books, 1973).
Davreux, Juliette, *La Légende de la Prophétesse Cassandre d'après les textes et les monuments* (Paris: Droz, 1942).
Ellmann, Mary, *Thinking about Women* (New York: Harcourt Brace Jovanovich, 1968).
Flügel, J. C., 'A Note on the Phallic Significance of the Tongue and of

The Castration of Cassandra   207

Speech', *International Journal of Psychoanalysis*, vol. 6, no. 2 (1925) pp. 209–15.

Foley, Helene, 'Sex and State in Ancient Greece', *Diacritics*, vol. 5 (1975).

Lyotard, Jean-François, *La Condition postmoderne: Rapport sur le savoir* (Paris: Minuit, 1979); trs. Geoff Bennington and Brian Massumi, *The Postmodern Condition: A Report on Knowledge* (Manchester: Manchester University Press, 1984).

Nightingale, Florence, *Cassandra*, in Ray Strachey (ed.), *The Cause* (London: Virago Press, 1978) Appendix I.

Pékary, Thomas, *Das römische Kaiserbildnis in Staat, Kult und Gesellschaft* (Berlin: Gebr. Mann, 1985).

Wolf, Christa, *Kassandra* (Darmstadt and Neuwied: Luchterhand, 1983).

——, *Voraussetzungen einer Erzählung: Kassandra* (Darmstadt und Neuwied: Luchterhand, 1983).

Index

210   *Index*

and black women's identity, 8–9,
121–42
and government policy, 20, 128,
133
see also black women (USA);
Civil Rights Movement
(USA)
Redbook magazine, 16
reportage, 77, 154–5
Rhoden, Emmy von, 44, 45
Rich, Adrienne, 16, 110
Rosenberg, Ethel and Julius, 104–5

Sade, Donatien-Alphonse-François,
marquis de, 196
Sappho, 203
Second World War, 14, 15, 19, 21,
80, 89, 91, 106, 128, 140
sexuality, 40, 41, 49, 89–90, 99,
119, 125, 136, 139, 141, 144,
153
language and, 141, 174, 184–90,
199, 203–4
lesbian, 141
taboos on, 49, 89, 150–2
see also abortion; contraception
Sielaff, Erich, 54
silence *see* speech, absence or
deprivation of
Sirens, 203
Smith, Stan, 6–7, 8, 21
socialism
and cultural policy in GDR, 154,
162–3, 167
and equality of sexes in GDR,
9–10, 147, 168
and feminism, 9–10, 30, 162–6
and politics in interwar Britain,
5, 73–5, 77–8, 80–5
Socrates, 200
Sophocles, 198
speech
and female subjectivity, 11,
24–5, 74, 104, 123–4, 127,
138, 147–9, 163–4, 173–5,
202–4
absence or deprivation of, 11,
24, 127, 129, 131–2, 139–41,
195–200

see also language
Speigner, Wulfram, 161
Spender, Dale, 176
Sphinx, 203
Spielberg, Steven, 129, 139
Stefan, Verena, 167
Stein, Gertrud, 70
Stendhal (= Henri-Marie Beyle),
69
stereotypes, 7, 10, 22–3, 27, 30–1,
48, 50, 52, 95, 99–100, 103,
105, 110, 116, 124–5, 127, 129,
135, 138, 157, 175, 184–92
Storm, Theodor, 43
Student Non-Violent Coordinating
Committee (SNCC), 128
suffrage, women's, 3, 4, 32, 39, 69
see also feminist movement;
entries under individual
countries
suicide, 95, 101–3
Sunday Times Magazine, 183, 190

Tamora, Queen of the Goths, 198
Tawney, R. H., 75
Taylor, Elizabeth, 99
Telegraph Magazine, 183
Tereus, 197–9
Tetzner, Gerti, 160
Thomas, Audrey, 8, 17, 108–18,
esp, 113–16
Traill, Catherine Parr, 111
Tubman, Harriet, 125
Tucker, Sophie, 141

United States of America
feminism in, 7, 105–6
women's position during 1950s in
6
women's suffrage rights in, 3
see also race issue (USA); Civil
Rights Movement (USA);
black women (USA)
Ury, Else, 46
Utopia, 91, 122–3, 139, 142

violence, 11, 24, 80–1, 116–17,
130–4, 141, 195–205